Using UseNet Newsgroups

Quick Start to UseNet Newsgroup Success!

W9-BIF-353

WinVN newsreader command reference

The WinVN Main window

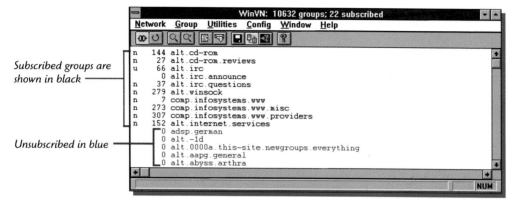

Subscribed groups are shown in black

Unsubscribed in blue

Action	How do I do it?
To subscribe to a newsgroup	Click the group name and then choose **Group**, **S**ubscribe selected groups
To find a group by name	Choose **Group**, **F**ind
To see the list of articles in a group	Double-click on the group name

The WinVN Group window

Article author

Article subject

Action	How do I do it?
To read an article in a group	Double-click on the article in the group's list
To post a new article in a group	Choose **A**rticles, New **A**rticle; or press Ctrl+L

201 W. 103rd Street • Indianapolis, IN 46290 • (317) 581-3500
Copyright © 1994 Que Corporation

The NewsWatcher Article window

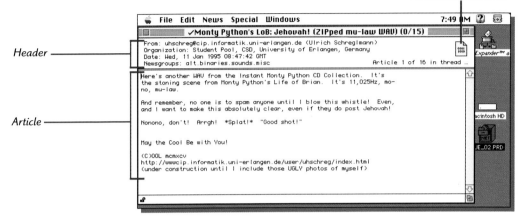

File Attachment icon

Header

Article

Action

To post a follow up to an article
you are reading

To decode a file attached to an article

How do I do it?

Choose News, Reply; or press ⌘+R

Click the File Attachment icon

The NewsWatcher New Article window

*To give your article a
subject, type a subject here*

*Enter the body of your
article here*

Action

To post an article you have written

How do I do it?

Choose News, Send Message or
click the Send button

NewsWatcher newsreader command reference

The NewsWatcher Group windows

The list of subscribed groups —

The full list of groups —

Action	**How do I do it?**
To subscribe to a group	Drag it from the Full Group List window to your subscribed group window; or click the group and choose Special, Subscribe
To Find a group by name	Choose Edit, Find; or press ⌘+F
To see the list of articles in a group	Double-click on the group name

The NewsWatcher Group window

To expand a thread, click here —

An expanded thread —

Action	**How do I do it?**
To read an article	Double-click on it
To post a new article in a group	Choose News, New Message; or press ⌘+N

The WinVN Article window

Header

Original message

Someone else's reply

```
Re: how to become a channel operator? (43 lines)
File   Edit   Search   View   Respond

Newsgroups: alt.irc
Path: dorite!news.sprintlink.net!howland.reston.ans.net!ix.netcom.com!netcom
From: slwork@netcom.com (Steven L. Work)
Subject: Re: how to become a channel operator?
Message-ID: <slworkD27nvt.5u3@netcom.com>
Organization: NETCOM On-line Communication Services (408 261-4700 guest)
X-Newsreader: TIN [version 1.2 PL1]
References: <haque.1.789771752@scs.unt.edu>
Distribution: inet
Date: Tue, 10 Jan 1995 22:31:04 GMT
Lines: 31

Saiful Haque (Mus Lab 3765) (haque@scs.unt.edu) wrote:
: I am new in irc. I was just wondering if anybody tell me how to become a
: channel operator?
: what's the process?
: Thanks in advance..

Just join a channel which doesn't exist.  You will create a channel with
that name and be an operator (and also have no one to talk to, so you will
have to have someone to invite).  In order to become an operator on an
```

Article

Action	How do I do it?
To post a follow-up to an article you are reading	Choose **R**espond, **F**ollowup Article; or press Ctrl+L
To respond by e-mail to an article you are reading	Choose **R**espond, **F**ollowup Mail; or press Ctrl+O
To decode a file in an article	Choose **F**ile, **D**ecode Article

The WinVN New Article window

To give your article a subject type a subject here

Enter the body of your article here

```
New Article
Post   Edit

Newsgroups:  news.software.readers
   Subject:  New book about UseNet
Attachments:

Que Publishing has just published a new book about UseNet titled Using
UseNet Newsgroups. If you'd like to find more information about this book,
visit our Web page at http://www.mcp.com.
```

Action	How do I do it?
To attach a file to an article you are posting	Choose **P**ost, **A**ttach
To post an article you have written	Choose **P**ost, **S**end

Using

UseNet
Newsgroups

PLUG YOURSELF INTO...

THE MACMILLAN INFORMATION SUPERLIBRARY™

Free information and vast computer resources from the world's leading computer book publisher—online!

FIND THE BOOKS THAT ARE RIGHT FOR YOU!

A complete online catalog, plus sample chapters and tables of contents give you an in-depth look at *all* of our books, including hard-to-find titles. It's the best way to find the books you need!

- STAY INFORMED with the latest computer industry news through our online newsletter, press releases, and customized Information SuperLibrary Reports.

- GET FAST ANSWERS to your questions about MCP books and software.

- VISIT our online bookstore for the latest information and editions!

- COMMUNICATE with our expert authors through e-mail and conferences.

- DOWNLOAD SOFTWARE from the immense MCP library:
  - Source code and files from MCP books
  - The best shareware, freeware, and demos

- DISCOVER HOT SPOTS on other parts of the Internet.

- WIN BOOKS in ongoing contests and giveaways!

TO PLUG INTO MCP: →

WORLD WIDE WEB: http://www.mcp.com

GOPHER: gopher.mcp.com

FTP: ftp.mcp.com

Using

UseNet Newsgroups

Noel Estabrook

Kate Gregory

Jim Mann

Tim Parker

que

Using UseNet Newsgroups

Library of Congress Catalog No.: 95-67119

ISBN: 0-7897-0134-0

98 97 96 95   6 5 4 3 2 1

Interpretation of the printing code: the rightmost double-digit number is the year of the book's printing; the rightmost single-digit number, the number of the book's printing. For example, a printing code of 95-1 shows that the first printing of the book occurred in 1995.

Publisher: *David P. Ewing*

Associate Publisher: *Stacy Hiquet*

Associate Publisher—Operations: *Corinne Walls*

Director of Product Series: *Charles O. Stewart III*

Publishing Director: *Brad R. Koch*

Managing Editor: *Sandra Doell*

Credits

Publishing Manager
Thomas H. Bennett

Acquisitions Editor
Beverly Eppink

Product Director
Jim Minatel

Product Development Specialist
Tracy Cramer

Production Editor
Heather Kaufman

Editors
Danielle Bird
Kelli M. Brooks
Noelle Gasco
Lisa B. Gebken
Thomas F. Hayes
Julie A. McNamee
Nanci Sears Perry

Figure Specialist
Cari Skaggs

Book Designer
Amy Peppler-Adams
Sandra Stevenson

Technical Editor
Discovery Computing, Inc.
Alp Berker
Anthony Schafer

Cover Designer
Jay Corpus

Acquisitions Assistant
Ruth Slates

Operations Coordinator
Patty Brooks

Editorial Assistant
Andrea Duvall

Production Team
Claudia Bell
Don Brown
Bob LaRoche
G. Alan Palmore
Kris Simmons
Mike Thomas
Jody York

Indexer
Kathy Venable

Composed in *ITC Century*, *ITC Highlander*, and *MCPdigital* by Que Corporation.

About the Authors

Noel Estabrook is currently a faculty member of the College of Education at Michigan State University after having obtained degrees in psychology, education, and instructional technology. He is heavily involved in delivering Internet training and technical support to educators, professionals, and laymen. He also runs his own training business part-time in addition to writing. Most recently, he has been involved in hypermedia authoring and completed an Internet compendium for educators last summer, which was published electronically.

Kate Gregory discovered UseNet in 1989, after hearing about it for years. She has written or contributed to over ten FAQs, assisted in the creation of new groups, and brought almost all her family and friends online. She has a computer consulting and software development business in rural Ontario, Canada.

Jim Mann is Director of Technology Resources at Antioch College in Yellow Springs, Ohio, where he is responsible for providing support for the college's Macintosh and Intel-based computer users, and running **college.antioch.edu**, the college's Internet connection. He is also president of Apple-Dayton, Inc. (one of the oldest Apple community user groups) and a strong believer in the idea of people helping people through user groups. He can be reached at **jmann@college.antioch.edu**, **jim_mann@adbbs.antioch.edu**, or **UG0056@eworld.com**.

Tim Parker started programming computers 20 years ago, and started writing about them 5 years later. Since then, he has published over 500 articles and 10 books on the subject. He has held roles as columnist and editor with some of the most popular computer magazines and newsletters.

Tim was a founding columnist and reviewer for *Computer Language Magazine*, a columnist for *UNIX Review*, and has contributed to dozens of other magazines. He is currently the technical editor of *SCO World* magazine, editor of the newsletter *UNIQUE: The UNIX Systems Information Source*, and a columnist with MacLean-Hunter Publications. He is the president of his own consulting company, which specializes in technical writing and training, software development, and software quality testing.

Acknowledgments

To Tom Davis—for introducing me to this wacky electronic world. To my wife, Anita—for helping me stay sane while I've been here. And to Jesus Christ, for keeping me through it all.

Noel

To my husband, Brian, and my wonderful children, Beth and Kevin. Thank you for putting up with my crazy working hours. Jan, thanks for showing me the Net in the first place. To the regulars in "my" groups, thanks for making the Net such a nice place to spend time and do business.

Kate

I'd like to acknowledge the work of John Norstad, Academic Computing and Network Services, Northwestern University and his team for developing and supporting NewsWatcher. Dr. Alan E. Guskin, Antioch University Chancellor, for his directive to make our Internet connection "look like America Online," which started my interest in way cool programs like NewsWatcher. The staff at Que who had the courage to use the Internet to seek out untried authors, and the patience to bear with us as we struggled to complete our projects. And, my wife Connie and my family who went many a night without being able to use the telephone.

Jim

Trademarks

Contents at a Glance

{Table of Contents}

Under–standing newsgroup names

see page 20

Chapter 3: How UseNet Works

Chapter 4: UseNet Culture and Netiquette

Business myths debunked

see page 52

Chapter 5: Frequently Asked Questions

Part II: Getting Connected

Chapter 6: Types of UseNet Access

Which newsreader is right for you?

see page 103

Getting news by CD-ROm

see page 135

Part III: Using WinVN

Chapter 11: Getting Started with WinVN

Familiarizing yourself with the WinVn Main Window see page 155

Chapter 12: Newsgroups in WinVN

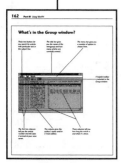

What's in the Group window? see page 162

Chapter 13: Reading Articles in WinVN

Searching for content in an article

see page 180

Chapter 14: Writing Articles and Responses

Posting your own articles

see page 193

Chapter 15: File Attachments

Part IV: Using NewsWatcher

Chapter 16: Getting Started with NewsWatcher

What are file attachments?

see page 204

Starting NewsWatcher the first time

see page 236

Chapter 17: Reading Articles in NewsWatcher

Chapter 18: NewsWatcher's Three R's: Read, wRite, Reply

Message windows
see page 268

Chapter 19: File Attachments

Creating a group in the Big Seven

see page 297

Part V: Your Own Newsgroup or Site

Chapter 20: Starting Your Own Groups

What you're going to need to download UseNet

see page 308

Chapter 21: Setting Up Your Own News Server

Part VI: Hot Newsgroups

Chapter 22: Hot Newsgroups

More groups than you can imagine

see page 349

Introduction

Does your local paper have a section that covers model railroads every day? Does *Entertainment Tonight* have a nightly segment for Jimmy Buffett fans? Does the local sportscaster let you come in and host the sports segment of the news and give your opinion on the coaches and players whenever you feel like it?

Yeah, right.

Welcome to UseNet. It doesn't matter what your interests are, you'll find a group discussing them. With over 10,000 groups and growing (when I started my news program this morning, 70 new groups had been added since last night!), there is truly something for everyone.

But the real miracle of UseNet is that you're not just reading the news: You can write it. The majority of the newsgroups allow anyone to jump in and say whatever's on their mind. Did you just finish watching the NCAA basketball finals and have an opinion about the officiating? Jump on **rec.sport.basketball.college** and tell the world what you think. Or maybe there's a missing child from your neighborhood and you want to get the word out to the rest of the country to be looking for him. Post the message to **alt.missing-kids**, maybe even post a picture along with the description, and maybe one of the readers will be able to help.

Using UseNet Newsgroups will help you find your way around the huge UseNet community. We'll provide the hands-on information you need to run the software and we'll also look at the cultural rules and pitfalls that you need to understand.

So if you're ready to begin the journey, read on. Don't worry about making a few mistakes along the way. Everyone on UseNet has made a few at some point. But then, they didn't have this book when they started, so you're already a step ahead of them.

What this book is

This is a book about UseNet. In it you'll find chapters about UseNet in general: what it is and how you can use it. You'll also find chapters on using two specific programs, WinVN for Windows and NewsWatcher for the Mac.

> Don't worry if you don't have one of these. Both of them can be downloaded for free from the Internet and we'll show you where to get them.

The most important characteristic of this book is that it is written for you, whoever you are. Here's what you can expect:

- If you are new to UseNet, you'll find that this book isn't going to intimidate you with overly technical descriptions or bore you with information you don't need to know. But, if you aren't connected to the Internet, you are going to need some help from either another book (read the note later in this section for a couple of suggestions) or from a friend or colleague who knows their way around the Net, a net.god, before you can explore UseNet.

- If, on the other hand, you have some experience with UseNet and you just need this book to help you with some of the mysteries and intricacies, you'll find that this book won't insult you by just repeating basics that you learned your first day on the Net. There is enough information that you'll find this of use. Of course, if you are already a net.god, you'll probably want to skip the first few chapters and jump right to the detailed directions on using a newsreader on your platform or creating your own newsgroup.

With that said, here's a brief description of each part of this book.

Part I, "Welcome to UseNet," provides an introduction to UseNet for those who need or want more background to bring them up to speed. We'll look at a little bit of history (not much!), the organization of UseNet, some cultural and etiquette issues that are vital to becoming a part of UseNet society, and some resources for further information.

Part II, "Getting Connected," covers one of the trickiest aspects of UseNet for new users: the various ways to get connected to it and what these options offer.

✱ {Note}

This book assumes that you know the basics about the Internet, what it is, and what you can do with it. While we do repeat a few essential points, you won't find a comprehensive Internet primer between these covers.

This book focuses on UseNet. In focusing on this and keeping the coverage here concise and to the point, we have not covered topics such as how you get connected to the Internet. This is covered in many other books that don't have the depth of coverage you'll find here on UseNet.

If you're looking for an introductory-level book about the Internet, you might have a look at some other books in Que's line-up, including *Easy Internet* and *Using the Internet*. Hayden's *Internet Starter Kit for Macintosh*, 2nd Edition is a good choice for Mac users.

Part III, "Using WinVN," shows you how to use one of the most popular (and FREE!) news programs for Windows: WinVN. You'll learn how to perform basic tasks such as getting the software and installing it, subscribing to newsgroups, reading the news, and even posting your own messages. And we'll look at more advanced topics including how to read newsgroups that include graphics and how to get the graphics from those groups.

Part IV, "Using NewsWatcher," shows you how to use one of the most popular (and FREE!) news programs for the Mac: NewsWatcher. You'll learn how to perform basic tasks such as getting the software and installing it, subscribing to newsgroups, reading the news, and even posting your own messages. And we'll look at more advanced topics including how to read newsgroups that include graphics and how to get the graphics from those groups.

Part V, "Your Own Newsgroup or Site," is for the more experienced user. (Even if you're just starting with UseNet, you'll be an advanced user in 6 months to a year, so this may come in handy for you too.) In this part we'll look at the basic procedure for starting your own newsgroup and we'll examine what you need if you are considering setting up a news server.

Part VI, "Hot Newsgroups," is for anyone who thinks that having 10,000+ newsgroups is a bit overwhelming. At most, you'll read a few groups regularly. This will tell you what some of the most popular and interesting groups are in a variety of categories.

Conventions used in this book

Throughout this book you'll see a number of highlighted sections designed to present different kinds of information to you in an easy-to-follow style.

① (Tip)

Keep your eyes open for tips that look like this; they can show you a clever shortcut or point out an interesting but obscure feature that can make your life easier.

✳ {Note}

A note often points out something subtle, yet important, that you should know. Even if you skip over tips, you should always read notes.

⊗ <Caution>

If you don't heed cautions, you may do something harmful without knowing it. Cautions are scarce, but they're *very* important

❓ Q&A

What's a Q&A box?

It's an informal question and answer section where we try to anticipate a question you're probably just itching to ask.

Sidebars take you aside for a moment and follow a tangent that isn't strictly necessary for the topic at hand, but might be inspired by it.

They let us share a personal anecdote or touch on something relevant but not crucial to the subject matter.

66 *Plain English, please!*

These notes define computer-nerd lingo when I'm forced to use it. If you already know a word, skip the definition and keep reading. **99**

Typefaces

In the many examples you'll find in this book, you'll see that when we want you to type something, we'll set that in **bold type**. On-screen text is in special `mono type`. Electronic mail addresses and important new terms that you should remember are also distinguished by **bold type**.

Part I:

Welcome to UseNet

1

Introducing UseNet

In this chapter:

- What is UseNet?
- The Internet in two pages
- A brief history of UseNet
- How UseNet fits in

"UseNet is the set of people who know what UseNet is." —Ed Vielmetti

Explaining UseNet is like explaining the phone system. Sure, all the phones in the world are connected by cables and wires and switches, but that's not what matters. What matters about the phone system is communication—people talking to each other, people doing business, people exchanging documents and computer programs, and people just passing the time of day. In the same way, the cables and wires and switches of UseNet are less important than what those connections allow people to do—communicate.

Is UseNet wires and cables? Is it the data and commands traveling over those wires and cables? Is it the computers that are connected by them? Or is it the people who use those computers? Although the hardware aspects of UseNet are certainly part of what UseNet is, perhaps Ed Vielmetti summed it up best when he said "UseNet is the set of people who know what UseNet is." And those people, collectively, can answer almost any question you ask of them, entertain you, teach you, listen to what you have to say, and broaden your horizons in ways you never dreamed possible.

What is UseNet?

To really understand UseNet, you need to understand traffic. **Traffic** is the lifeblood of UseNet. It is millions of messages (also called posts, postings, and articles) traveling from one computer to another—sort of an electronic rush hour.

Basically, a message will travel from one machine to another machine and to another machine where it can be read by someone on yet another machine. For example, when you place a phone call, your call doesn't go directly through to the person you're talking to. First, it stops at a switching station from your calling area, then it's electronically forwarded to another switching station at the destination, and then directed on to the person you're calling. UseNet's workings are very similar to this process.

 Q&A

Why is it called UseNet?

The name is modeled after Usenix, the UNIX users' conference series. It was supposed to mean UNIX Users Network, since all the early sites were UNIX machines, and many of the early discussions (even the first flame war) were about the UNIX operating system.

The Internet in two pages

Is UseNet part of the Internet? Strictly speaking, no. But the majority of people who access UseNet do so through the Internet, and most of the traffic flows over Internet connections, so the Internet is a good place to start.

The Internet was originally developed by the U.S. Department of Defense to link its many sites around the country. It uses a technique called **packet-switching** to send data and commands between machines. The connections between machines look like a web, as shown in figure 1.1.

Before you walk across a busy street, you look both ways, right? Well, your network does the same thing. Basically, the information you send is bundled into little "packets" that take up small amounts of room. Then, your computer looks to see if there is any incoming electronic traffic. If not, it sends the packet out; if there is traffic, it waits for a bit (actually, the time it waits to look again is almost too small to even measure) and then tries again.

The advantage to this is obvious. Imagine trying to merge into traffic if your car was 500 feet long—you'd need a lot of space to get in, right? It's the same on the Net, little packets need less room to "merge" into the vast amount of electronic traffic out there.

Fig. 1.1
This 9-machine network is connected in the same web-like manner as the Internet.

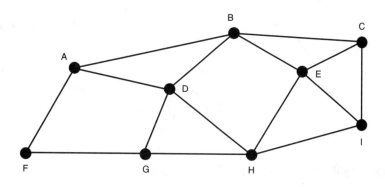

When a machine is connected to the Internet, the user of that machine can access any other machine on the Net almost effortlessly. Programs called **clients** are designed to provide a (hopefully) easy- to-use interface that takes care of information transfer. Some popular clients include:

- **E-mail:** Send electronic mail to any user on any machine. Even machines not on the Internet can often exchange e-mail with machines on the Internet through a **gateway**—an electronic "doorway" onto the Internet. Just as a TV let's you look at an event far away, a gateway can allow you to "look at" the Internet in various ways.

- **FTP (File Transfer Protocol):** Retrieve files from another machine. Some sites allow you to retrieve or upload files to it even if you don't have an account there. This is called **anonymous FTP**. Thousands of freeware and shareware programs are available for distribution in this way.

- **Gopher:** Retrieve catalogs, indexes, and public documents from other machines via a menu-driven interface.

- **World Wide Web (WWW):** See graphics, hear sounds, and access information from other machines. This is very similar to Gopher but with "guts"—as easy as point and click.

- **Telnet:** Log onto a machine from anywhere with no long distance charges. You can check your mail while traveling on business, log onto library computers all over the world and look for the one book you need, or run a program that is only available on a handful of computers in the world.

- **Internet Relay Chat (IRC):** Join a CB-radio style discussion on a variety of topics.

- **UseNet news:** Join an ongoing public discussion where many conversations are going on at once. Find out how your favorite sports team is doing, do some biological research, or discuss the latest election.

A brief history of UseNet

UseNet started in 1979 in North Carolina, with just three sites exchanging messages over phone links by using software called UUCP to copy files between UNIX machines. It wasn't very organized and it wasn't developed to be what it is today. The original developers estimated that the traffic would grow to one or two messages a day. In 1995, a large site processes about one message per second.

In the beginning

A simple organization of groups developed early on. Each machine had local groups, with names like "general" or "announce," and messages from these local groups did not travel to other machines; they were what is now referred to as "local" groups.

(Tip)

Newsgroup names have dots in them. You can pronounce the dots or not, but do not pronounce them as "period." net.general is either "net general" or "net dot general." Newsgroup names are discussed in more detail in chapter 2, "How Newsgroups Are Organized."

There are two basic ways to get news transferred across the Net. The first is by means of a mailing list. Basically, a **mailing list** is a way of distributing news via e-mail. One e-mail address acts as a clearinghouse for all messages and sends out any messages to anyone who's subscribed to the mailing list. The downside of this method is that everything is dumped in your mailbox. This was the way that ARPANET, the network that eventually became Internet, worked.

The second way to get news is to have a machine that is dedicated solely to storing and disseminating news. This way, when a user wants news, he goes to the source using a newsreader and reads what he wants, when he wants—instead of having everything clog up his mailbox. These dedicated machines, called **servers**, organize, distribute, and keep track of thousands of messages—a task that a mailing list can't do as well. This is the direction the ARPANET eventually went.

❝ *Plain English, please!*

A newsreader is a client that accesses a news server and presents the user with news in an organized, readable format. This entire book will deal with various newsreaders to access UseNet. **❞**

Mailing lists versus newsgroups

When two people on the same machine read the same newsgroup, there is only one copy of each news article on the machine. The software keeps track of which articles each user has read in a small file for each user. When two people on a machine both subscribe to the same mailing list, each person gets their own copy of every message.

If your site is large and several hundred people all subscribe to a popular mailing list, this can be an important issue. All those hundreds of copies of each mail message take time to transfer over the communications link and take up space on the server. To fix the problem, the local system administrator sets up a fake newsgroup and arranges for only one copy of each mail message to arrive and to be put into this newsgroup. The subscribers are then asked to remove themselves from the mailing list and instead read the newsgroup. The load on the server machine is thus significantly reduced. This process started almost as soon as the first news transport software was available and is still in use today.

But what happens when people start using a newsgroup or mailing list inappropriately? If people become openly confrontational or obscene, a perfectly good newsgroup can go downhill fast. When this started occurring in newsgroups (or mailing lists), the technique of moderation entered the scene. Quite simply, in a **moderated group**, each piece of mail (or posting) goes to an individual instead of directly to the group. This person, called the moderator, checks the message to make sure it's appropriate and then sends it on to the group.

✴ {Note} _____ | Some newcomers to UseNet are shocked to hear of moderated groups and think of them as a form of censorship. But all a moderator can do is prevent a posting from appearing in one particular newsgroup; there are over 10,000 unmoderated newsgroups and any rejected posting can easily be posted somewhere else instead. On the other hand, some newcomers are shocked to hear of unmoderated groups, and expect a sysop or other authority figure to remove offensive, obscene, or wildly off-topic material. That won't happen. UseNet is a cooperative anarchy, and the vast majority of groups muddle along well without any authority figures in sight.

The Great Renaming and the death of the Backbone Cabal

In the early days, as mentioned above, UseNet traffic was carried over long distance telephone links. Some people were better than others at persuading their managers to pay the phone bills, and those sites started to carry more and more of the traffic. Eventually, the chain of high-traffic sites became known as the **Backbone**, and the administrators of the backbone sites gained the sarcastic nickname The Backbone Cabal. If a backbone site didn't carry a group, the group was essentially dead, and the Cabal generally discussed and decided among themselves whether or not they would carry a group.

By the mid-eighties, the number of newsgroups was growing rapidly, and newsgroups were still organized rather haphazardly. The Backbone Cabal decided that all the existing groups should be reorganized into a topical hierarchy, so they chose seven categories that reflected the sort of traffic the Net was seeing at that time: computer science (comp), social issues (soc), recreation and hobbies (rec), science (sci), arguments (talk), UseNet news itself (news), and miscellaneous discussions (misc). Each hierarchy would then have sub-levels. For instance, a discussion on the hobby of horse training might be located in the group **rec.horse.training**.

✱ {Note}

The "Big 7" groups (those whose names start with comp, soc, rec, sci, talk, news, and misc) are considered by many purists to comprise all of UseNet, though a more practical definition of UseNet is all the traffic that uses UseNet software and protocol, regardless of the hierarchy name. There are many more hierarchies besides the "Big 7," such as the alternative (alt) groups.

Existing groups had their names changed to fit into the new hierarchy, and some of the new names had three levels rather than the previous two. Names suddenly became very important, as sites were rejecting entire hierarchies as frivolous, making propagation a real issue. The classic illustration of this is comp.women.

There was a desire expressed for a group to discuss women's issues. The natural name seemed to be soc.women, since the discussions would mainly be around social issues. But many sites were no longer taking groups in the soc hierarchy, so soc.women would not reach all the people on UseNet. Because almost everyone on the Net was in the field of computing, someone proposed the name comp.women to discuss women in computing. Every site was taking the comp hierarchy, and so this group would be available to everyone. A bitter argument among the Backbone Cabal ensued, which was not eased by a proposal for comp.society.women. A vote of sorts was held and the group passed, but was not created on many sites and never became a real, thriving group. The Backbone Cabal was never the same again.

At the same time, new software called NNTP was allowing people to use the Internet to carry UseNet traffic. This meant that if two sites on opposite sides of the continent both wanted a certain group, it no longer mattered if the Backbone carried it or not; the traffic could go over the Internet. The **interest poll**, commonly called a vote, became a far more important method of deciding whether a group would exist or not, and the Cabal faded away as an entity, though some individuals from the old backbone sites are still active on the Net today.

Commercialization of the Net

In the late '80s and early '90s, more and more companies began to discover UseNet, perhaps because they were hiring people who missed the access they had as students. What had been an academic and research network began to include people working at small computer companies, then larger computer companies, and finally **service providers**, sites that sold accounts to people who wanted UseNet access.

Gateways were set up to allow e-mail exchange between people on large commercial services like CompuServe and America Online and people on the Internet, or connected to Internet sites as in figure 1.2. Subscribers to those services could not access UseNet newsgroups, but they soon wanted to. Finally, the four largest commercial providers, CompuServe, America Online, Prodigy, and Delphi, all joined UseNet, bringing hundreds of thousands of subscribers with them.

Not all these subscribers were well-intentioned, friendly people who wanted to join conversations, and not all of them were prepared to play by the rules of UseNet, which were long-standing and for the most part unwritten. Many of the new subscribers weren't clear on the difference between the Internet and UseNet, and pointed to the commercialization of the Internet as a justification for the commercialization of UseNet. These culture clashes are still going on, and are discussed in more detail in chapter 4, "UseNet Culture and Netiquette."

How UseNet fits in

UseNet traffic is enormous, comprising hundreds of megabytes per day. In the beginning there was far less—not even one megabyte per day—and was all passed over telephone links, many of them long distance. This was a natural barrier to the growth of UseNet. As the traffic increased, managers started to notice larger phone bills, which usually meant no more news at that site, or at least a lot less of it. So the people in charge of UseNet news at most sites tried to keep the traffic low enough so that no one would notice.

But in the late '80s, use of the Internet as a way to transport UseNet news messages grew by leaps and bounds, and not surprisingly, the traffic did too. Since the Internet doesn't rely on long distance phone lines, but rather on networks that go with fixed rate phone lines or fixed rate communications services, the high long distance phone rates were decreased. Just like you can get groceries cheaper at those big outlets with lots of stores around the country who buy in bulk, so too can electronic traffic become cheaper as there become more, bigger providers closer together. Thus, the high traffic experienced on UseNet today resulted.

Fig. 1.2

Some UseNet sites are connected to each other by the Internet (solid lines); others have non-Internet connections (dashed lines).

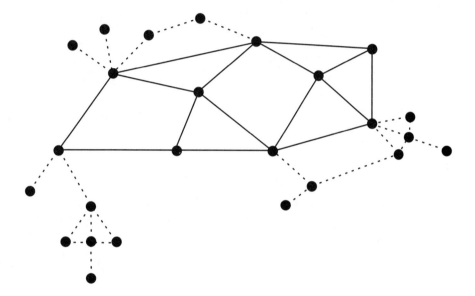

So the Internet has facilitated the growth of UseNet, and UseNet has returned the favor: People are buying Internet access just so that they can read news. Just one piece of information gleaned from a UseNet newsgroup can save hours or days of expensive time, and that persuades companies to join UseNet. And even if you're not in it for business—it's just plain fun!

2 How Newsgroups Are Organized

Imagine picking up your morning newspaper, only to find the whole paper is one big section with articles on different topics arranged any which way. You'd be confused, right?

On many systems, the UseNet hierarchies are the only clue to what the appropriate topics of discussion are in each newsgroup. Some names are cryptic (some deliberately and some thoughtlessly), but all are written in a code that experienced Netters can decipher easily. With a little practice and help, you will be able to recognize a newsgroup's topic just as easily as you determine a magazine's content by the name on the cover.

Imagine picking up your morning newspaper, only to find the whole paper nothing but one big section with articles on different topics arranged any which way. You'd be confused, right? Just multiply that by a thousand and you'd have UseNet without hierarchies. With thousands of newsgroups, it is vital that there be some sort of organization, otherwise, users would spend more time finding groups than they would actually reading them.

Understanding newsgroup names

All newsgroup names have dots in them—for example, **rec.boats.paddle**. The UseNet namespace is a **topical hierarchy**, which means the name of a particular group gets more specific from left to right after each dot, or period. In the example we're using, the first level of the newsgroup name is the hierarchy name, rec., which indicates this group is for discussing recreation and hobbies. The second level, boats., means this group is for discussing recreation and hobbies involving boats. The final level, paddle, does not necessarily mean the group is for the discussion of paddle boats, but for boats that are paddled—including canoes, kayaks, and rafts.

Hierarchy names not only indicate what kind of traffic to expect in a group, they also help sites determine whether or not to carry a group. There are over 12,000 newsgroups with the number increasing every day; so rather than listing all the groups each site wants to carry, administrators list hierarchies from which to receive or not receive. For example, an administrator might choose to receive all the groups in the comp. hierarchy, none of the groups in the talk. hierarchy, and none of the groups in the rec. hierarchy except **rec.boats.paddle**.

⚙ *{Note}*   When talking about newsgroup names, the asterisk character (*) has a special meaning. It's a shorthand way to refer to an entire hierarchy or subhierarchy. For example, misc.kids.* indicates all the groups whose names start with misc.kids. The asterisk doesn't have to be last—*.answers would denote all the groups whose name ends in .answers.

Since the introduction of "The Big 7" hierarchies many years ago, it became apparent that even this organizational scheme would become too crowded and unwieldy with time. Today, with thousands of newsgroups on UseNet, there have been many more hierarchies added. Most of the new hierarchies were created due to different categories of news. Some of the more important ones are:

- The Big Seven

- The alternative hierarchy

- ClariNet

- Bionet, vmsnet, and other worldwide hierarchies

- Local and regional hierarchies

The Big Seven

The seven hierarchies created in the Great Renaming are the heart of UseNet. As was explained in chapter 1, the Big 7 consist of those hierarchies that were most used at the time UseNet really got off the ground. When newsgroups first began to proliferate, these seven hierarchies were sufficient to handle hundreds of possible topics in a relatively organized manner.

comp.

Groups in this hierarchy are for discussion of computer-related matters. Important subhierarchies include **comp.sys.***, for discussion of topics specific to one hardware platform or system (for example, **comp.sys.ibm.pc.*** for PCs and compatibles), **comp.lang.*** for programming languages (but only to the extent the conversations are relevant to any machine, operating system or compiler), and **comp.os.*** for topics specific to different operating systems.

Examples: **comp.lang.c++** discusses the C++ programming language; **comp.object** discusses object-oriented programming

news.

The news. hierarchy contains groups that discuss UseNet news. Everyone should read **news.announce.important**, which sees about one message per year; and all newcomers to UseNet should read both **news.announce.newusers** and **news.newusers.questions**. In addition, if the inner workings of UseNet, the creation of new groups, and the way administrators handle problems on UseNet interest you, look around the news. hierarchy. UseNet contains much information to explain itself. Most newsgroups contain a document that answers frequently asked questions (called a FAQ) and information is being provided on newsgroups constantly. Since all the information in the news.* hierarchy is about UseNet, reading these groups will turn you into a seasoned veteran very quickly.

Examples: **news.groups** discusses the formation of new newsgroups; **news.software.readers** discusses newsreader software

rec.

This is the "R&R" hierarchy, and these groups are intended for discussion of recreation and hobbies. Major subhierarchies include **rec.arts.*** and **rec.sport.***.

Examples: **rec.arts.tv** discusses television shows (primarily American ones); **rec.food.preserving** discusses pickling, jam-making, and other ways of preserving food

sci.

Groups in the sci.* hierarchy are for discussion of scientific and related topics. Many disciplines that are not usually thought of as actual "science," such as biology and chemistry, are represented in the sci. hierarchy of UseNet. These sub-hierarchies include such scientific disciplines as mathematics and engineering. Most of the second level names are abbreviations: **sci.med.*** for medical topics, **sci.engr.*** for engineering topics, and so on.

Examples: **sci.med.diseases.viral** discusses viral diseases; **sci.geo.petroleum** discusses petroleum geology

soc.

Perhaps the most volatile of the Big 7 hierarchies are the soc.* groups, which are given for the discussion of social issues. The two biggest subhierarchies are **soc.culture.***, which covers various cultures around the world, (most are associated with specific countries), and **soc.religion.***, which has moderated groups for discussing religious issues. Soc. has a great number of second level groups because social issues are hard to classify.

Examples: **soc.culture.new-zealand** discusses New Zealand and its culture; **soc.org.nonprofit** discusses the operation of a nonprofit organization

talk.

Groups in this hierarchy are for discussion of any topic on which tempers are likely to flare and minds are unlikely to change. Just about any topic is fair game and reader discretion is advised.

Examples: **talk.abortion** for arguments about abortion; **talk.politics.guns** for arguments about guns and gun control.

②Q&A

What's special about the Big Seven? How are they different from all the rest?

Two things set the Big Seven apart—propagation and rules.

Propagation is the number of sites that receive a group. Many groups in comp.* have almost 100 percent propagation; they are received by essentially every site on the Net. Groups in other hierarchies have much lower propagation.

Every hierarchy has its own rules for creating new groups, changing the moderator of a group, deleting groups, and so on. Some hierarchies, like alt., have no rules at all—anyone can do anything. Others have very strict rules, allowing one or two people to do anything they want and no one else to do anything.

The Big Seven UseNet hierarchies hold discussions and votes, called RFDs and CFVs—Request For Discussion and Call for Votes, respectively—to gauge the desire for a group. If the vote passes, the group is created and carried by almost every site that receives the hierarchy. This discussion and voting process is discussed further in chapter 20, "Starting Your Own Groups."

misc.

Groups in this hierarchy are for discussion of any topic that doesn't naturally belong in any of the other six. This hierarchy is home to the oddest group on UseNet—misc.misc.; this group can literally involve discussions on anything—have you ever wondered what those two little lines that connect your nose and your upper lip are called? Misc.misc might have the answer.

Examples: **misc.kids** discusses child raising; **misc.rural** discusses rural living.

The alternative hierarchy

The alt.* hierarchy was formed when Brian Reid, a recipe newsgroup moderator, took objection to the placement of the group he moderated, in which recipes were posted and discussed. He formed alt.gourmand as a replacement group as sort of a "renegade" hierarchy. In addition to Reid's group, the Backbone Cabal refused to create other groups that users wanted, such as rec.sex and rec.drugs, so even more "alternative" groups began springing up. At the time, many sites would not carry these "alternative" groups, and some, such as companies who provide UseNet for business purposes, still won't today. However, probably the most popular hierarchy in use today is the alt.* hierarchy, due mainly to the fact that service providers realize the great profits that carrying this hierarchy can bring.

There are no rules in alt.*, which has led to a very poor image for this hierarchy. Many alt. groups could never be created anywhere else because they are for discussing topics that are illegal, immoral, or generally unacceptable. But many alt. groups are home to perfectly normal conversations; someone just decided it was quicker to form an alt. group than to go through the three month creation process for a Big Seven group. A good example of this is **alt.computer.consultants**, where computer consultants discuss the business of consulting.

⊗**<Caution>** Many names in alt.* make no sense because they were created by people who didn't understand the hierarchical naming approach used in UseNet. Some groups are created only to have a funny name—not to actually be used for discussions—and then end up with discussions in them.

ClariNet

The ClariNet hierarchy, clari.*, is the first hierarchy that providers incur an additional cost to receive—even though the normal end-user never sees this cost, the provider that carries this hierarchy does. It distributes articles normally found in newspapers, but much faster, and is organized by topic. Founded and run by Brad Templeton, it runs with UseNet software and can be read with any newsreader (if your site receives it), but is considered not to be part of UseNet by many because of the commercial aspect of the distribution.

Examples: **clari.feature.miss_manners**, for the syndicated column Miss Manners; **clari.living.books**, for book reviews from Associated Press and elsewhere.

Other worldwide hierarchies

Several other hierarchies are widely distributed across the world of UseNet. These include such hierarchies as **bionet.***, which is used by biological and biochemical researchers including those involved in the Human Genome Project; **vmsnet.***, which is used for discussion of VMS systems; and **biz.***, which is used for business discussion including advertising and other commercial traffic.

Examples: **bionet.molbio.hiv** discusses the molecular biology of HIV; **biz.books.technical** discusses books for a technical audience.

Local and regional hierarchies

Over 100 hierarchies are designed for use by people in a restricted geographical area, though many of them are read by people who have moved away from an area and want to stay in touch. Almost every country represented on UseNet (one notable exception is the U.S.) has a regional hierarchy, as do many regions, provinces, states, and cities. The reason that America does not have a regional hierarchy is because of its size and UseNet usage. France, for example, has a regional hierarchy because there are still not a lot of UseNet users there. It wouldn't make a whole lot of sense to make a *.us hierarchy, because such a hierarchy would be hopelessly crowded. Regions within the U.S., however, do have regional hierarchies. The discussions held in these groups should be specific to their area, and items of nationwide or worldwide interest should be discussed elsewhere.

Examples: **can.politics** discusses Canadian politics; **ba.general** for general discussions about the Bay Area in California; **ne.general** for general discussions about the New England area.

Other special parts of newsgroup names

There are other common words and phrases that you will see in newsgroup names. This section discusses a few of those.

.binaries.

A group with binaries anywhere in its name is not for discussions. Instead the postings contain binary files.

66 *Plain English, please!*

A **binary file** is a file that is not intended to be read by human eyes, but rather to be understood and translated for use on another computer. A GIF file of an image, a WAV file of a sound, and an EXE executable computer program are all examples of binary files.

Binary files can't be transmitted by the UseNet software unless they are first **encoded**. The most common method to encode a binary is to use a process called **uuencode**. The "uu" in the name stands for UNIX-to-UNIX, because the process was first developed to work with UUCP, UNIX-to-UNIX Copy. Uuencoding changes the characters in binary files into combinations of ASCII characters, which can then be posted to UseNet. Anyone who reads the posting and wants to see the image, hear the sound, or execute the program needs to save the posting to a file, and then use a uudecoding utility to transform the saved file into a copy of the original binary. 99

In the early days of UseNet almost all binaries posted were executable programs, posted in the comp.binaries.* groups. These days alt.binaries.* carries an immense volume, almost all are image files (GIF, JPEG, etc.), and almost all are images of naked or near-naked people. Many sites won't carry the groups, not from any objection to nudity but because of the huge volume, and because so many of the pictures are copyright violations, having been scanned from magazines or captured from videos.

*.d

Any group whose name ends in .d is a companion group to another newsgroup . The .d group is the place for discussion about postings to the main group. For example, **alt.binaries.pictures.d** is a newsgroup for the discussion of the pictures that have been uploaded to **alt.binaries.pictures**. Not all groups have companion discussion groups, but many do.

*.info

Any group whose name ends in .info is a moderated group for announcements, FAQs, and other important material. It is always part of a hierarchy and usually anyone who reads one group from the hierarchy will read the .info group as well. For example, **rec.arts.startrek.*** has seven groups, including **rec.arts.startrek.info**.

❝❝ *Plain English, please!*

Because the population of any newsgroup is transient to say the least, there is often information on a group that may be well-known by some but new to others. There is still other information that seems to be asked for again and again and again, but is not worth continually using space on the newsgroup to discuss. This is where the invention of the **FAQ**, or **Frequently Asked Question**, came in. Any user can subscribe to almost any newsgroup, and by simply reading that group's FAQ can save a lot of time and space asking a question that's been asked a hundred times before. ❞❞

*.answers

The *.answers groups are for FAQs and only FAQs. They are discussed in more detail in chapter 5, "Frequently Asked Questions."

*.misc

Any group whose name ends in .misc is the "catchall" group of a hierarchy. For example, the **rec.pets.dogs** hierarchy consists of rec.pets.dogs.activities, .behavior, .breeds, .health, .info, .misc, and .rescue. The .misc group is for any discussion on dogs that doesn't fit into the other five categories. For instance, since seeing-eye dogs don't really fit into any other categories, a discussion about them might be found in the .misc category.

Moderated groups

As mentioned earlier, some newsgroups are moderated—no one can post directly to the group. Instead, a post is mailed to a moderator, who then decides whether or not it will be posted. Although most newsreaders make it appear as though the post is being submitted directly to the group, it is actually being forwarded to the group's moderator. Posts to a moderated newsgroup can sometimes take up to a day to actually appear on the group (if they're accepted).

Some moderators reject more postings than they approve (for example, about 20% of submissions to **rec.humor.funny** are approved); others have only a gentle rein on the group. In some groups, submissions are sent to one member of a team of moderators, and in others they are circulated to an advisory committee.

 Q&A **What can I do if my posting is rejected?**

In many cases, the moderator will include suggestions along with the rejection notice (for example, "Fix up the formatting so this is more readable") and encourage you to resubmit your posting after revisions. In other cases, you will be told that your submission is off-topic for the moderated group. The moderator may suggest another group that would be appropriate for your posting.

Sometimes, though, you just have to accept rejection. For example, if someone posts a simple request for information, the moderator will post the first submission received and reject all the rest as duplicates.

As noted in chapter 1, people unfamiliar with moderated groups may be uncomfortable having their submissions scrutinized for approval, while people familiar with moderated groups may feel uncomfortable reading articles that have not been scrutinized. This mix of moderated and unmoderated groups is one of the hallmarks of UseNet.

Choosing groups to read or post to

Here are seven ways to find a group whose content is likely to interest you:

- Look at a list of all the newsgroups carried on your site. Finding a list of all the newsgroups carried on your site, especially if you can search it electronically, is probably the best way to find a group, assuming its name describes it well.

- Look at a list of all the Big Seven newsgroups and some other world-wide hierarchies.

- Read a newsgroup designed to help you find the group you want.

- Bump into interesting groups by chance, or find them by reading about them in other groups.

- Ask someone at your site for help.

- If you are on a UNIX system, use the search capability of your newsreader to locate groups

- Many non-UNIX newsreaders also allow you to access a list of valid newsgroups. Check the documentation for topics on finding a group, searching for a group, and so on.

A number of periodic postings contain lists of newsgroups. These are posted regularly to **news.lists**, **news.groups**, **news.announce.newgroups**, and **news.answers**, and list all the known groups in the Big Seven, the alt. hierarchy, and other worldwide hierarchies. Look for the following postings:

- List of Active Newsgroups, Part I
- List of Active Newsgroups, Part II
- Alternative Newsgroup Hierarchies, Part I
- Alternative Newsgroup Hierarchies, Part II

❗(Tip)

> Don't save copies of these postings for longer than a week or two. First, newsgroups come and go at such a rapid pace that such documents become obsolete in a relatively short period of time. Second, these documents are reposted to the appropriate newsgroups very often, so they can be retrieved at almost any time you wish.

Several newsgroups—such as **news.answers**, **news.groups.reviews**, and **news.groups.questions**—are excellent places to find out where specific topics are discussed.

News.answers and the rest of the ***.answers** groups not only lead you to interesting groups, but they house the FAQ lists for many groups, which might answer some of the questions you had been planning to ask. FAQs and the ***.answers** groups are discussed in chapter 5.

The moderated group **news.groups.reviews** contains short reviews of Big Seven and alt. groups, written by a regular reader. This is an excellent place to find out if a particular group will really interest you or not.

If neither of these groups has led you to a group that discusses the topic you seek, try posting a question in **news.groups.questions**. Helpful, experienced regulars will point you in the right direction.

Sometimes none of the formal channels will help you because you don't really know what you're looking for. During your first few months of reading UseNet, pay special attention to any mention of newsgroup names. For example, imagine you are reading **rec.boats.paddle** and you see an article cross-posted to rec.backcountry. Now you have the name of a new group to explore, and perhaps you'll find some material that interests you.

If the topic that interests you is a local one (finding a good restaurant, or some aspect of local politics), ask someone on your own site to help you find a group. But make sure you have exhausted all other ways to find a group first, before you impose on a local system administrator.

3 How UseNet Works

In the first two weeks of December 1994, 1.3 million articles totaling 3,443 MB of traffic passed through a single UseNet site.

The basic element of UseNet is called a message, also referred to as a posting, a post, or an article. UseNet connects a large number of computers, each of which is known as a site. The messages travel between sites with the help of a transport system. This transport system requires a standard format for UseNet postings, which is described later in this chapter.

News sites

News sites refer to the places where the news is stored for your reading. Much like the publication plant of your local newspaper, a news site (or UseNet site) holds the electronic "newspaper" until it's "delivered" to you via a newsreader client.

Just as a newspaper production plant has a production manager, so too does a news site have a manager. An individual UseNet plant manager is usually called a **system administrator**, or **sysadmin**. In addition to basic management, the sysadmin decides which groups to carry and handles many disciplinary matters.

News articles arrive at your site from another machine that can be thought of as an electronic newsfeed—similar to the AP Wire Service that many newspapers use. Your news site then files all the news into the appropriate newsgroup or newsgroups. Once the news is at your news site, it's ready for you to read!

Time lags

The process of getting news, organizing it, feeding it, and getting it ready to read can take time. Uunet, the site that takes more traffic than any other, estimates the average time for a posting to reach it is 11 hours. Some articles take as long as two weeks to arrive. Why? There are many possible reasons:

- Your site may not continually check for new news. If the site feeding news to your local news site only sends news occasionally, you just have to wait. In addition, if your news site only checks the newsfeed site occasionally, a delay will occur.

- A site on the route between the submitting site and your site is down or has taken news down for a day or two to solve a problem or install new hardware.

- A phone line on the route between the submitting site and your site is down or cannot carry a high-quality signal.

There are two implications of this delay. First, if you need a quick answer (perhaps for your 4:00 p.m. meeting today), you may not get one. There are better ways to get quick answers to emergency questions, but if you've tried everything, go ahead and post, but mention your deadline clearly (and don't just say "4 p.m. today," because you don't know what day or time zone people will be reading your article; say "4 p.m. EST Tuesday," or whatever time you need the answer). Accept the fact that replies will continue to trickle in long after they could be useful.

Second, whenever you see a posting, you know it was posted some time ago and that many other people have already seen it. A good idea is to check the Date/Time header. That way, you won't bother answering an urgent post that was submitted a week ago. Knowing this can help you in doing your part to reduce needless traffic on the Net.

❶ (Tip)

Before answering any posting, always scan the whole group to see if any answers have been posted, and then re-read the article with the question. If it's a simple question that many people will know the answer to and you don't know the whole answer, leave it for someone who does. If you do know the whole answer, e-mail it to the person who asked. Only post a reply to the group if it's a complex question and you think others will be interested.

Expiring articles

In the first two weeks of December, 1994, 1.3 million articles totaling 3,443 MB of traffic passed through Uunet, a large service provider that tries to carry every article of every group. No site can afford to keep every article from every group forever, so UseNet software clears out old articles from time to time, a process called **expiring**. Most news site software can expire different groups and hierarchies on different schedules. For example, many sites keep articles in news.* for two weeks, but articles in alt.* for only a day or so.

If articles seem to be disappearing from your site when you know they should be there, they have probably been expired. Many sysadmins will agree to keep a group's articles longer on request; simply send e-mail to your news site's sysadmin and ask.

Not all disappearing articles have expired; other reasons include:

- The article may have been canceled by the poster. You can cancel an article you sent if you notice an error, change your mind, or find the article is no longer relevant. If the cancel reaches a site before your article, people at that site will never see your original article. If your article arrives before the cancel, it will disappear when the cancel arrives.

- The article may have been deleted by your sysadmin. It may contain a copyright violation or other material your sysadmin does not want stored on your site. This is very rare, as most sysadmins don't have enough time to look at every article that is posted at their sites.

- Someone other than the poster may have canceled it. This is generally frowned upon, and most newsreading software makes it very difficult, but in certain cases of unacceptable postings, third-party cancels will be issued. One example of an unacceptable posting is the classic Make Money Fast, a chain letter that everyone on UseNet has seen innumerable times. When it is posted, it is usually canceled immediately to prevent the flood of follow-ups complaining about it and to prevent other naive users from saving it to repost later.

⊗<Caution> Posting the Make Money Fast chain letter or anything else that is likely to be canceled by a third party will probably cost you your UseNet access. Chapter 4, "UseNet Culture and Netiquette," covers this in more detail.

Censorship

It is probably important to talk about censorship a little. Censorship per se doesn't really occur that often on UseNet (although many disgruntled Netters often complain that it does!). What more often occurs is a strict enforcement of the rules or acceptable practices on the Net.

For instance, when a group moderator refuses to post a submitted article, this is not censorship. More likely, the submitted post was simply against the newsgroup's charter (or purpose for existing) and wasn't relevant. When a sysadmin deletes an article from their site it is most often because the post contained copyrighted, obscene, or inappropriate material.

Again, this isn't censorship, but rather an enforcement of what is acceptable use of the medium. Just as the local editor of your newspaper probably won't put a picture of a nude centerfold on the front page, neither will moderators or sysadmins allow such things on their groups or systems.

It would also be helpful to point out the biggest reason why censorship doesn't really exist on UseNet—choice. There are multiple ways of seeing that just about anything is open to you (though maybe not in the place or form you would most prefer). A few of these techniques:

- You can post any rejected articles to an unmoderated group.

- You can create your own alt.newsgroup to carry the material that has otherwise been rejected.

- If your sysadmin can't or won't carry the traffic you want, you can buy access at a site that will.

Delivering the news

The software that is responsible for moving news articles from one machine to another, deleting duplicates, and expiring old articles is called the **transport software**. The specifics of news transport software aren't really important to you as long as it works! There are various types of transport software that are constantly being changed and revised.

If you are interested in finding out more about transport software, there's a FAQ on news software (UseNet Software: History and Sources) that you can read once you have access (FAQs are discussed in chapter 5, "Frequently Asked Questions"). For now, it's enough to know that the software that moves news around from machine to machine exists and is fairly standardized throughout the Net.

What's in an article?

A news article is built from standard parts into a fairly standard form. An article is a collection of lines of ASCII text. The first few lines are called the headers. Next comes the body, separated from the headers by one blank line. Many newsreaders can also add a signature after the body of the article. A sample posting is shown in figure 3.1.

Fig. 3.1
A sample posting.

Header

Double-quote text

Quoted text

New material

Body

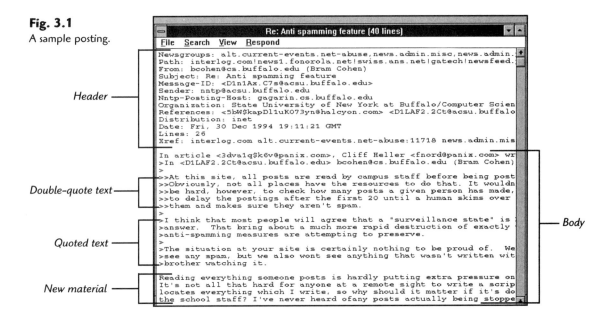

Headers

Every news article is delivered with a header, like the address information on your snail-mail's envelope, only more extensive. All header lines start with a single, capitalized word that is the header name followed by a colon (:), a single space, and information about the header. For example, a posting with the subject "What brand of disk is best?" would have among its headers, this one:

> Subject: What brand of disk is best?

There are 19 standard headers that can be included in a UseNet posting. Many of them are unimportant and are only present for system or other technical purposes. A few of them are handy to be familiar with. They are:

- *Date:* The date, time, and time zone when the article was first posted. This header is automatically generated by your news software.

- *Distribution:* At one time, this was used to restrict a posting to a specific geographical area and was very useful for seminar announcements, for-sale ads, and so on. These days, with so many commercial service providers taking and passing on all distributions, it has become meaningless.

- *Followup-To:* Used to direct follow-up articles to a different newsgroup than the one the article is posted to. Make sure you read this header before following up, or you could end up quite surprised if your article is in a completely different newsgroup. If an article has Followup-To: posted, most newsreaders will not prepare follow-up articles to it but instead will send a private e-mail response.

- *From:* The name and e-mail address of the person who posted the article. This is also generated automatically.

- *Keywords:* A list of words or phrases the poster provides to help people select or reject this article automatically.

- *Newsgroups:* This header lists the one or more newsgroups the article belongs to. If more than one newsgroup is listed in this line, the article is said to be crossposted. Crossposting is discussed in the next chapter.

- *Organization:* The name of the site from which the person posting the article accesses UseNet.

- *Reply-To:* The e-mail address of the person to whom replies should be directed if the address in the From: header is not correct.

- *Sender:* The e-mail address of the person who posted the article if the address in the From: header is not correct. It is generated automatically.

- *Subject:* A succinct description of the topic the posting is about. It should be as specific and simple as possible. If the Subject: header starts with "Re:," the article is a follow-up to a previous article.

- *Summary:* A short summary of the contents of the article.

The three most important ones are Subject:, Newsgroups:, and Followup-To:, as they provide vital information that you need to know. Other headers, such as Reply-To:, Keywords:, and others can be helpful but aren't vital.

Body

The body of a UseNet article is fairly free-form unless the article is a follow-up to another article. When posting an original article however, make sure you keep your line length under 70 characters. Many newsreaders don't automatically word wrap, so if your line is longer than the standard terminal size (80 characters), the message will appear choppy and hard-to-read. Failure to do this will annoy almost every experienced editor out there.

Follow-ups have a fairly standard format. First comes the attribution line. It explains what article prompted the response, identifying it by Message-ID and author. For example:

> In article <121394-aftr@somesite.com>, Some User (someone@somesite.com) writes:

Then comes the quoted text. This is some (but not all!) of the text from the original article, with a quoting character inserted at the beginning of each line. The standard quoting character is > (greater-than symbol). An example line of quoted text:

> >Can anyone send me the 800 number for Chinaberry books?

Finally comes the response text. It stands out because it has no quoting character at the beginning.

When an article is a follow-up to a follow-up, the original follow-up lines are double-quoted (>>) and the most recent follow-up is single-quoted (>). With each level of follow-up, an additional > is added. Attribution information is not uniform since many posters edit this information.

It can be confusing to read the same material several times as people quote it in follow-ups. Just remember to look for a quoting character at the start of the line. Not everyone uses > (colons are also popular quoting marks) as the quoting character, but if all the lines at the beginning of the article start with the same character, the person is probably using it as a quoting character.

Signatures

Many newsreaders can add a standard signature to any posting, which saves you the trouble of typing your name and contact information at the end of each article you post. Signatures on UseNet have become an art form, and there is even a newsgroup, **alt.fan.warlord**, dedicated to reposting spectacular signatures.

Many people like to include a funny or inspiring quote, a song lyric, or a little piece of ASCII art in their signatures. They may also list personal or business information that helps to place them in the community of the newsgroup.

ⓘ (Tip) — Two rules about signatures: If you create one for yourself, limit it to four lines; and when responding to a post with a signature, delete the original poster's signature.

Newsreaders

A **newsreader** is any software product that you use to read UseNet news. There are newsreaders for almost any operating system: UNIX, Macintosh, DOS, Microsoft Windows, OS/2, even CMS, VMS, and TSO/ISPF. Prices range from free to hundreds of dollars.

New newsreaders are being released every month as the Internet software market explodes. There are at least 15 newsreaders for Windows and 5 for Macintosh available now. All of them allow you to do similar things with the news.

The most common function a newsreader accomplishes is (obviously) news reading. Most newsreaders offer advanced functions for reading news, such as how articles are presented. Some newsreaders let you read articles with the click of a mouse, some by having you press a key.

Many newsreaders also allow you to manipulate articles. In other words, they give you options as to how you can select articles to actually read. Are the articles to be displayed by date? By subject? By poster? Newsreading can be easily customized to fit your needs by using these functions.

There are many options that newsreaders offer at the group level, as well. How many groups you can view at once, how to search for new groups, and how to update group information are only a few of the functions that newsreaders let you control.

There are a myriad of other functions most newsreader software accomplish. Fonts, colors, and display settings, news server and connection settings, article saving settings, and many other procedures are present in most newsreading software. Specific newsreaders are discussed in some detail later in this book in chapters 7 through 19. But before you start posting articles, or even replying by e-mail, you need to learn about the culture of UseNet, as discussed in the next chapter.

4

UseNet Culture and Netiquette

People all over the world are interested in solving a tricky programming problem, but not in the cheapest price for the Microsoft Visual C++ compiler in Boston.

U seNet is, in many ways, a community. People who are "on the Net" have heard many of the same jokes, remember many of the same incidents, and have heard of many of the same people. If you want to join that community, you can! But join slowly, and carefully, so that you are less likely to fall on your face.

Lurking

Since we're talking about joining this electronic community slowly, this would be a perfect place to talk about lurking. **Lurking** is the practice of reading newsgroups without posting to them. For a beginner, this is excellent practice. Lurking gives you a feel for the group, let's you know who's an expert, who's a loudmouth, who's a leader, and what the group is all about. *Never* start posting to a newsgroup as soon as you subscribe to it—lurk some first. If you don't, you will end up looking foolish—or worse!

Language

Like any specialized group, UseNet has its share of jargon. For example, we've already defined posting, sysadmin, site, signature, and third-party cancel. The following sections cover a few others. As a user of UseNet, you are somewhat behooved to learn some of that language. Would you go to Africa with the Peace Corps and tell the tribal chief he looked "way cool"? Probably not—you'd learn some of their customs and language first and try to communicate with them in a way they could relate to. Failure to do this on the Net is just as insensitive and unacceptable.

Newsgroup titles

A newsgroup is usually referred to as a newsgroup or a group. Groups are also sometimes referred to by abbreviations. For instance, many people on the Net refer to the newsgroup **rec.humor.funny** simply as "rhf." However, on the Net, newsgroups are never called boards, bboards, bbss, forums, chat areas, conferences, echos, nets, or channels. These phrases are reserved for commercial services that offer newsgroup-type alternatives.

Gender specifications

Gender is often not obvious in postings, and many people use an invented gender neutral pronoun in their postings. If you see the word "sie" it means "she or he" and is pronounced "see." The word "hir" means "his or her" and is pronounced, well, "hir." No one is saying you have to use these words, but you should know what they mean.

!(Tip)

> The "he is a gender neutral pronoun" / "no it isn't" debate is one of the top ten for both frequency and tedium in almost every group on the Net. Leave it alone.

Acronyms

Because everything has to be typed, acronyms are popular on UseNet. They cut down on the number of words you must type and most are easily understood by the UseNet community. Several groups list acronyms in their FAQs, but some of the universal ones are:

- BTW: By The Way

- FAQ: Frequently Asked Question

- FOAF: Friend Of A Friend. Usually the source of some pretty unbelievable stories.

- FWIW: For What It's Worth

- IMO: In My Opinion.
  IMHO: In My Humble Opinion.
  IMNSHO: In My Not So Humble Opinion.

- LJBF: Let's Just Be Friends

- OTOH: On The Other Hand

- IOW: In Other Words

- Re: Regarding

- IRT: In Regards To

- ROTFL: Rolling On The Floor Laughing. There are many variants, but anything that starts ROTFL is describing a humorous incident.

- RTFM: Read the F*#@$!* Manual

- TIA: Thanks In Advance

- YMMV: Your Mileage May Vary. Used when giving advice to remind readers that the same advice does not work for everyone.

UseNet is global

Although Americans make up the large majority of UseNet users, people from countries all over the world read UseNet, and you can't always tell where they are from by their e-mail addresses. Never assume English is someone's first language. Never assume anyone lives in the same country as you do or that their countries have the same laws as yours. Though you probably believe that your country is the best in the world, exercise a little caution in the way you make that belief known.

Before you post, ask yourself if people in Holland will gain anything from reading this? Or people in South Africa? Japan? Australia? People all over the world may be interested in solving a tricky programming problem, but possibly not in finding the cheapest retail outlet price in Boston for the Microsoft Visual C++ compiler. They're interested in toilet training children, but not in a vacancy in a northern California daycare center. They're interested in policy and administration issues concerning UseNet, but not in the availability of a feed of alt.* in the Midwest of the United States. If you do have a post that is very location-specific, find a local or area group to post it to, or, put the location reference in the Distribution: header.

People who read UseNet come from all walks of life. They may, of course, be students or computer professionals, but more and more Netters are doctors, stock brokers, mechanics, writers, freelancers of every stripe, retired people, or people taking a break from the workplace for a few years. Anybody can buy an account from a service provider or sign up with a Freenet. Once again, never assume.

Getting your point across

Have you ever heard one of those computer-generated voices giving you directions or information? If you have, you realize that there's no way to get any meaning from what they say other than the factual information. There's no sparkle in the eye to indicate good humor, no tears to show sadness. Now take even the voice away and limit your communication to a bunch of pixels on a screen. It must be real tough to get anything but factual information across, right? Wrong. Users have come up with several ways to express feelings of all sorts.

Emphasizing techniques

It's hard to convey emotion with nothing but the ASCII character set, but most long-time Netters have learned some ways to do it. Some examples:

- Putting a *single* word in stars to emphasize that word. Putting under-scores _around_ a word accomplishes the same thing. Yet another way to accomplish this is to merely CAPITALIZE that word.

- Putting a *series* *of* *words* in stars suggests that you are speaking slowly and emphatically, perhaps to make a point to someone who hasn't yet grasped the obvious.

- Putting a SINGLE word in capital letters is another form of emphasis.

- Putting a whole sentence, or your whole post, in capital letters is shouting. DON'T DO IT.

(Tip)

It's a bad idea to post in all capital letters, no matter how strongly you feel about the subject. It's hard for others to read and is considered extremely rude. If you don't want your mailbox filled with hate mail, don't do it.

Smileys

This :-) is a **smiley**. If you look at it sideways, it's a happy face. You can find entire lists of smileys on the net, but :-) and :-((happy and sad respectively) are enough for most people. Using a semicolon instead of a colon makes the smiley wink ;-). Some people omit the nose :), have a pointy nose :^), or give the smiley glasses 8-) as a form of self portrait. Others add a beard :-)## or mustache :-{) or silly hair =:-), but you will be able to work these out as you see them. Smileys are often more formally referred to as emoticons (EMOTional ICONS), but are most often referred to as smileys.

Some other online systems use <> to enclose stage directions, so someone might type <grin> or <ducking out of reach> or <g> or <rotfl>. UseNet, in general, doesn't.

<Caution>

Just because there is no :-) does not mean the poster is serious. Many people post sarcastic replies that they think are funny and do not flag them with a smiley. Never fly off the handle in response to something that might have been a joke.

Signatures

Signatures are exactly what they sound like—they are something that is used to indicate you as unique. Signature files can be created using most newsreader software and then be automatically appended to all your posts. At their most basic, signatures include general information such as your name, e-mail address, snail-mail address, or phone number. More creative individuals include little drawings using ASCII characters or clever little sayings—all with the intent of helping them stand out a little bit in the world of pixels.

Flames

Flames are heated, intemperate, and insulting articles. They are also an art form on UseNet for those who enjoy them. There are many groups devoted to flaming (some, but not all, have flame in the newsgroup name) and many more that are home to frequent flame wars. But not every nasty response is a flame.

 Q&A

What sets a flame apart from a nasty response?

Flames are written as much for everyone else reading them as for the person they are directed to. They are witty and literate and show a sense of style. They go beyond simple name-calling and disagreement, while still showing very clearly just how angry the flamer is.

Crossposting and spam

One of the neatest features of UseNet is **crossposting**. Heres how it works. Imagine you have a question about canoe and camping equipment. You know that **rec.boats.paddle** is the place to discuss canoeing, and **rec.backcountry** is the place to discuss camping, so you decide that you would like to post your question to both of these groups. On many systems, such as commercial bulletin boards, you would post two messages, one to each group or chat area (on UseNet that's called multiposting). Crossposting lets you post one message to both groups at once. Some of the advantages of crossposting over multiposting include:

- You don't have to prepare your message twice. You know that readers of both groups will see exactly the same question.

- The volume of news is reduced: only one copy of the message is transferred around the Net.

- Most answers will appear in both groups, so that other interested people will read all the answers, not just the half that appear in their regular group.

- In most newsreaders, when you read a crossposted article in one of its groups, it will be marked as read in the other group too, and you will not have to read it twice.

If you do not specify a Followup-To: header on a crossposted article, most newsreaders will crosspost any follow-ups to the same groups. This is usually a good thing, so that everyone who saw the question can see the answer. However, if you are going to crosspost, you should know the times when it's best for you to set followups to a slightly different set of groups.

Kill files

You like the newsgroup—you really do. But you can't *stand* that loudmouth who likes to share his "wisdom" with the group 27 times a day—at the top of his lungs! What do you do? Well, most UNIX-based newsreaders have the capability to create what is called a **kill file**. Simply put, a kill file is something created to eliminate the need to read a post from a particular person or on a certain topic if you don't want to. In essence, you tell your newsreader, "Look, if any article in this group is by Loudmouth Joe, don't show it to me." The syntax of a kill file is obviously different, but the concept is the same.

Kill files are very handy when a person on a group is particularly obnoxious, as in the example above. Kill files are also very handy for dealing with threads that may have been interesting to begin with but turned into flame wars. Keep in mind that many of the Windows and Macintosh newsreaders do not have this function. However, since you can actually see the subject headers and don't have to look at an article unless it looks interesting, kill files aren't really needed.

- When an article is posted to a low-volume, moderated group (especially a .answers or .info group), set follow-ups to a higher-volume, unmoderated group. When doing this, however, it is a good idea to post the original article to the high-volume group as well so people on that group will know what is being responded to.

- When an article is likely to generate a great deal of traffic that will not be of interest to some of the groups (for example internal company discussion in response to an announcement), use the Followup-To: header to make sure the responses appear only in groups that will be interested.

- When an article is to be crossposted to groups with a sense of community who are historically unfriendly to each other, set follow-ups to only one of the two groups. You may even choose to multipost if the groups are truly hostile.

①(Tip)

Whenever you followup to a crossposted article, your article will be destined for the groups listed in the Followup–To: header, or the Newsgroups: header. Most newsreaders will allow you to change the Newsgroups: line, so if you don't believe your response is appropriate for all the newsgroups, delete the inappropriate ones from your Newsgroups: line.

It is possible to post the same article to hundreds or even thousands of newsgroups, either as individual postings or as a number of crosspostings. This is called **spamming** and it is not acceptable behavior. There is no topic that is relevant to 20 or more newsgroups. If everyone on the Net simply must see it, it should be posted to **news.announce.important**, the group everyone on the Net should read. The moderator of **news.announce.important** approves one or two postings every year that really should be seen by everyone on the Net.If you choose to spam anyway, someone will cancel your posts, and chances are your site will revoke your UseNet access as well.

The green card lawyers

In May, 1994, Laurence Canter and Martha Siegel made the infamous Green Card Post that brought the word spam into the vocabulary of almost every Netter. Using an ingenious combination of crossposting and multiposting, they posted copies of the same message to over 6,000 newsgroups, including many groups not carried on the commercial site where they bought access. The message was aimed at people born outside the U.S. who might want to apply for a green card, and it offered to help (for a fee) with the application. There were three main objections to the posting:

- It was a commercial advertisement.

- It was off-topic for nearly every group it appeared in, with the possible exceptions of **misc.immigration** and **alt.visa.us.**

- The same announcement was posted over and over again, causing a noticeable jump in traffic for that day.

Of these objections, by far the most serious was the spamming, posting the same thing over and over again. Canter and Siegel were certainly not the first to do this, though they reached more newsgroups than any of their predecessors. In the past, spams have always been greeted with howls of outrage, even when they are non-commercial. (One famous non-commercial spam warned readers in every newsgroup that the end of the world was imminent. The poster was the sysadmin of a university site.)

Many of the angry people on UseNet went to great lengths to punish Canter and Siegel for what they had done. They received thousands of pieces of e-mail, so many that the service provider could not keep the machine up. Some of these were angry flames, others were phony requests for information sent in an attempt to waste the lawyers' money sending information packets. But some Netters went well beyond sending e-mail responses. For example, their address and phone number were posted to the Net, and Martha Siegel reported receiving harassing phone calls and hundreds of magazine subscriptions she had not ordered. Complaints were launched with a number of regulatory bodies and Bar Associations.

Other suggestions made in public included tying up their fax line hour after hour by having Netters who lived near them fax them junk mail constantly, filling their U.S. mailbox with flyers and newspapers so that they could not find their own mail, leaving so many nonsense messages on their answering machine that they could not find their real business messages, and other schemes to attempt to demonstrate that 6,000 copies of the same post is not appreciated.

The legal team defended their actions through the American media, and announced plans to form a company to help others use UseNet for business purposes. A few small subsequent spams were met immediately by third-party cancels (see chapter 3) and vanished without a trace. They have since concentrated their efforts on a World Wide Web site and a book about doing business on the Internet.

Netiquette FAQs

There are many good FAQs about netiquette out there. Probably the most well-known and popular is the Emily Post FAQ (available at **ftp.iastate.edu** /pub/netinfo/netiquette among other sites). This is a somewhat light-hearted FAQ that succeeds very nicely in getting across what you should and should not do on the Net.

Another helpful, though more serious, FAQ is the **newusers.questions netiquette** FAQ. You can easily find this FAQ and other useful information by subscribing to the **news.newusers.questions** newsgroup and reading it. However, this FAQ is located at many sites, including freebsd.cdrom.com /.9/ inet/rtfm/de.newusers.questions/news.misc.

Doing business on UseNet

Now that you know what you can't do, it's time to find out what you can do. Remember, the problem that most people had with the lawyers wasn't that they had advertised, but that they had violated UseNet integrity by posting their advertisement everywhere without regard for where it was being sent. There are certainly some legitimate ways to use UseNet in a business capacity—as long as they aren't overused.

Business myths debunked

UseNet is not the Internet. Doing business on the Internet is a very good thing and is well accepted; the myth that doing business on the Net isn't acceptable is simply not true. However; blatant hucksterism will bring on a blizzard of angry mail and phone calls, and typically make your sysadmin very annoyed. It could even cost you your account.

There are several ways to use UseNet to make money if you have a business or if you do freelance work. You can gather information for your business, develop a good reputation by posting wisely, send e-mail responses to posts that solicit help, advertise your business in your signature, or post outright advertisements (although you need to be careful with this one).

Signature advertising is generally accepted on UseNet. It is generally considered good netiquette to limit your signature to four lines. Because some people pay for their online time, it costs a lot of money for some people to download and wade through lots of intricate 20-line signatures. However, four lines, if used wisely, is still plenty of room to advertise your business. Figure 4.1 shows a few sample signatures.

If you have a WWW site or files available for FTP, or if you will send brochures to those who e-mail you, including a single line in your signature advising readers of this is a great way to advertise, while giving potential customers a choice as to what and when they want to check you out.

Posting outright ads needs to be handled with great care. Some rules to follow when posting an ad:

- Post a one-time announcement when you first join the Net or release your product, and never again. Limit yourself to signature ads or e-mail responses after that. If you release a new version or change your service significantly, you can post again.

- Avoid blatant hype and instead make simple, verifiable claims. List a few features of your product or a few of your services. Summarize the table of contents of your book.

- Never criticize your competitors.

- Make it clear from the start that this is an ad and that you are selling this product or service. Never pretend to be an objective third party.

- Never lie or even fudge the truth a little bit.

- Post only to relevant newsgroups. If the group's FAQ states that advertising is not welcome, don't post there. Chapter 5, "Frequently Asked Questions," covers finding the FAQ for a group.

Fig. 4.1

Most signatures, such as these found in alt. computer.consultants, contain contact information and some indication of the type of business of the poster.

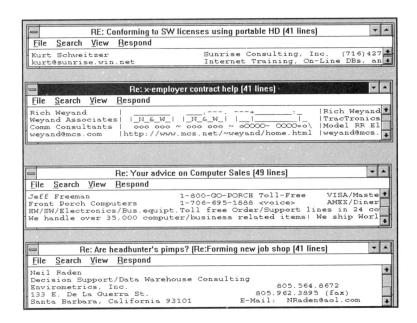

Making a good reputation for your business

Developing a good reputation is an excellent technique for improving your business. Find the newsgroups where people discuss your business topic (computer consulting, sheep farming, or whatever) and become a well informed regular, so that other people look forward to your posts. A good reputation is your most valuable asset, and you can build one by your own postings.

⊗<Caution> Don't assume that because you are posting to a group as an individual and not as a business that you can do or say what you want—especially if you have your business information in your signature. Nasty, inflammatory postings in any group can damage the reputation you have worked to build. Anyone could be reading: your boss, your mother, or your customers.

E-mail responses to posts asking for services or equipment are generally accepted, since the person requested responses. Make sure your response is on topic. For example, do not send information on your multi-level marketing system suggesting they won't need a job if they join your system to everyone who posts a resume to **misc.jobs.resumes**. Similarly, e-mailing an ad for a children's product to everyone who posts to **misc.kids** is not appropriate. However, if someone posts to **alt.computer.consultants** asking for experience and advice about a customer newsletter, e-mailing some information about your newsletter service is appropriate.

Legal implications

The legal issues surrounding UseNet have not been clarified by legal statute or tested in a court of law in any country. The most important thing to keep in mind is that it is impossible to prove beyond a reasonable doubt that a posting came from any specific individual.

Pornography

Stories about sex and image files of sexual activity contribute a great deal to the volume of UseNet, taking the more inclusive definition of UseNet as all the traffic that uses UseNet software and protocol, regardless of the hierarchy name. Most of it is in the **alt.sex.*** and **alt.binaries.pictures.erotica.*** hierarchies. Depending on where you live, some of the material in these newsgroups may be illegal. If your site carries the groups, copies of stories and images that may violate local law will be stored on your machine, even if no user on your site looks at them. Some sysadmins choose not to carry these hierarchies as partial protection from liability.

If you don't want to read sexually explicit or pornographic material, be sure to stay away from groups whose names make it clear that they contain such material. Efforts to prevent others from reading such material usually fail; even if you get your site to stop carrying the group, those who really want the material need only get another account at a site that carries the group. There are usually better uses for your time than trying to shut down parts of UseNet, especially since you won't succeed anyway.

Copyright

Most people believe that anything posted to UseNet is automatically copyrighted by the person who posts it. In the past, the general belief was that anything posted is in the public domain. It has yet to matter enough to anyone to make it to court.

> 66 ***Plain English, please!***
>
> **Copyright** applies only to words, not ideas. You cannot copyright short-bread cookies, but you can copyright your exact recipe and instructions for shortbread cookies. That copyright won't stop anyone from following your recipe to make terrific cookies, but it might stop someone from including your recipe in their book or magazine article without your permission. 99

A more serious matter involves people posting material that they do not hold the copyright to. Examples include:

- Typing in a magazine article, news article, or book excerpt.
- Scanning a picture from a magazine and posting the resultant GIF or JPEG for others to view.
- Capturing a frame from a commercially available videotape, converting it to an image file, and posting it.
- Writing and posting a work of "fan fiction" in which the characters of a famous movie or TV show figure prominently.

When sysadmins become aware of copyright violations, they usually remove the articles from their sites. Third-party cancels are sometimes used to remove the articles throughout the Net. Many sysadmins who care about copyright violation will not carry the **alt.binaries.pictures.erotica.*** hierarchy because almost none of the images posted in that hierarchy belong to the people posting them.

Other people's secrets

UseNet makes it easy to blab secrets that should have been kept and to ensure that thousands or even millions of people read those secrets. There is very little you can do to be sure that your secrets won't end up posted in public. A disgruntled former employee might post your proprietary information. An angry former lover might post private information. And you can't prove who posted it because it might have been a forgery. And keeping your company off the Net won't help because these revenge-seekers can always buy an account of their own.

In Ontario, Canada, the courts imposed a publication ban on material presented at the trial of Karla Homolka, who was convicted in the deaths of two young schoolgirls. Almost immediately a newsgroup was formed as a joke, but it was then used to discuss the many rumors swirling around. The police in Ontario asserted that posting to these groups and carrying these groups was publishing, and therefore violated the ban. Most universities and other large sites dropped the groups, though they carry the replacement groups ostensibly to discuss the ban itself. Although the system did its best to stop the discussions, they soon discovered it was impossible.

Harassment

Posting private information, as mentioned above, is the simplest way to bring misery to another person. Sometimes people post requests for others to join them in harassing another person. Occasionally these requests are disguised: For example, a man might post that his girlfriend collects postcards and suggest that everyone mail her one. Most seasoned Netters are skeptical of requests like these, and with good reason.

More experienced Netters can use UseNet itself against other posters. They can forge embarrassing postings so that they seem to be from the victim, usually resulting in an avalanche of mail. They can forge a special posting called a **sendsys** that will produce one mail message to the victim from each machine on the Net (in December 1994, articles were posted from over 60,000 different sites). They can set up third-party cancels to cancel everything their victim posts. These schemes are eventually discovered, usually with no lasting consequences other than embarrassment and a very full mailbox.

Anonymous posting

UseNet discussions are held in public. Most participants use their full, real names in all discussions. The use of "handles" in general conversation is not considered polite. However, there are groups in which many or even most of the participants feel a need to post anonymously.

There have been a number of systems set up to allow anonymous posting on UseNet. Most of them disappear within weeks or months of their creation. One long-term survivor, created in 1993, is the **anon.penet.fi** server. You send mail to special addresses on this site, and your name and e-mail address are replaced with an address on that machine, such as anon123@anon.penet.fi, and then the mail is sent to another anonymous user's real address, or posted to a newsgroup, depending on the special address you chose.

❶ (Tip)

> Send e-mail to help@anon.penet.fi for full instructions and information about anonymous posting.

There are other, less popular servers available, but the important thing to remember is that no anonymous server is completely foolproof. Your sysadmin may read your mail before it leaves your site: sysadmins of sites between you and the server may also read your mail, or mail on its way to you. People who forge mail in your name to the server may discover your anonymous ID (this can be prevented with a password on the penet.fi server, though many users fail to set the password). Still, most people can't be bothered to read your mail or crack your identity, so if there's something that's too personal to discuss under your real name, the anonymous servers are a viable alternative.

5 Frequently Asked Questions

People have been known to argue back and forth over mathematical or logic puzzles for weeks, while all the time the argument was summarized in the FAQ.

In this chapter:

- What are FAQs?
- What can you learn from FAQs?
- Where do you get FAQs?
- What if a group doesn't have a FAQ?
- Who can write a FAQ?

What are FAQs?

FAQ stands for Frequently Asked Question. A FAQ is a list of questions that are asked again and again, with their answers. Chances are, the simple question you planned to ask of the group may have already been answered in the FAQ.

In many groups, the FAQ is a comprehensive introduction to a very specific subject (the 10-part FAQ "Law Related Resources on the Internet and Elsewhere" totals almost 14,000 lines). Some FAQs contain personal anecdotes and experiences not to be found in any book or reference material. And it's all provided as a public service by the FAQ authors and maintainers.

Q&A

How do you pronounce FAQ?

Very few people pronounce all three letters (*ef–ay–kyoo*). Most often, FAQ is pronounced "fak."

FAQ lists were developed for two main reasons. First, some people were making lists and collecting information on various topics related to particular newsgroups. As a public service, they started to post this information. Second, FAQs were developed to reduce cycles of increasingly boring postings like the cycle that follows:

- Someone discovers the newsgroup **alt.fan.pratchett**, where people discuss the books of Terry Pratchett. So this person decides to ask the group for a list of all Terry's books.

- Several group regulars send e-mail to the original poster describing how to find the FAQ files that include a comprehensive list of Pratchett books, including translated editions.

- Several people who don't know about the FAQ post incomplete lists, and several others post complete lists. These *first generation* follow-ups appear over the course of a week or so.

- The same group of regulars sends e-mail to the first generation posters telling them about the FAQ.

- A different group of posters follows up to the first generation postings that were in error, reminding people which books were forgotten. This carries the conversation for a second week.

- On occasion, a third generation of follow-ups occurs as people post corrections to corrections or thank you's for corrections. This can be responsible for a third week of traffic.

- In all likelihood, this scenario will replay itself within a month or so. And on and on....

When the answer to a FAQ is not a simple fact (such as a list of books), the situation is even worse. People have been known to argue back and forth over mathematical or logic puzzles for weeks, only to see the same argument take over the group just a few months later (when the argument was summarized in the FAQ).

①(Tip) _____ | Never post to a group until you have read the FAQ or are sure there isn't a FAQ for the group, even if you have a question or believe you know the answer to a question.

What can you learn from FAQs?

Most FAQs contain some or all of the following:

- *Charter for the newsgroup.* The charter for a newsgroup is written as part of the group creation process, described in chapter 20, "Starting Your Own Groups." It is usually a paragraph or two that describes the topics the group was created to discuss.

- *Moderation policy for the newsgroup (if it's moderated).* The moderation policy for a group may be a single sentence (the **comp.os.research** moderation policy, as described in its FAQ, is eight words long), or may span pages (the **soc.history.war.world-war-ii** FAQ contains 50 lines on the moderation policy).

- *Examples of topics that are welcome in the newsgroup (and those that are not).* Many newsgroups list topics that are welcome, as well as those that are not. Do not try to convince yourself that your case is a worthy exception. If this group states in the FAQ that ads, requests for help with homework, surveys, or any other material should be posted elsewhere, do not post it to the group. It's rude, and you'll probably regret it.

- *Pointers to newsgroups or mailing lists for related topics.* Many newsgroups cover similar material; it can be difficult to tell from the name alone which newsgroup you should post to. A number of FAQs list related newsgroups and which topics belong in each (see fig. 5.1).

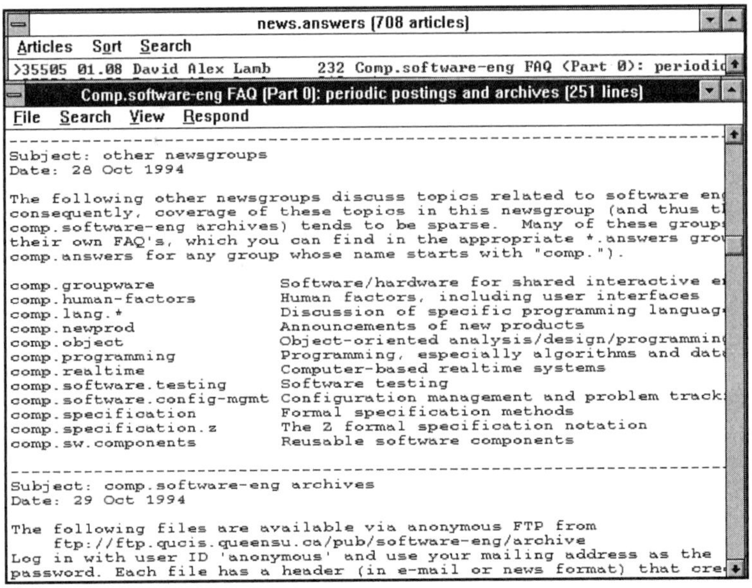

Fig. 5.1

The **comp.software-eng** FAQ lists other newsgroups that may be of interest to people interested in PC and compatible hardware.

```
┌──────────────────── news.answers [708 articles] ─────────────┬─┬─┐
│ Articles  Sort  Search                                       │▼│▲│
│ >35505 01.08 David Alex Lamb    232 Comp.software-eng FAQ (Part 0): periodic │▲│
├──────── Comp.software-eng FAQ [Part 0]: periodic postings and archives [251 lines] ─┬─┬─┤
│ File  Search  View  Respond                                  │▼│▲│
├──────────────────────────────────────────────────────────────┼─┤
│------------------------------------------------------------- │▲│
│Subject: other newsgroups                                     │ │
│Date: 28 Oct 1994                                             │ │
│                                                              │ │
│The following other newsgroups discuss topics related to software eng│
│consequently, coverage of these topics in this newsgroup (and thus t│
│comp.software-eng archives) tends to be sparse.  Many of these group│
│their own FAQ's, which you can find in the appropriate *.answers gro│
│comp.answers for any group whose name starts with "comp.").   │ │
│                                                              │ │
│comp.groupware          Software/hardware for shared interactive e│
│comp.human-factors      Human factors, including user interfaces│
│comp.lang.*             Discussion of specific programming languag│
│comp.newprod            Announcements of new products         │ │
│comp.object             Object-oriented analysis/design/programmin│
│comp.programming        Programming, especially algorithms and dat│
│comp.realtime           Computer-based realtime systems       │ │
│comp.software.testing   Software testing                      │ │
│comp.software.config-mgmt Configuration management and problem track│
│comp.specification      Formal specification methods          │ │
│comp.specification.z    The Z formal specification notation   │ │
│comp.sw.components      Reusable software components           │ │
│------------------------------------------------------------- │ │
│                                                              │ │
│Subject: comp.software-eng archives                           │ │
│Date: 29 Oct 1994                                             │ │
│                                                              │ │
│The following files are available via anonymous FTP from      │ │
│     ftp://ftp.qucis.queensu.ca/pub/software-eng/archive      │ │
│Log in with user ID 'anonymous' and use your mailing address as the │
│password. Each file has a header (in e-mail or news format) that cre│▼│
└──────────────────────────────────────────────────────────────┴─┘
```

- *Instructions for retrieving by FTP, e-mail, or the Web.*

- *Conventions the group uses for spoilers.* Many groups list information they consider to be spoilers in their FAQ, along with instructions for you to follow when posting spoilers.

66 *Plain English, please!*

Spoilers are pieces of information that some people may not want to read; for example, the ending or plot twists to a movie, book, sporting event, or TV show. 99

- *Frequently asked questions about the group, and their answers.*

⊛ {Note}

If you are posting about a TV show right after it has aired, remember that it may not have aired in another time zone, and that some people may have taped the show to watch later. Treat major surprises as spoilers.

When you have spoiler information you want to post, be sure to respect the wishes of the group as reflected in the FAQ.

Finally, after reading all the introductory *about this group* and *about this FAQ material*, you will discover that they are all handled differently. Some contain long answers to questions, others are more terse (see figs. 5.2 and 5.3).

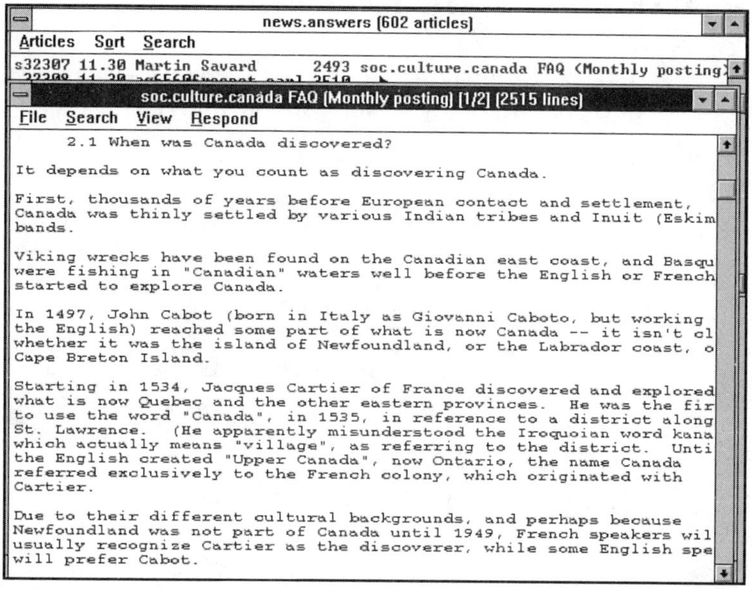

Fig. 5.2
The **soc.culture.canada** FAQ gives long and comprehensive answers to short questions.

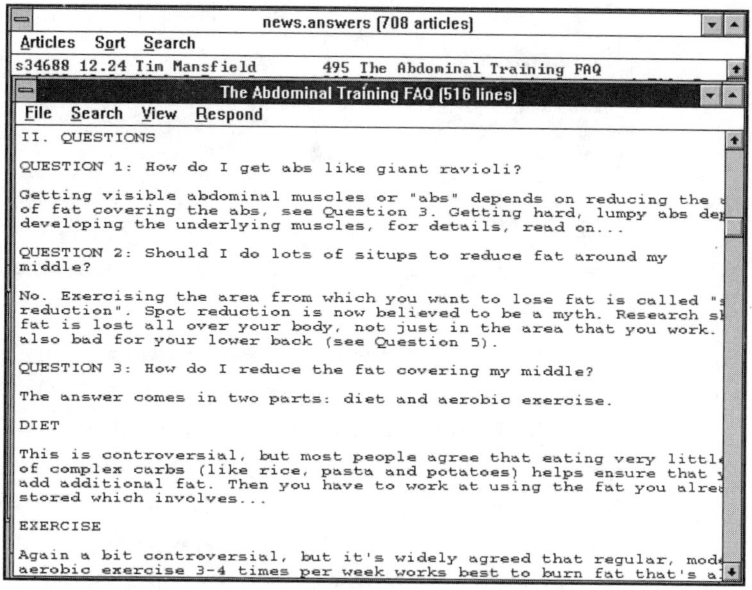

Fig. 5.3
The abdominal training FAQ starts with short answers to short questions.

Most FAQs follow the question and answer format, but there are essays and survey results available as FAQ files as well.

Where do you get FAQs?

Most FAQs are posted to their newsgroups regularly. The frequency of the posting varies from group to group. Read the newsgroup for a few weeks and you are likely to see a FAQ.

Some groups have developed FAQs that are too large to post. In these groups, a pointer to the FAQ with instructions for retrieval by FTP or e-mail is posted (see fig. 5.4). Follow the instructions carefully.

Fig. 5.4
The misc.kids FAQs are available individually, most only by e-mail.

```
                        news.answers (637 articles)              ▼ ▲
 Articles  Sort  Search
>32679 12.05 Diane Lin              466 Welcome to Misc.kids/FAQ File Index <Upd
─────────────────────────────────────────────────────────────────────
         Welcome to Misc.kids/FAQ File Index (Updated 11/22/94) (481 lines)  ▼ ▲
 File  Search  View  Respond
                                                                           ▲
                   *** Index to FAQ Files ***
 ==============================================================
 NOTE:  Some/many of the files listed below are available via the
 Web.  Use URL "http://www.internet-is.com" to get a listing of what
 available.
 ==============================================================
 If you are interested in any of the following topics, please
 e-mail the contact person directly, who will then
 send you a copy of the file.  Please be specific when requesting
 files, as some folks maintain more than one FAQ file.  If you would
 to add something to the files listed, please also do so via e-mail,
 and indicate that you would like your comments added to the
 FAQ file.  Please read the instructions carefully.  If a notation
 follows the person's e-mail address, e.g. (Subject "send toys"),
 the subject line should read "send toys", *WITHOUT* the quotation
 marks, of course.  Such files are sent out automatically, and if yo
 don't put the correct subject line in your e-mail, it will not be
 processed as quickly.  Also, please do *not* request FAQ files usin
 an anonymous address--files will most likely bounce or get truncate
 because of the automatic stripping of the headers by the anonymous
 mail server.

 If you ask for an FAQ file and don't get it within a week, it
 may have bounced.  When you ask again, please be sure to include yo
 e-mail address in the body of your request, in case 'reply' doesn't
 work.  ("Rec." = "Recommendations")  Please also keep in mind that
 some of the files are quite long, which might confuse/bollux some
 mailers.                                                               ▼
```

Many FAQs are crossposted to **news.answers**. Even if your site does not get a specific group, you may be able to read its FAQ in **news.answers**. All articles posted to **news.answers** are archived on the FTP server **rtfm.mit.edu**. (RTFM, you may recall, stands for Read The Fine Manual, though many people use a word other than fine.) The articles are in a directory called /pub/usenet/<*groupname*>, where <*groupname*> is the name of the group you are interested in. For example, /pub/usenet/misc.rural contains archived FAQs for **misc.rural**. If you are on the Internet and can use FTP, it may be quicker for you to FTP the FAQ directly from **rtfm.mit.edu** than to search through your group or **news.answers** for the posted version.

If your site doesn't carry **news.answers** (it's a very high volume group), it may carry **alt.answers**, **comp.answers**, **misc.answers**, **rec.answers**, **sci.answers**, **soc.answers**, or **talk.answers**. Only FAQs for groups in the comp.* hierarchy are crossposted to **comp.answers**, and so on.

What if a group doesn't have a FAQ?

First, make sure it really doesn't. If you've read the group for a few weeks without seeing one and checked the **rtfm.mit.edu** archive, that doesn't mean there is no FAQ. If your group is part of a hierarchy, the FAQ might be posted only to the parent group, or to a subgroup just for FAQs.

For example, discussions on raising children take place in the misc.kids hierarchy, which consists of 7 groups, including **misc.kids**, **misc.kids.health**, and **misc.kids.info**. Each week, a list of the FAQs and instructions for retrieving them is posted to **misc.kids** and **misc.kids.info** (refer to fig. 5.4). If you read only **misc.kids.health**, you might not be aware of the many children's health-related FAQs available. Always check the parent group if there is one. If all else fails, it never hurts to post to the group asking if there's a relevant FAQ.

Who can write a FAQ?

Anyone who has read the group for some time (probably months or years). You need that experience to know what material to include and what to leave out. But you don't need any special qualifications or permission to put together a FAQ or to arrange for it to be posted to news.answers. How to write a FAQ is covered in chapter 21.

Part II:

Getting Connected

Types of UseNet Access

Not all access methods will let you access UseNet as much as you want. Getting the most bang-for-the-buck is not difficult: it just takes a little knowledge.

Now that you've decided you want to use UseNet, how do you get to it? There are many different ways to connect to UseNet, not all of which may be feasible for you because of geographical or economic restrictions. In this chapter we look at the different methods by which you can access UseNet.

Simply put, unless you are a large corporation with enough money to purchase a dedicated interface to the Internet, you will have to use a third-party service to get to the UseNet newsgroups. Even that's not a simple process, as there are several different ways to connect through third-party services.

To simplify the subject, we can divide the access methods into three categories:

- **Direct access:** You dial in through a dedicated service that is directly connected to the Internet.

- **Commercial online service providers:** You dial into an online service that offers Internet access as part of its package.

- **Other access methods:** You can't get to UseNet directly, instead you rely on another company to send you items of interest.

Hopefully, by reading about the services each type of access offers (as well as factoring in your own experience level), you will be able to determine the best method for you to access the wonderful world of newsgroups!

Direct access

Direct access is when you connect to the Internet either directly or through a company that offers dial-in access to the Internet. A direct connection (often called a **dedicated connection**) is an expensive proposition that requires you to devote a machine (called a **gateway**) to interface with the Internet, as well as providing a high-speed telephone line. The administration this type of connection requires is often far more complex than an individual would want to be involved with. Usually, dedicated Internet gateways are used only by large organizations.

If you happen to be a student, you may have direct access to UseNet through your university or college. Most educational institutions are directly connected to the Internet, and many allow students to dial-in to their Internet system from home. Connecting through your school's Internet gateway is the most economical and least limiting option available, as most schools provide full access to all Internet services. If you have graduated (or are about to), try befriending someone in the department that controls the gateway so that you won't lose your access when you leave school, or stay in touch with a friend who's still in school!

For the rest of us, we must access UseNet some other way. One way is to use a service provider. Service providers are companies that have an Internet gateway they make available to individuals and companies who pay a fee for the access.

There are two common types of access through a service provider: **dial-up** (in which you dial into an Internet gateway and connect straight to the Internet) and **shell accounts** (where you use the service provider to indirectly access the Internet). After you have connected to the service provider using either method, you can download the UseNet newsgroups that interest you.

There are hundreds of service providers throughout the country. Most of them charge users a flat monthly minimum fee, and then add on a charge for the amount of time you are online. This can be a problem for users who want full access to UseNet, as there is a huge volume of information to be downloaded every day. If you want all the newsgroups, for example, you are faced with transferring about 90 MB of data every day! Even with high-speed modems, this takes quite a while to transfer. If you only want a few newsgroups, though, direct service providers can be reasonably priced.

So you want your own Internet gateway?

Assuming you have lots of money and even more time for experimenting, you can directly connect to the Internet. You must work with the Internet Network Information Center (NIC) to obtain a domain name and set up the proper gateways on the Internet backbone. If you are considering this type of access, obtain a copy of the Internet RFC (Request for Comment) 1359, "Connecting to the Internet" to see what steps to follow.

To obtain a copy of RFC 1359 by e-mail, send a message to **service@nic.ddn.mil** with the subject 1359. You can also get the RFC from the NFSNET Network Service Center by addressing the message to **info-server@sh.cs.net** and set the first two lines of your message to:

REQUEST: RFC

TOPIC: 1358

Don't put anything else in the message. The automated system reads only the RFC number and your e-mail address in the mail header.

If you want to use FTP to obtain the RFC, log in to the NIC archive, **nic.ddn.mil**, using the login "guest" and the password "anonymous". Change to the RFC directory and transfer the RFC with the command "get RFC1358.txt".

If you don't have electronic access, you can obtain a printed copy of the RFC by calling the Internet Network Information Center at 1-800-235-3155 and giving them the RFC number.

SLIP and PPP accounts

SLIP (serial line interface protocol, a public domain version of TCP/IP) and **PPP** (point-to-point protocol, a more advanced version of SLIP) allow you to connect your computer through a normal telephone line (not a dedicated line) to the Internet. Most SLIP and PPP users have their own domain names that are set up by the Internet's Network Information Center.

66 *Plain English, please!*

A **domain name** is a unique identifier for you or your company. If you directly access the Internet, you must have a domain name. Domain names are used to identify your computer or network so that mail can get routed to you properly. Your domain name is also attached to all outgoing mail, along with your user name.

Only a few individuals bother to apply for and set up their own domains, but they are viewed as the ultimate status symbol on the Internet. 99

If you are using SLIP or PPP from a machine on a network, other machines on your network can go through that machine to connect to the Internet, too. Unfortunately, heavy use of the Internet can result in a lot of network traffic, potentially bogging it down.

Both SLIP and PPP allow full access to all Internet features, although the relatively slow speed of even the fastest modems means that some services like downloading the entire day's newsgroup feed or accessing graphics-heavy applications like Mosaic are slow. With both SLIP and PPP, the Internet connection doesn't have to be maintained all the time. The connection to the Internet can be completed and dropped whenever you want.

(!) *(Tip)*

Don't even consider using SLIP or PPP with anything slower than a 9,600 baud modem. Even that should be considered a minimum, with the faster speeds and compression methods preferable.

SLIP and PPP are good when you are using the Internet a lot, but the costs of a SLIP or PPP account can be considerable. For example, it is not unusual to have monthly bills of $150 to $400 for the connection. Naturally, you will also need software on your computer that supports SLIP or PPP.

✱ {Note}

> Of course, these prices will depend a lot on where you are in the world. In a decent-sized city in the U.S., you'll probably be able to shop around and find monthly SLIP access at about $20–30 per month plus a small fee (ranging from $1–$5 per hour) for online time. In some areas, you'll find bargain basement costs. For instance, in Indianapolis, where the publisher of this book is, SLIP access costs $15 for a 14.4Kbps connection and that includes *120* hours of connection time per month.

There are many companies offering SLIP and PPP connections, including most of the direct service providers like UUNET Technologies and NetCom.

Shell accounts

Shell accounts are more reasonably priced than SLIP and PPP, although you do not have direct access to the Internet. Essentially, you are given an account with the service provider and use their machine to download newsgroups (and access other Internet services such as e-mail). Many shell account systems do not allow you to Telnet or FTP files, so if you need this type of Internet access, make sure the service provider you are considering offers all the services you want.

With a shell account, you have your modem call the service provider's computer (you don't need SLIP or PPP) and transfer the information you want. Most of the process is transparent to you, as you don't actually communicate with the service provider's machine using direct commands. Instead, a script will handle it all for you.

There are many service providers offering shell service, with some offering a mix between shell accounts and SLIP/PPP support. UUNET Technologies and NetCom are two of the largest. Typically, for a shell account you can expect to pay a minimum monthly fee of $10 to $25, with additional charges for connection time. If you find your requirements increasing, you can often switch to a SLIP or PPP account with a minimum of bother.

(Note) You cannot use shell accounts if you want to download the entire UseNet newsgroup feed every day, as the sheer volume of data will bog your machine down for the whole day (and run up your charges accordingly). If you want to download only a few newsgroups, though, shell accounts work well.

A very popular service provider is Freenet, an expanding international organization that gives users a unique username through the Freenet domain with very low (if any) connection charges. At the moment, Freenet is available in only a few cities, but it is expanding quickly. Most Freenets offer full Internet access, including UseNet, although you read messages online instead of downloading them to your computer.

Online services

Online services (such as America Online, CompuServe, Delphi, and Prodigy) were popular before Internet access became important. Online services offer electronic mail and message capabilities between users, as well as libraries of files available for downloading. As the Internet became more popular with individual users, the online services started making limited access available. Now most offer almost complete access to the Internet.

All the online services now provide electronic mail both to and from the Internet, and most offer (or are developing) UseNet access, FTP access, and World Wide Web facilities. The online services are ideal for the casual UseNet reader who wants to browse a few newsgroups at irregular intervals. Most online services charge a basic monthly fee as well as a connect-time rate, so low-volume users find their monthly bills quite reasonable. However, UseNet access can be addictive, so the bills can quickly mount.

 (Tip) If you are using an online service to access UseNet and don't want to use the service's other features, it is often cheaper to arrange a shell account with a service provider.

An online service is the easiest method of getting to UseNet because all you really need is a modem, a communications software program, and an account with the service (which can usually be set up with a telephone call or online registration). Most online services have local access numbers in large urban centers, or an 800 number in some rural areas.

✖ <Caution>　Make sure the online service you are considering offers either a local number or a toll-free 800 number. Long distance numbers add considerably to your usage costs. Most online services have an 800 number but add an extra cost to pay for it. Some services also require you to access the system through a packet-switched network (like Tymnet, Datapac, and SprintNet), which have their own connect charges. Make sure you understand exactly how much access to UseNet is going to cost you through each service!

Life isn't completely trouble free using online service access. Not all the services offer complete access. Only Delphi, BIX, and the Whole Earth 'Lectronic Link (WELL) offer complete access to the Internet at the time of writing, although the others are rushing to catch up. (Delphi and BIX are owned by the same corporation.)

Most online services offer UseNet newsgroups, although some services filter newsgroups to remove subjects they consider too controversial (such as any newsgroup with "sex" in its title). If you contact the providers to ask about their services, make sure you find out if full UseNet access to all newsgroups is available.

✱ {Note}　Which online service is best? The general consensus on UseNet is that Delphi offers the best total Internet package, while CompuServe offers additional services (besides Internet). America Online's graphical newsgroup front-end to newsgroups is winning a lot of support, though. Of course, the choice is up to you. Try to get a trial membership and check out each service. All four of the major online services have special offers with several free hours of connect time for you to check out their systems.

CompuServe

CompuServe is the most widely used online service. Although originally a character-based service, a graphical interface is available for Windows. CompuServe provides UseNet access through a set of submenus that can be frustrating to work through, as there are many pages of warning and instructional material about newsgroup contents that must be paged through each time you access the Internet services. Once past all the text, though, you can create lists of your favorite newsgroups and scan them each time you log in (see fig. 6.1). You are billed for access time, but CompuServe doesn't add any extra charges for newsgroup access.

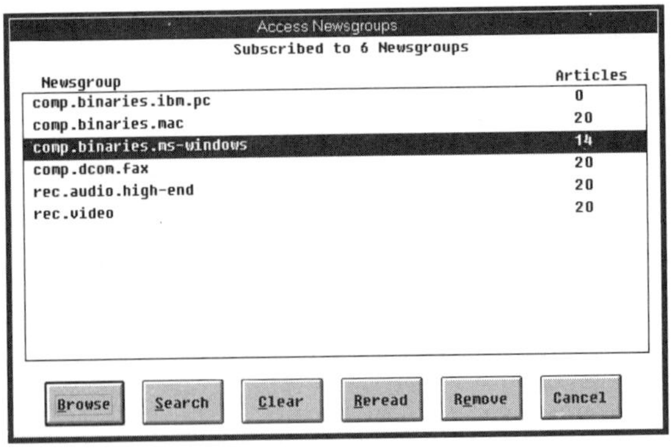

Fig. 6.1
The CompuServe UseNet menu lets you build a list of your favorite newsgroups to simplify catching up with messages.

To access CompuServe's Internet facilities, type **GO INTERNET** at any prompt. The on-screen instructions will guide you through the rest of the steps, as well as offering you useful hints and a library of FAQs and advice. You can post to newsgroups without any limitations.

⊛ {Note}

Some users find it awkward to randomly scan newsgroups through CompuServe. The system almost forces you to add newsgroup names to your subscription list to browse them. If you decide you don't want to regularly read the newsgroup, you must delete it from your subscription list. A browse capability would have been preferable.

Delphi

Delphi is considered by many users to be the best online service for Internet access. They were one of the first services to provide full access (except for graphical World Wide Web pages, which are due in summer 1995). Delphi's Internet access is also reasonably priced, with a $3 per month fee on top of the normal Delphi charges. Only heavy users pay a premium, which is imposed when transferring large amounts of files through FTP.

Delphi uses a menu-driven, character-based system for all user interactions. Delphi does offer a Windows-based package called the InterNav, but it simply has a window that shows the character-based menus and a few shortcut icons that issue commands automatically for you (see fig. 6.2).

Fig. 6.2

The InterNAV Windows-based navigator is an icon-driven front-end to Delphi's Internet services, which offers UseNet access to all newsgroups.

To get to the Internet services, issue the command **internet** at any prompt. From the Delphi Internet menu, you can create a list of your favorite newsgroups, as well as browse any newsgroup you want to check out.

America Online

America Online has become popular in the last couple of years because of its Windows-based interface and the signing of many widely-read magazines to offer online versions of each edition. America Online's Internet access includes almost the full range of services.

Through its Window-based software, America Online makes extensive use of icons to navigate its services. Once you have figured out what they all mean, using the service is quite easy. Many veteran Internet users find the menu-driven system cumbersome and awkward to move through, but it seems to be very popular with new users.

America Online's Internet section provides for newsgroup browsing as well as posting. Other Internet services are available through a menu item, too.

Prodigy

Prodigy is a graphically based online service, which makes it attractive to Windows and Macintosh users. A character-based system is also provided, but isn't used by many people. Prodigy's access to Internet was limited to e-mail for a long time, but they started providing most of the other services when demand became significant.

Prodigy is the smallest of the four online service providers discussed, primarily because of intense competition and limited access to the service. The UseNet services offered by Prodigy include newsgroup browsing, posting, and a library of popular FAQs, discussion threads, and other items of general interest.

Other types of access

Online services or direct connections are not for everyone. If you have no interest in checking newsgroups on a regular basis (relying on them only occasionally for information or as a casual hobby), paying monthly fees may not make much sense. Also, access can be a problem in remote locations. There are a few alternatives that provide elements of UseNet access, albeit late and sometimes abbreviated.

Filtering services

The Computer Science department at Stanford University has developed the Database Project, which provides news filtering services for UseNet. Essentially, you create a profile with the system that includes keywords of messages you are interested in. At regular intervals the system will e-mail you all the messages that matched your keywords. You can select sophisticated contents and "hit" probabilities, too.

✱ {Note}

For more information about the Stanford news filtering service, send e-mail to **netnews@db.stanford.edu** with the word "help" as the body. By return e-mail you'll get instructions about the service and how to create and use your own filtering profile.

Several other systems are beginning to provide newsgroup filtering capabilities, too. Unfortunately, with most of them you must have an e-mail account that can be reached by Internet, although a mail-out service is currently offered by some clipping agencies (although they are expensive). For users who are only interested in scanning the newsgroups for certain subjects without spending hours manually paging through messages, news filtering is an invaluable service.

❗ (Tip)

Many users now couple news filtering services with their normal browsing of newsgroups to get the best of both systems. This lets you satisfy both casual and professional requirements.

Computer Witchcraft's WinNET

Computer Witchcraft provides a nationwide UUCP-based access method for Internet. A Windows product, called WinNET Mail, can be used to access newsgroups as well as the usual e-mail purposes and a mail-based version of FTP. The WinNET Mail software is distributed free of charge, essentially because Computer Witchcraft recovers their costs when you use their provider service. Computer Witchcraft also provides 800 service, with the costs factored into your bills.

WinNET Mail lets you subscribe to UseNet newsgroups. A pull-down menu lets you enter the name of the newsgroups you want to subscribe to, as well as showing you any groups that are already subscribed. When you subscribe, a message is sent to the Computer Witchcraft server indicating that it should send you the news feed.

When you have subscribed to a newsgroup, you get new articles sent to you when you connect to the server. Unfortunately, this can be a time-consuming process (and hence expensive) with busy newsgroups, or if you subscribe to many of them. For light newsgroup use, though, this can be an effective method.

> Avoid newsgroups that allow binary files to be sent as messages, as they can take many minutes to transfer a single large file.

CD-ROM distribution

A few enterprising companies recognize that not everyone wants access to newsgroups online. To provide a good dose of the information available through UseNet, these companies distribute a newsfeed on CD-ROM at regular intervals. The CD-ROMs can be a summary of FAQs and sample threads, or they can contain the full newsgroup message base on a weekly or monthly basis.

> For more information about CD-ROM-based timely access to UseNet, contact Common Knowledge Publishing about their DiscNet service. They can be reached at (610) 433-6866, or by e-mail at **ckp@server0.cybernetics.net**. A sample of the service containing one current issue disk and a disk of general information is available for $15.

Summary CD-ROMs are released several times a year by a few companies that specialize in CD-ROM distribution of public domain archives. These CD-ROMs typically include all the FAQs from the period, as well as a sizable dose of traffic within each newsgroup. Some services only provide FAQs and archived message bases, so check the contents of the CD-ROM carefully to make sure you are getting what you want.

For convenience, you can subscribe to a bimonthly or monthly service that will send you the entire contents of the UseNet newsfeed on CD-ROM. The services are available from a number of companies, most of whom advertise in the popular computer magazines. Typically, a yearly subscription can cost $200 to $500.

Why would you want to get a CD-ROM feed? It is certainly more convenient to store the information on a CD-ROM, as well as permanent. The downside, of course, is that you are stuck with many messages that you will never read or only read once. The amount of material that you would want to keep permanently is a very small percentage of the total. Still, CD-ROMs provide a useful alternative for many users.

Bulletin board systems

Bulletin board systems (BBSs) have been around for many years, offering users a local (and usually free) place to communicate, transfer files, and access file archives. Many of the more popular and heavily used BBSs have added some Internet access to their system, while a few even act as gateways to the Internet.

Typically, a BBS may carry a restricted selection of newsgroups (primarily because of the sheer volume of messages involved in daily updates) and may provide other newsgroups on request. If you can find a local BBS that does offer newsgroup access, this can be a very cost-effective method of reading the news. Since most BBSs are privately run, though, regular access to read news may be difficult to arrange.

A few dedicated Internet BBSs have begun appearing. These provide free or low cost access to daily newsgroup feeds, e-mail, FTP, and World Wide Web services. The number of Internet-dedicated BBSs is still small, but the growth of the Internet and the popularity of the service will probably spur more users to offer the service.

Newsreader Software for Windows

7

This chapter is designed to help you make an informed choice about which newsreader best fits your needs. It won't make the choice for you. But, hopefully, it'll help.

In this chapter:

- WinVN virtual newsreader
- Trumpet for Windows
- NewsXpress
- Chameleon 4 from NetManage
- InterAp Internet software

Y ou have your cup of coffee and doughnut and you drop by your favorite newsstand to pick up the paper on your way to work. The only problem is, there are 10 papers to choose from. Which one do you pick? One has the sections laid out clearly, another has a more readable typeface, and yet another has staff writers you like better than those on the other papers. Decisions, decisions. And no matter which one you decide on, there will be plusses and minuses; as soon as you pick the *Daily News*, someone standing next to you will inform you that *State Journal* would've been a far better choice.

In actuality, the example used above is not a bad one in determining what factors to consider when deciding on a newsreader. The only factor you won't have to worry about when choosing a newsreader is the content of the news—that'll be determined by your NNTP server. Many of the other factors will come into play, though.

For instance, the authors of a particular newsreader may have a style that you prefer over those in other newsreaders. One newsreader may handle windows one way, while another one handles them another way. As an example, WinVN let's you have multiple windows open anywhere on your screen, whereas Trumpet limits the location of its windows to its own application window. One newsreader may group functions just so—maybe you can't
put your finger on why you like it, but you know you do. Still another may present material in a unique way.

Picking software to connect

Although this isn't a networking handbook, it'd be helpful to talk about one of the most important aspects of your Internet connection in Windows—your Winsock. A Winsock simply allows your Windows applications to talk to the Internet in a language it understands. There are really two basic ways to go when deciding how you want to make a connection.

The first is to choose a Winsock client—that is, a piece of software that acts like a mediator between your computer and a server. Some good Winsock clients are FTP's PC/TCP or Trumpet Winsock, among others. These packages are designed solely to establish a connection—nothing more. Once they're configured and set up, you should be able to run any TCP/IP-compliant Internet client available.

The other option is to buy a commercial package with the Winsock software built into the Internet

clients. Some of these packages will also want you to buy your actual account through them, and still others may be too generic to fit your already existing connection. If you do consider this option, make sure you read the fine print and do some research.

Of course, you can also combine these two basic options. For instance, you may really like a particular commercial client, but are unhappy with the Winsock software provided. In this case, you may want to go with a stand-alone Winsock client and also use a commercial newsreader. Again, pick the option that best fits your needs and wants.

For more information on picking and setting up a Winsock, you may want to look at *Special Edition, Using the Internet, 2nd Edition* from Que. This book examines several popular Winsocks.

All these elements must be taken into consideration. Do you like multiple windows? Do you want all your Internet clients to be included in one piece of software or do you want each one to be separate? Do you want to configure your own Winsock or do you want the newsreader client to try to do it for you? And out of all these questions, and others, which factors are most important to you? If you insist that all your Internet clients come in one package and you don't have the time to find them on your own, you'll probably opt for a commercial package. If price is your main concern, perhaps a freeware or shareware version will be best. All these aspects must be carefully weighed—only you can choose.

Other software you'll want

Newsreaders are not yet to the point where they'll do everything for you. There are some additional applications you'll want both in order to obtain a good newsreader and then to fully utilize it once you have it. As was mentioned before, you first need Winsock software and an Internet account; these are the two prerequisites to reading news effectively.

If you choose to go the public domain route, you will need a good FTP client. WS_FTP is an excellent one. This should allow you to retrieve any public domain software you'll need. Since most software available on FTP sites is compressed using PKZip (sometimes referred to as ZIPped files), you'll also need an uncompress utility. Because many IBM-compatible files use this compression method, software such as PKUNZIP or WINZIP is best. If you want to compress files for upload, you may want to obtain a copy of PKZ, as well.

Depending on which newsreader you choose, you'll also want to get a copy of WinCode. This is an encode/decode package for Windows that allows you to manipulate, split, and code uuencoded files, the standard coding protocol on the Internet.

Finally, you should obtain some type of graphics viewer, such as LView (**ftp.switch.ch** /mirror/ win3/desktop). These applications will allow you to utilize some of the graphics newsgroups. For full-motion video, which is being uploaded more and more today, you'll need a "player" like DMFW from Xing Tech. These files are often in the MPEG format and are often rather large. In addition, you may want to have some type of audio capabilities installed on your machine, although audio files are still fairly uncommon on the Net. Macmillan Publishing keeps most of these applications available at its FTP site— **ftp.mcp.com**.

WinVN virtual newsreader

WinVN is public domain software and is available via FTP. The authors of WinVN have given up all claim to their copyright and others can distribute, modify, and use the software in any way they wish. This book includes several chapters on how to use WinVN because it has been found to be the best public domain (and possibly commercial) newsreader client on the market. WinVN is powerful, has many features, and is constantly being updated and improved. Version .93.10 is discussed in this book, but new versions are constantly being released. It would be a good idea to regularly check for recent releases, which may contain new features and capabilities.

⊗<Caution>   Shareware is not freeware. Unlike freeware, which does not cost anything to use, shareware usage requires a fee. In most cases, shareware fees are very nominal—shareware fees can be anything from a postcard of your home town to $50. However, when compared to the hundreds of dollars most commercial packages cost, the shareware fee is usually a bargain. If you find yourself using a shareware application on a regular basis, remember to send in the shareware fee, as this is the only way the author can continue to develop software.

WinVN offers several powerful features that make it a particularly good newsreader. For binary newsgroups, WinVN provides on-the-fly uudecoding—no external decoding applications are necessary. This means that you won't have to worry about whether or not you'll be able to view the pictures posted to your favorite graphics newsgroup. As part of the decoding capabilities of WinVN, a smart filer is provided to allow you to customize how decoded files are to be stored and referenced according to your unique needs (see chapter 15, "File Attachments").

WinVN also provides a way to customize how you read the news. You tell WinVN how many articles to display, which groups you want to see, or how to thread articles—not the other way around. WinVN offers a great deal of flexibility in utilizing the news. In addition, WinVN has the most accommo-dating interface, allowing you to set fonts, colors, and other aspects for different windows according to your own taste.

Stylistically, WinVN provides an attractive user interface, making use of a multiple-window design that lets you accomplish many tasks at once— including the capability to compose and post mail and news articles offline (see fig. 7.1).

Fig. 7.1

WinVN makes use of a multiple-window interface for ease of use. With WinVN, you can compose mail and read different groups and multiple articles all at the same time.

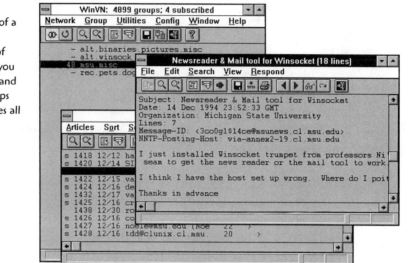

In addition, WinVN is easy to install and use. Simply unzip WinVN, tell it who you are, and you're ready to go. There are no complicated registration or configuration procedures to complete before you can begin reading the news. Just tell WinVN your mail and NNTP server addresses and you're off!

Trumpet Newsreader for Windows

Trumpet Newsreader for Windows originally started as a DOS newsreader and was then developed for Windows and released in 1992. Trumpet, like WinVN, is available via FTP, listed under the name wstsk###.zip. The latest version is 1.0 Revision B, and so would be called wstsk10b.zip. It can also be found under the name Wintrump or Wintrumpet (**csuvax1.murdoch.edu.au** /pub/pc/windows).

⊗<Caution> Do *not* confuse Trumpet Newsreader with the Trumpet Winsock client. If, for instance, you do an Archie search for "trumpet," you will find the Winsock software. Trumpet for Windows Newsreader, or WinTrump as it's sometimes called, is software for reading news only. Make sure you retrieve the correct one.

There are several nice features that make reading the news with Trumpet an enjoyable experience. First, Trumpet takes advantage of Windows accessories to help in executing binaries. For example, Trumpet will automatically display a graphic using Paintbrush as soon as the binary is extracted—this can save you several steps. And as with WinVN, no external uuencoding utilities are necessary.

Also, Trumpet has a very effective server updater. Articles that have already been read or marked as read are no longer displayed, making navigation quite easy by eliminating having to look at previously read or discarded articles. In addition, Trumpet was created as a "double-sided" application—with one side acting as an e-mail client and the other as a news client. While on the news "side," the full Trumpet newsreader is activated (see fig. 7.2). With the click of a button, however, you can switch to the e-mail side of Trumpet, allowing you to look at logged mail, send mail, and have a mini mail client at your disposal while maintaining access to news (see fig. 7.3).

Fig. 7.2
While on the news "side" of Trumpet, all newsgroup information is displayed.

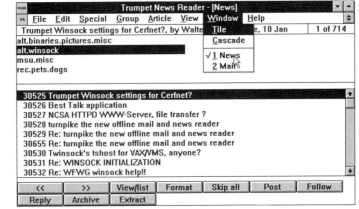

Fig. 7.3

Even though the user has access to news at all times, the mail side offers the ability to use mail functions separately with the click of a button.

```
┌─────────────────────────────────────────────────────────┐
│ ═          Trumpet News Reader - [Mail]           ▼ ▲    │
│ ▭  File  Edit  Special  Group  Article  View  Window  Help  ▼│
│ Re: MAC system $399, by Noel Estabrook, Tue,  Tile   :43:24 +1000 │ 1 of 118│
│ Incoming Mail                          Cascade                  │
│ News: alt.quotations                                            │
│ Outgoing Mail                          1 News                   │
│ Outgoing News                          √2 Mail                  │
│─────────────────────────────────────────────────────────────  │
│ N Noel Estabrook        Re: USENET News reader for all    We ▲ │
│ N Noel Estabrook        Re: USENET News reader for all    We   │
│ N Noel Estabrook        Re: MI -> YellowStone             Thu  │
│ N Noel Estabrook        Re: Suggest a good breed          Fri, │
│ N Noel Estabrook        Re: Asking for advice             Fri, │
│ N Noel Estabrook        BREEDS: several, advice, ??s       Sat,│
│ N Noel Estabrook        Re: compuserve gateway            Sat, │
│ N Noel Estabrook        Re: BREEDS: several, advice, ??s   Sun │
│ N Noel Estabrook        Info on, breeders of Norrbottenspets?  Sun ▼│
│  ┌────┐ ┌────┐ ┌────────┐ ┌──────┐ ┌─────┐ ┌─────┐ ┌──────┐  │
│  │ << │ │ >> │ │View/list│ │Format│ │Fetch│ │Mail │ │Reply │  │
│  └────┘ └────┘ └────────┘ └──────┘ └─────┘ └─────┘ └──────┘  │
│  ┌────┐ ┌──────┐ ┌─────┐                                    │
│  │Move│ │Delete│ │Print│                                    │
│  └────┘ └──────┘ └─────┘                                    │
└─────────────────────────────────────────────────────────────┘
```

Despite its ease-of-use and attractive features, Trumpet still has areas for improvement. First of all, Trumpet attempts to squeeze everything into one window—newsgroups, headers, and articles. You can choose to cascade or tile windows, but doing so only succeeds in making each window so small as to be almost unusable. And because it is impossible to change the front-end fonts, there is no way to increase the amount of information available in each window. In any event, the comfortable feel of a true multi-window interface certainly isn't present.

Also, there is not the continual revision and updating of versions that one might expect with public domain software—so if there's a feature you particularly like and Trumpet doesn't have it, you might be waiting a while before it's implemented.

Finally, there aren't as many user options available, so customization to your needs is more restricted and alternatives are less flexible. For instance, only the article text font can be changed—everything else is pre-set. There are also fewer configurations available for article and group retrieval, file management, and settings. Many other options give you fewer choices, as well. These factors make Trumpet an adequate but restrictive newsreader.

In short, if you want a simple, easy-to-use newsreader without too many bells and whistles that will handle a majority of newsreading tasks with ease, Trumpet may be for you. If you would like a high level of customization and added power in your newsreader, you may want to look elsewhere.

NewsXpress

This section deals with NewsXpress—the "new kid on the block." NewsXpress was only released to the public domain in November, 1994, but it shows promise as a very effective newsreader. It has an interface slightly reminiscent of NewsWatcher for Macintosh—threads are represented by folders that you can open to reveal them fully and the graphics and windows representations are very Mac-like (see fig. 7.4). If you've used a Macintosh before and are comfortable with the interface, this could be the perfect newsreader for you. In any event, it's definitely worth a look.

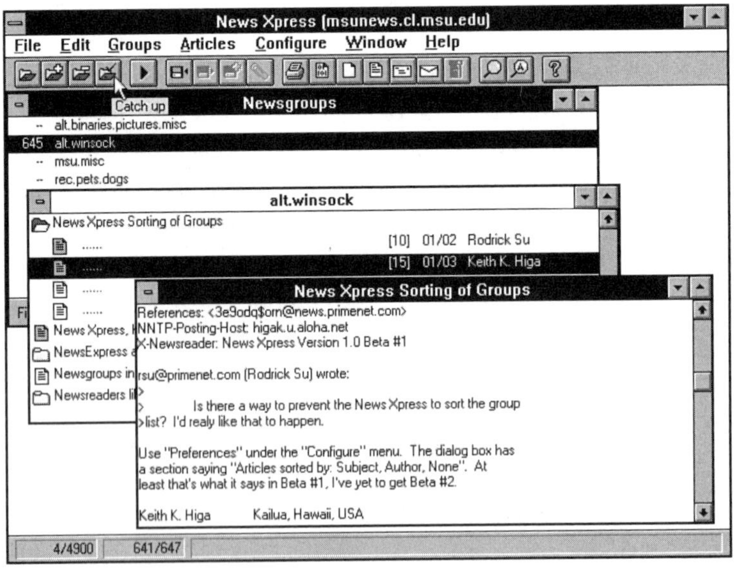

Fig. 7.4
NewsXpress has a very easy-to-use interface with fonts and configurations set to get the maximum amount of information on the screen at any one time.

Probably the most striking characteristic of NewsXpress is its attractive interface. It seems to take up a small amount of space while at the same time offering a lot of different options. It only has one toolbar containing buttons to accomplish any task you would like.

Decoding and filtering are done on the fly almost flawlessly. There is a fair amount of customization available for unique configurations, but much more needs to be done in this area. There is also a handy status bar at the bottom of the screen that tells you how decoding, group and article retrieval, and any other time-consuming function is progressing. In many other newsreaders, status notification takes up a whole window, but NewsXpress' built-in status bar saves this space.

Most new entries into the public domain software game are usually somewhat lacking in areas and NewsXpress is no exception. For instance, NewsXpress doesn't yet do ROT13 encryption. In addition, routine functions such as showing group lists, articles, and using word wrap can still be quite clunky at times.

The documentation for NewsXpress is also very skimpy and is at this time incomplete, so if you are unsure of how something works, it may take some experimentation before you figure it out. On the bright side, there are future versions of NewsXpress are expected to be released, so you can figure that many of these problems will be taken care of in the coming months.

So far, it appears that NewsXpress has been very well-received. If you want to find out the current status and availability of NewsXpress, subscribe to **alt.winsock**, where NewsXpress seems to be getting a lot of attention. It is currently available via FTP at **ftp.cyberspace.com** in /pub/ppp/Windows /newsreaders and a few other sites, but expect it to come to an FTP site near you soon.

Commercial products

In addition to the public domain software we have reviewed so far, there are many commercial newsreaders that have recently entered the marketplace. In this section, we will look at two of them—**InterAp** and **NetManage Chameleon 4**. Both of these packages are intended to be integrated Internet clients. In other words, both packages include software to read news, surf the Web, access FTP and Gopher sites, and more. As was also mentioned earlier, these clients also come with their own Winsock software, which is intended to give your Windows machine Internet access.

The commercial package reviews will contain a little more technical information—such as RAM, storage, and software requirements—than the public domain overviews did. Public domain software is usually intended to be usable by a wide range of users. However, commercial software is often written with more requirements in order to run effectively.

In these sections, we will be dealing with issues related to the newsreader portion of these software packages. Other areas, such as configuration and connectivity functions, will also be discussed when appropriate.

InterAp Internet software

InterAp is an integrated Internet client package (see fig. 7.5). It offers many options from which to choose. If you do not already have Internet access, it furnishes you with information on Internet service providers to get you started. It also offers such capabilities as online help, autoconfigurations, and integrated customization of each application.

Fig. 7.5
InterAp gives you access to every Internet client and function from one window. Configure global settings, conduct network diagnosis, or access an individual client at one time.

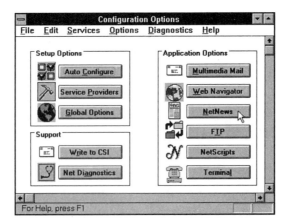

Before talking about the newsreader client, there are several general aspects of InterAp that are worth noting here.

First, the installation is very easy and flexible. During setup you can choose which Internet clients you would like to install. If you don't want to surf the Web, you don't have to install the Web client. Once the desired applications are installed, though, you have the option of returning to the setup program to add the ones you didn't install at a later date. This feature can save time and space while allowing you to decide what you would like to do on the Internet.

InterAp also provides the best of both worlds when it comes to multiple interfaces. Although InterAp avoids the inherent problems in trying to do everything with one application by using different clients for different types of access, it also provides a one-click front end.

66 *Plain English, please!*

An application's front end is comprised of what the user actually sees when using the program. For instance, instead of seeing each individual client that may be in an application, the user will see the front end, which acts as a "buffer" to make the application easier to use. 99

The LaunchPad, as InterAp calls it, is a single mini-Window (more like a toolbar, really) that contains an icon for each client and function (see fig. 7.6). With a single click, you can move between clients and other applications with ease. This feature avoids the confusion of having a large window with lots of applications to deal with.

Fig. 7.6
InterAp offers an easy-to-use front end called LaunchPad, from which any application or function can be accessed.

InterAp also proved to be the easiest commercial package to configure and use as well as install. It integrates very well with any Winsock stack—the setup program is even designed to detect an already existing Winsock. Overall, getting InterAp operational is relatively trouble-free and will work quite nicely whether you need help getting online is or already have access but just need a client package to help you take full advantage of your connection.

For its newsreader, InterAp chose NetNews, which in reality is the same newsreader as WinVN. Therefore, many of the information in chapters 11 through 15 in this book will apply to NetNews. There are exceptions to this, however. WinVN always releases to the public domain first and has no responsibility to InterAp. In addition, the makers of InterAp provide support and resources for their software.

Remember we said earlier that WinVN was public domain software? Well, InterAp took advantage of this fact and packaged it with their Internet service, and despite the delays in new version releases, it makes for a very effective newsreader. The only difference in the two (besides version release) is in the area of support—if you use NetNews with InterAp, you will contact InterAp for support.

What does this mean to you? Quite simply, it means that the version of WinVN you receive with InterAp will probably be old and outdated to some extent. Because any new version of WinVN will be released in the public domain first, it will take InterAp some time to get the new version, integrate it with their already existing Internet package, and then make it available.

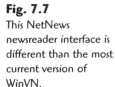

Fig. 7.7
This NetNews newsreader interface is different than the most current version of WinVN.

Chameleon 4.1 from NetManage

Chameleon is the self-proclaimed "Instant Internet" client. This is a lofty claim that may not be altogether true, as there were several glitches encountered when installing and configuring the software. As an example, the 800 number used for electronic registration can take several attempts before a solid connection is established. Once past the frustrations of setup, however, Chameleon delivers an easy-to-use newsreader client that might be worth it to you if you are willing to spend a little time and effort.

Like InterAp, Chameleon is a multi-application Internet client. After your Instant Internet is registered, you are presented with 14 different applications to choose from—allowing you to access FTP, Archie, news, mail, and a variety of other resources.

Chameleon is unlike InterAp, though, in that there is no launch program that integrates the different clients; each one must be used and managed by the user. This could become a bit tricky once you have several clients open at once, but this is not an insurmountable problem for most Windows users.

Chameleon 4.1 requires at least 4 MB of RAM to run. You will also need 7 MB of storage on your hard drive, as well as DOS 5.0 and Windows 3.1 running in enhanced mode. If you happen to have access to an ISDN line and your computer has the proper hardware, Chameleon supports the new WinISDN driver standard in addition to supporting COM speeds as high as 115.2kbps. Although NetManage offers a 30-day free trial to test Chameleon, the licensing fee will be $120 if you decide to keep it—and NetManage asks for your credit card number up front.

Chameleon's newsreader is called NewtNews and offers a simple and elegant user interface. Provided at the bottom of the NewtNews window is a status bar with quick help information to guide you through toolbar buttons and menu options. However, progress regarding group and article retrieval, as well as other time-consuming functions, is not monitored and displayed with the status bar.

Of particular usefulness is the fact that every NewtNews option is displayed, either by menu item or toolbar button, at the main window. If a button or menu item is not available at a particular moment, it is simply deactivated and cannot be used. This gives the user a very clear idea as to what can be accomplished at any time while using NewtNews.

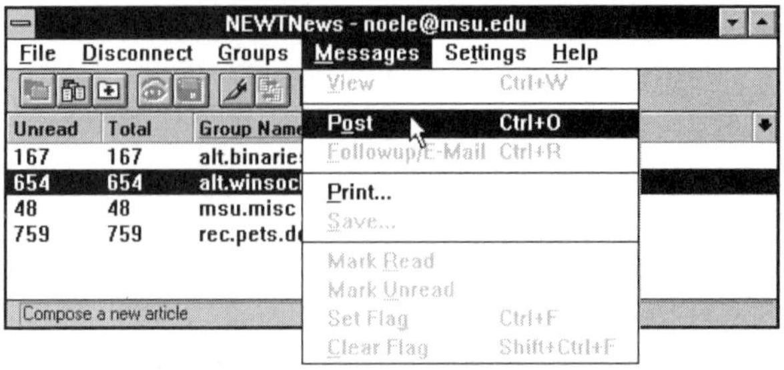

Fig. 7.8

NewtNews displays every available option at all times during your newsreading session. Options that cannot be executed, however, are deactivated. In this example, the article options are not activated while the user is in the Group window.

One of the first things you notice about NewtNews is that it doesn't make use of true multiple-window display. Although article and composition windows are unique, only group lists or article lists can be displayed at any one time. This can be a hindrance to quick function changes while using NewtNews.

Although easy to use, NewtNews is somewhat lacking in the areas of flexibility, customization, and power. There are a very limited number of settings and configurations the user can set. So if you're happy with what NewtNews has to offer, it will work well for you, but if you desire a little more, you may be out of luck. Many of the functions that are standard on many newsreaders, such as ROT13 crypting and uuencoding, are not available on NewtNews.

If all you want to do on the Internet is read news, NewtNews probably won't be for you. If, however, you want a commercial package with every available Internet client available on one set of disks, looking at Chameleon might be worth your while. Some of the other newsreaders we have looked at seem to be more flexible and powerful and, though easy to use, NewtNews falls short in some of these areas.

Choosing a Macintosh TCP Newsreader

In this chapter:

- The Macintosh software and hardware you'll need

- Where to get the most popular Macintosh TCP newsreaders

- How to set up MacTCP

- How to choose between Macintosh shareware newsreaders

- Whether a commercial program is for you

A newsreader allows you to do three basic things: Read news, post new articles or reply to articles, and download files.

If you're an experienced Mac user and you already have MacTCP and your SLIP or PPP connection properly configured and working, you may want to jump ahead to the reviews of the most popular MacTCP newsreaders.

If you're new to this or you want a quick review, follow along as we outline how to go from scratch to reading the news.

Before you can get started using any MacTCP newsreader, there are a number of things you need to do. But what order do you do them in? Like anything else, there's the easy way, and the hard way.

This chapter makes a number of assumptions:

- One assumption is that you'll be connecting to your Internet provider via a modem. If you're connecting via a networked Mac, your local system administrator should be able to provide you with support.

- Another assumption is that you've already selected an Internet provider and have established a SLIP or PPP connection and have some type of e-mail account.

- A final assumption is that you have mastered the Macintosh basics of "point, click, and drag," creating a new folder, and opening and closing an application.

If these assumptions don't fit you, you might want to take some time to check out Hayden's *Internet Starter Kit* to select an Internet provider, or review the manuals that came with your computer.

What you need

This section covers some of the basic requirements that you will need. If you have established a SLIP or PPP connection and have MacTCP installed, you can be assured that your machine can probably handle any of the newsreader software talked about in this section. Keep in mind, of course, that the faster and more powerful your computer and related peripherals, the faster and easier newsreading will be.

- *Classic II/Performa 200 or better.* Avoid using an SE, as there could be some incompatibilities with some of the software we'll talk about.

- *System 7.0.* System 7.5 has lots of extras (including MacTCP) but still has some bugs.

- *8 MB of RAM.* The more memory you have, the more you'll be able to accomplish. If you're running System 7.0, you can get away with 4 MB, but 8 MB will still serve you better.

- *80 MB of storage.* This is an absolute minimum. If you plan on down-loading or storing files, plan on at least doubling this figure.

- *9600 baud or faster modem.* There are many 14.4k modems for under $100.00 through mail order and even the high-speed 28.8k modems can regularly be found for under $200. Of course, spending the extra money on a faster modem won't do you much good if your connection limits how fast you can connect—make sure to check.

①(Tip)

> Dealers who create custom systems often buy minimum basic systems and upgrade them with third-party RAM and hard drives. What that means to you is that, if you know where to look, there are a lot of 4 MB SIMMS and 250 MB hard drives floating around at really reasonable prices. Don't expect to find these "pulls" at the computer store in the local mall. Instead, look for a type of dealer called a VAR—Value Added Reseller—they're the people building custom solutions for local businesses. Mail order prices are also very competitive in today's market.

What software will you need?

At the minimum, you'll need MacTCP, a SLIP or PPP "client," and the newsreader of your choice. But, you're also going to need programs to get other files, programs to view pictures, and so on.

- MacTCP (included in System 7.5)

- InterSLIP (or other SLIP tool) or MacPPP

- The newsreader of your choice:

    NewsWatcher

    Nuntius

    Internews

    The News

- Stuffit (Lite, Expander, or Deluxe)

- Disinfectant (or other anti-virus program)

- Anarchie

- Fetch

- uuUndo

- JPEG viewer, such as JPEGView

- GIF viewer, such as GIFConverter

- SoundApp for sound files

- Sparkle (for viewing MPEG movies)

- Eudora (for sending e-mail)

Where to get the software you need

You can find everything you need freely distributed at "all the usual places." But how do you find these places, and how do you get there from here? You know, you "just FTP it from sumex!"

Here's another assumption. If you want to take the time to gather this software yourself, you'll need to know how to log in to your Internet computer and either FTP or Gopher the software from a large site like Stanford's Info-Mac archive—the famous **sumex-aim.stanford.edu**—or the University of Michigan's Macintosh FTP site, **mac.archive.umich.edu**.

 **{Note}**

Looking for "all the usual places?" Here's a brief list of the most popular Mac FTP sites:

> **ftp.apple.com**
>
> **ftpbio.bgsu.edu**
>
> **ftp.support.apple.com**
>
> **ftp.utexas.edu**
>
> **mac.archive.umich.edu**
>
> **sumex–aim.stanford.edu**

If you have an established PPP or SLIP connection, you should also be able to use FTP to get these files. Once you have the above software, you'll have everything you need.

When you do go about downloading the needed software, it might be a good idea to get Anarchie first. Since Anarchie will both find FTP sites and software, you can save yourself a lot of time by using it as opposed to another FTP client.

Begin by locating Anarchie and double-clicking to start the program. (*Note:* Anarchie is shareware and you should send the shareware fee to the author. You can do this by opening the registration form and filling it in.)

If your connection has been established, double-clicking on Anarchie will activate MacTCP and InterSLIP or MacPPP will dial your modem, connecting you to your host.

Anarchie opens a list of **bookmarks**, which are pointers to many of the more useful FTP sites in the world. Scroll down the list until you find Info-Mac and its **mirrors**. Select an Info-Mac mirror and double-click.

66 *Plain English, please!*

Mirrors are directories that contain information from another site. For instance, since everybody who wants to can't log onto sumex at the same time, other FTP sites put a mirror of sumex, with all of sumex's software on it, at their site so that more people can get to the information. 99

Getting helper software in one place

As this chapter is being written, there is an inane flame war going on UseNet regarding how shareware should be available in the marketplace.

It seems that a fellow on the Net came up with an idea. He created a couple of disks filled with the most popular Mac newsreaders, translators, viewers, and movie players and offered to sell these disks to "newbies" for his costs plus postage.

The response? Flames from Net guru wannabes blasting him for trying to make money off of something that was available for free. "You can get this stuff from all the usual places," began one flame, "Why should you make a profit!?"

Whatever you think of the idea, the disks are available. In fact, Apple-Dayton, Inc. (which is one of the oldest community user groups for Mac and Apple II users) offers this software on two high-density disks. If you're interested, send your name, address, and $10 to Apple-Dayton, Inc., P.O. Box 3240, Dayton, Ohio 45401-3240, and they'll send you their Internet Disks-of-the-Month.

(Tip)

> You might want to try an info-mac mirror in a different time zone, such as the Hawaii mirror. The more popular ones are often full during normal business hours. Many of the foreign mirrors are usually accessible but can be slow.

Anarchie next opens a window showing the Info-Mac "directories" as folders. To download newsreaders and any other communications software such as Fetch, double-click on the Communications folder. Next, double-click on the MacTCP folder.

You are now in the mirrors/info-mac/Communications/MacTCP directory (see fig. 8.1). When the new window opens showing a list of files, find the files you'd like to download and double-click them. This directory contains NewsWatcher (newswatcher-20b22.hqx), Nuntius (nuntius-12.hqx), InterNews (inter-news-105.hqx), Fetch (fetch-212.hqx), and many more communications packages. But you still need some of the helper programs we talked about earlier.

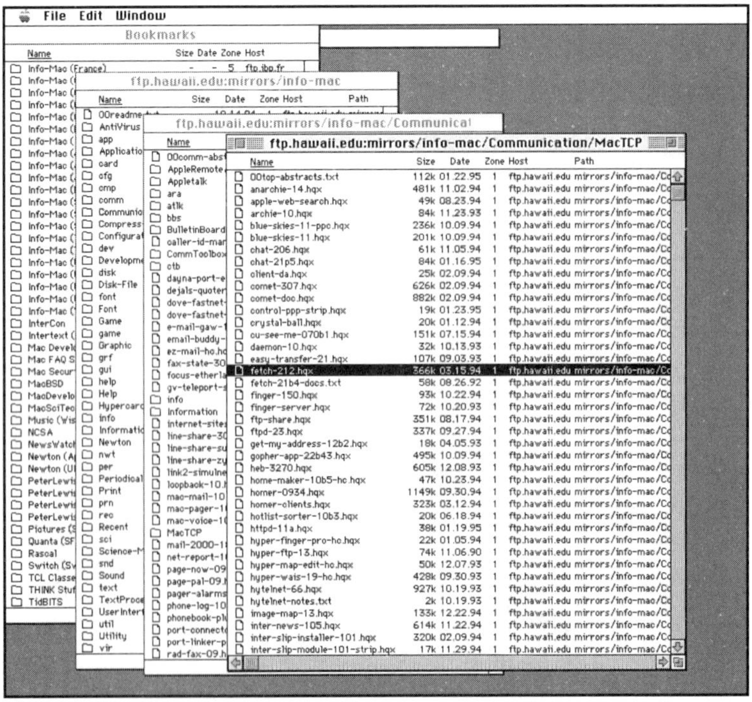

Fig. 8.1
With Anarchie, getting the software you need from all the usual places is as simple as double-clicking on the file you want.

To download graphics programs like JPEGView (jpeg-view-331.hqx), GifConverter (gif-converter-237.hqx), and Sparkle (sparkle-231.hqx), you'll need to get to the mirrors/info-mac/Graphic/Utility directory.

As mentioned before, you'll also need some applications to uncompress files on the Mac. Many of these applications, such as Stuffit Lite (stuffit-lite-35.hqx), Stuffit Expander (stuffit-expander-352.bin), and uuUndo (uu-undo-10.hqx) can be located and downloaded from the mirrors /info-mac/Compress-Translate directory.

(!) (Tip)

> If you have a copy of Stuffit Expander installed on your computer, Anarchie will use it to automatically debinhex (take the .hqx ending off) applications you choose to download.

Which newsreader is right for you?

The wonderful thing about using a Mac is that you have the ability to choose a work environment to suit your needs. The same holds true for MacTCP newsreaders. As I said before, a newsreader allows you to do three basic things: read news, post new articles or reply to articles, and download files. The difference between the three newsreaders reviewed in this section is in how they handle these basic tasks.

NewsWatcher, from John Norstad (the author of the popular anti-virus program Disinfectant), is far and away the best MacTCP newsreader available today. It's free, it's elegant, it has wonderful documentation, and as of this writing it is still described as "beta" with a To Do list of more features to come!

Chapters 16 through 19 are devoted to NewsWatcher. If you want to jump ahead, that's okay.

Nuntius 1.2

If you buy into the Mac macho concept that the best Macintosh programs are those you can use without reading the documentation, you'll love Nuntius. There is no documentation.

Nuntius is freeware, and is available at most mirrors, such as the one described in the last section.

Early versions of the program contained a readme file from Speck with the advice to subscribe to a Nuntius mailing list (NUNTIUS-L at **listserv@cornell.edu**), and a note (perhaps a plea) that if you want better documentation (or any documentation), you can help by writing some.

The latest version 1.2 takes a giant leap forward and offers a FAQ gathered by Aaron Freimark (**aaron@med.cornell.edu**), who administers the NUNTIUS-L list, and pointers to some documentation at **ftp.css.itd.umich.edu** in the directory /users/mikek, where you'll find a Word 5 document called new-nuntius.word5.hqx, and at **ftp.cit.cornell.edu** in directory /pub/mac/bear-access/docs/glued, where you'll find a glue document by Freimark.

Despite the lack of documentation, Nuntius is way cool. Once you get it set up, it's easy to use, pretty quick, and offers two features available in no other newsreader:

- When you post a message to a newsgroup, Nuntius will call your favorite word processor—Word, WordPerfect, MacWrite, Nisus, whatever—to create the message.

- When you reply to a post via e-mail, Nuntius will call Eudora—the most popular Mac e-mail program—to compose and send the e-mail.

Pretty slick, eh? Remember back in the setup portion of this chapter we suggested you needed System 7.5 or 7.x and 8 MB of RAM? One big reason is that you'll need the memory to have Nuntius and a word processor like WordPerfect or Word running.

Getting started with Nuntius

To get started, create a folder and name it Nuntius or something that suits your fancy. Drag the nuntius.sea icon into this folder and double-click. The self-extracting archive will open and you'll get four files: Nuntius, the FAQ, notes, and the latest bug list.

1 To start Nuntius, double-click on its icon.

2 You'll first be prompted for the name of your news server—you should have it committed to memory by now from setting up MacTCP and InterSLIP in the previous section. You can use either the IP numbers, i.e., 192.131.123.11 (see fig. 8.2), or the server name, i.e., **college.antioch.edu**. Since a name is easier to remember, you might want to enter the name.

Fig. 8.2
You'll need to know the name or address of your news server before Nuntius will start.

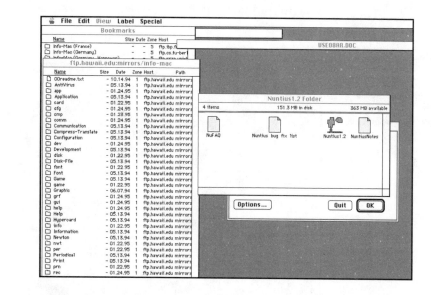

3 After entering your server address, click OK or press Return. Nuntius will connect with your host and begin to gather a list of all the newsgroups available. Be patient. At 9600-baud, it can take some time. The more newsgroups you have available, the longer it will take.

Nuntius now presents you with two windows: All Groups and Untitled. It also presents you with your first set of challenges.

The good news is that the All Groups list is sorted in alphabetical order into folders with the familiar click-down arrowhead. The bad news is that if you don't know that the Mac newsgroups are in the "comp" folder, which is in the "sys" folder, which is in the "mac" folder, you're going to spend a lot of time browsing through the newsgroup list. And if your host offers a large news feed, this time adds up to extra online costs. To save yourself some time and money, have your handy-dandy newsgroup list (see chapter 22, "Hot Newsgroups") available.

Once you find the group or groups you're interested in, simply select them and drag them from the All Groups window into the untitled window. You can drag individual groups or entire folders (see fig. 8.3). When you've made your first selections, go to the File menu and save the result as "your newsgroups" or something similar. The next time you run Nuntius, you'll want to start up from this file to reduce the time necessary to connect to the host.

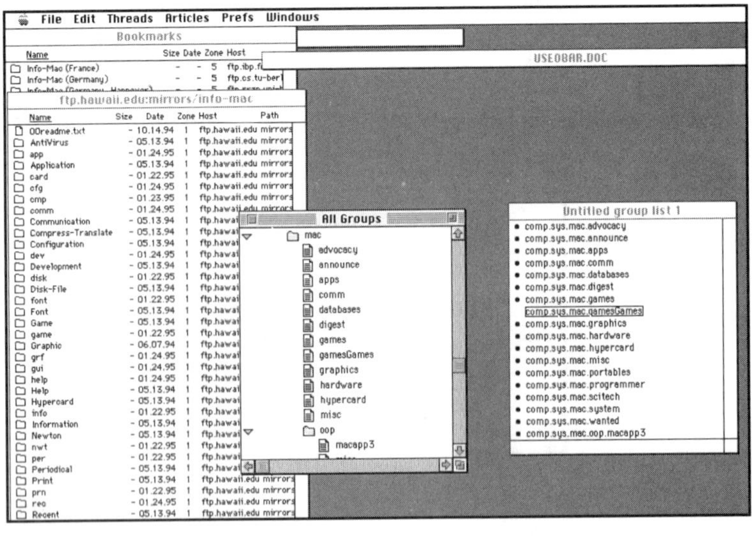

Fig. 8.3
You create your personal newsgroup list by selecting and dragging a group or a folder from the All Groups list to your group list.

Setting your preferences in Nuntius

At this point, you can read messages in your newsgroup selection, but you won't be able to post messages or e-mail replies until you configure your personal preferences. You do that by pulling down the Prefs menu and going through the various choices.

Setting the font style and size is a matter of personal preference. You'll also have to fill in your name and e-mail address and make a decision about how you're going to handle binaries.

The really cool part comes when you tell Nuntius how you want to edit articles (see fig. 8.4) or send mail (see fig. 8.5).

Fig. 8.4

A really cool feature of Nuntius is that you can select your favorite word processor to edit your posts.

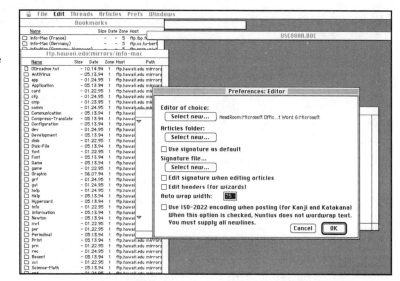

Nuntius allows you to pick your favorite word processor for editing articles. This means that you can use your spell checker, grammar checker, macros, or whatever when you create or follow up on a post. Frankly, this is Nuntius's best feature. A trap, however, is that you have to click and drag through an article to select it before you can activate the Transfer menu, but that's an inconvenience you quickly get used to. Another problem with this is the extra time it can take to switch applications to perform these functions.

Nuntius only supports Eudora as an e-mail program. But, again, the convenience of using a familiar mail tool—especially a full-featured one like Eudora—makes this worthwhile.

A final feature that makes Nuntius worth the hassle of learning it by trial and error is its ability to handle binaries. To download a binary, you simply select all its parts, press the command key (that's the one with the picture of the apple on it next to the space bar) and **e.** The binary file is downloaded to the folder you select on your hard drive.

Fig. 8.5
You can choose to send mail with Eudora, and even use Eudora's default settings, by configuring the Mailer settings under the Prefs menu.

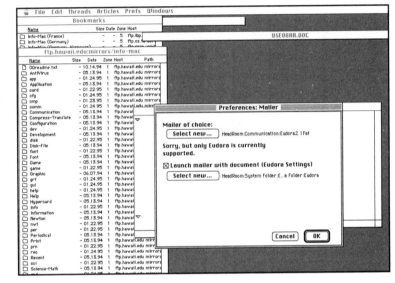

If you're going to use Nuntius, make sure that you take the time to download one of the documentation files and to subscribe to the mailing list, or do us all a favor and write some good documentation.

InterNews 1.0.5

InterNews, from Dartmouth College's Computer Services, gets a three-apple rating out of a possible four. It loses half a point for the way it handles binaries and another half point for its multi-paned window front-end.

InterNews comes with complete documentation, and is easy to set up and use. Its multi-window front-end is something you either love at first sight or simply hate.

InterNews is shareware and is free for educational and nonprofit users. For government and commercial enterprise, its prices range from $25 for a single user to $5,000 for an unlimited number of users. I'll let you figure it out, but I think that means for most of us it's free.

InterNews requires no installation. Simply locate the icon of the
InterNews.sea self-extracting icon, double-click on it, and the program
creates a folder with the program, a quick start, and a user's manual. If you
downloaded this using Anarchie with Stuffit Expander installed, the entire
folder should be ready to use.

The user's manual alone is worth the price of admission, and you should take
the time to print it out and read through it before you run the program.

To start InterNews, double-click its icon. You'll be presented with a dialog
box that asks you for the IP number (or name) of your news and mail hosts
(see fig. 8.6). The only trick in this setup dialog is that InterNews asks you
what type of authentication your host requires, and, if it's required, for
your login name and password. Authentication is often set up by system
administrators to ensure that only authorized users are allowed to
post or reply to messages. (This prevents you from posting a message
as kirk@enterprize.starfleet.fed.) If you're unsure about authentication,
ask your service provider.

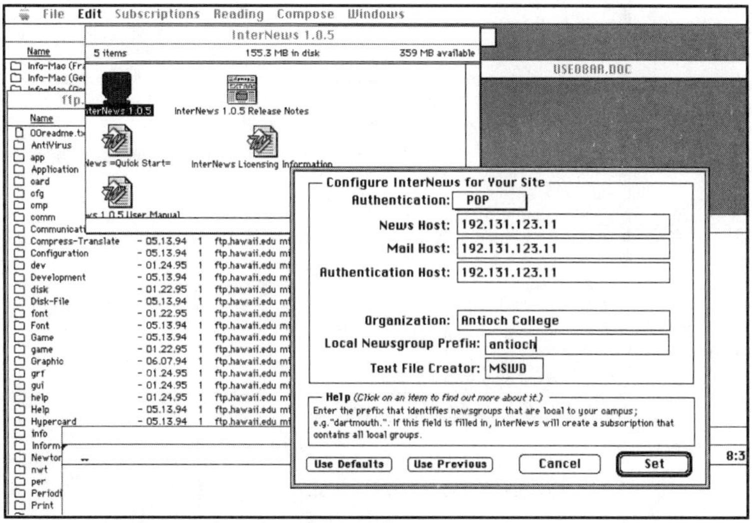

Fig. 8.6
The hardest part of
configuring InterNews
is determining whether
or not your host
requires authentica-
tion. If you're not
sure, ask your system
administrator.

InterNews now goes to your host and gathers a list of all newsgroups and any
local newsgroups. At this point you can double-click on either of these icons
to see a list of newsgroups offered by your host. Breaking the group list into

all groups and local groups is a great feature, and is especially helpful for users at educational sites who may only want to use a newsreader to check out items of local interest.

Creating your own "subscription" only seems obvious if, A) you read the manual, or B) you think in terms of subscribing to newsgroups from a command-line newsreader. Anyway, go to the Subscriptions menu, pull down to New Subscription, and you'll get an icon for an untitled group.

To build your own list, you must scroll through the entire list of all newsgroups and drag them one-at-a-time onto the untitled group icon (see fig. 8.7). You can find newsgroups using InterNews without having to scroll through all groups, however. Simply choose the Find option under the Reading menu. For instance, you could type **comp.** to get all the comp.* groups. When you're finished, save this file as "my newsgroups" or something familiar.

Fig. 8.7
Once you create a custom newsgroup list, you can speed up the process of contacting the server and gathering newsgroups by clicking on the icon for your group list. InterNews also creates an icon for local newsgroups, which is a time-saver for people who only want to read news of local interest.

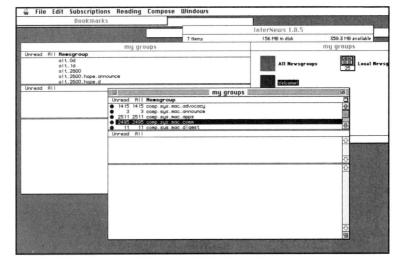

A nice feature of InterNews is its ability to call Fetch or Anarchie to transfer FTP files that are mentioned in news articles that you read (see fig. 8.8). The way it works is like this: When someone mentions an FTP site in a post, you click and drag over it to select it, pull down the Windows menu, select FTP Access, and a dialog box opens asking you for a file name or directory at the FTP site you've selected.

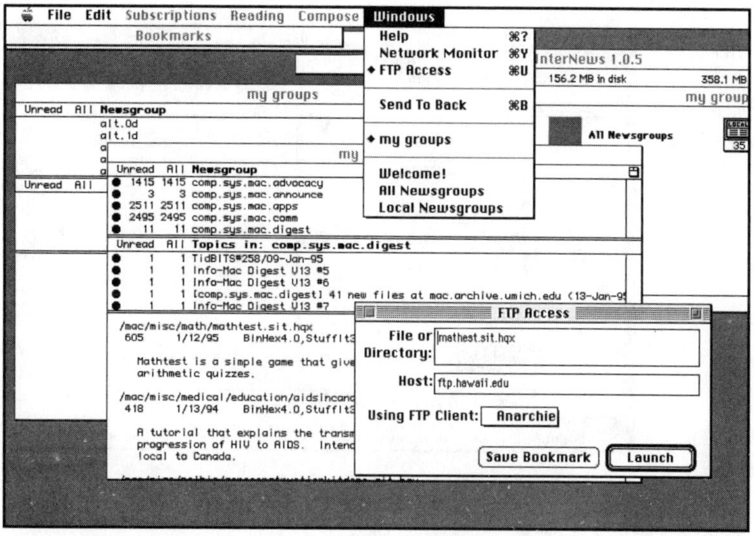

Fig. 8.8

InterNews lets you use Fetch or Anarchie, or any other Mac FTP client, to retrieve files mentioned in posts.

Click Launch and InterNews sends Fetch or Anarchie to get the file you requested.

This works most of the time, and the times it doesn't work are usually the fault of the original poster, not your FTP client. You see, most people just make off-hand references to "all the usual places." For example, someone might respond to a question by saying "The file's at sumex." We know that means **sumex-aim.stanford.edu**. So, compose a mail reply or follow-up article and edit the reference to provide the correct URL, **ftp://sumex-aim.stanford.edu/**. Now select it and Fetch will know exactly where to go.

Downloading binary files in InterNews is a bit klunky, but you can do it. You select the first message in a thread and save it, and then you append the other messages to that file. The end result is a binary file that you can decode with Stuffit. InterNews' Help file contains detailed information on how to download binaries.

My personal favorite InterNews feature is the warning you get before you post a message to news (see fig. 8.9). Everyone should read it and take it to heart before posting to news.

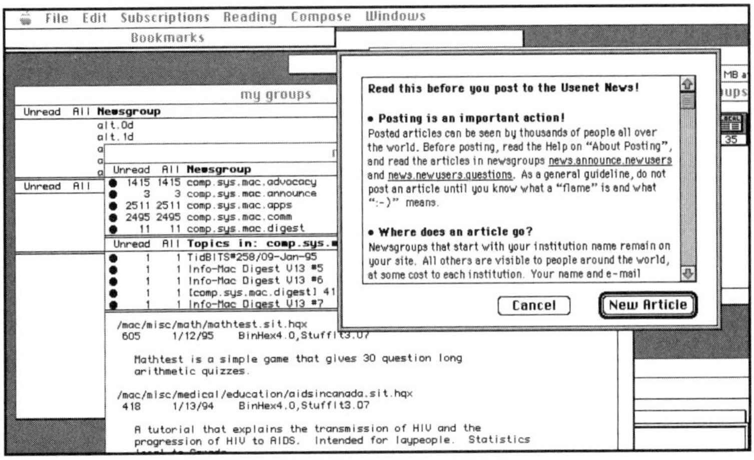

Fig. 8.9
Every Internet user should read and take heed of the advice in InterNews's Before You Post dialog box.

The News 2.36

The News, authored by Bill Cramer, is a shareware program. This means that you may try it for 30 days, but if you decide to use it, you must send Cramer $25.

All in all, The News is not a bad program. It comes with good documentation, is pretty easy to use, and runs quickly over a modem connection.

The News comes as a Stuffit .sit archive, so you have to go through a bit of extra effort to uncompress it. Once you get all the pieces into a folder, you'll find the program, the user's manual, and a quick start.

You should print out the manual before you get started. Although the manual is saved in Word 5, you should be able to translate it into another word processor if you're not using Word.

To start the program, double-click on its icon (again no installation is required). The News opens and presents you with a blank screen. This is a bit unnerving (unless you've read the manual). So the first step is to pull down the File menu and select Preferences. This brings up a dialog box where you fill in your personal information, provide the address of your news "NNTP" host, and your mail "SMTP" host. You can start by leaving the upper boxes checked, and unless your host requires authentication, you don't need to provide your user name or password.

Now it's back to the File menu (sigh). Select New, and The News will contact your host and gather a list of all the available newsgroups. But, the window you see on your screen is blank. So, go up to the Groups Menu, select Edit Group List, and finally (hooray) you're presented with a list of the available groups.

To create your own group list, you scroll through the list, select a group you like, and click on the Subscribe button.

The author suggests you may want to only subscribe to a few groups at first—not a bad idea since you've been racking up online charges throughout this tedious process. Mercifully, you can Shift+click on a number of groups to add them to your personal group list all at once.

Once you've built your personal list, click on the Done button, and go back to the File menu and select Save As to name your group list.

A nice feature of The News is that if you pull down the Articles menu and drag down to Sort, you can sort articles in a group by subject, date, or author. This is a help in prioritizing posts in a large group by date, or putting threads together by subject, or searching for (or ignoring) an author.

To read a news item, simply select it and double-click. The News opens a double-tiered window with the header at the top and the body of the message at the bottom. This actually is pretty slick if you want to copy and paste when you quote in a reply. And it makes quick work of scrolling through long headers in posts.

The News makes getting involved pretty easy. The Articles menu allows you to post a new message or reply via e-mail. And the keyboard commands, while not mnemonic, aren't hard to learn.

Posting a follow-up or sending an e-mail reply opens a pretty standard screen.

To download a binary file, you select the first part, go to the File menu and select Save, and then Append the other parts to the original file. You then must use Stuffit to de-hqx the file before you can view or run it.

Is The News for you? That's your choice. A side benefit, and an aside really, is that The News is the best UUCP newsreader available. If you've somehow gotten this far, and just discovered that you have a UUCP news connection rather than a TCP connection, consider using The News as your front end. But, that's the subject for a different book.

Commercial programs

The two main commercial programs on the market as this book was being written are VersaTerm from Synergy Software and TCP/ConnectII from InterCon Systems.

These programs take an integrated "works" approach to accessing the Internet, and as in any works-type program, the sum of the parts is greater than the value of any single feature.

The advantage of either of these programs is in their integration, where the cost of installing and supporting a single program is less than the hassle of gathering, updating, and training users in multiple applications.

At around $150 for the VersaTilities package and from $200 to $500 for TCP/ConnectII, you, as a stand-alone user, will have to weigh the cost versus the potential benefit of using a single program for your e-mail, news, and other Internet activities.

Contact:

Synergy Software
(215) 779-0522
Tipmaxwell@sales.synergy.com

InterCon Systems
950 Herndon Pkwy
Herndon VA 22070
(703) 709-5500

(At this writing, you can download an evaluation copy of TCP/ConnectII from Intercon. Use Anarchie and open their folder and look in the sales folder. To activate the software, you have to call InterCon's sales office and get an authorization number.)

Text-Based Newsreaders

Even if you can use a Windows- or Mac-based GUI newsreader, you may choose a text-based newsreader for some of the powerful features available in no other readers.

The very first newsreaders were text-based; the millions of people who access UseNet through a UNIX system still use these systems. Even if you can use a Windows- or Mac-based GUI newsreader, you may choose a text-based newsreader for some of the powerful features available in no other readers. Ask your service provider if one of these programs is available on your system.

❋{Note}   The text-based newsreaders discussed in this chapter do not run on your computer, but on your service provider's computer.

What is a text-based newsreader?

Simply put, a text-based newsreader is not a GUI newsreader. The output on the screen is made of characters rather than graphics. The user interacts with the program using only the keyboard, and never the mouse. The program regularly prompts for input (after reading each news article it might prompt what next?). Also, the user can only do one thing at a time.

Q&A

> **Why should I care about old-fashioned newsreaders when I use a much better one?**
>
> Even if you have access to the most recent and exciting newsreader, with a totally intuitive interface and every powerful feature you could ever want, you should still know a little about text-based readers because so many Netters are using these readers to compose the articles you read, and to read the articles you post. Don't assume everyone has the features you have in your software. One simple example: Your software may automatically wrap long lines, but many newsreaders don't, so if your postings include lines over 80 characters, other Netters will find them difficult or impossible to read.

This chapter describes three popular text-based newsreaders: trn, tin, and nn. They have many similarities, but are not identical.

Can you choose your newsreader?

On many systems there is only one newsreader available. If your access is free from your employer or university, you are unlikely to have a choice. The sysadmin will not have the time and energy to support multiple programs, and will simply choose one and stick with it.

(Tip)

> If you pay for your access through a commercial provider, you may be able to choose from a variety of text-based newsreaders. If you can't find a specific one, ask your support contact if it can be installed on the system.

All three newsreaders discussed in this chapter use a hidden file called .newsrc to keep track of what groups you are interested in and what articles you have read. If your site has more than one of these newsreaders, you can switch among them for a while until you know which one you prefer, and your information will be available to all of them.

trn

trn is a threaded newsreader. Threading shows you articles in a more logical order than the order they arrived at your site. The References: header is used to determine which articles are follow-ups to previous articles, and to arrange the articles into threads. You are shown a tree diagram of the threads in each group, so that you know when you are reading an article if there are any follow-ups to it, which is important if you plan to follow-up to it yourself.

You start the newsreader by typing **trn** at the UNIX prompt. As shown in figure 9.1, trn first displays the number of unread articles in each of the first five groups. Then it asks if you want to read the first group. If you answer no, it asks if you want to read the second group, and so on.

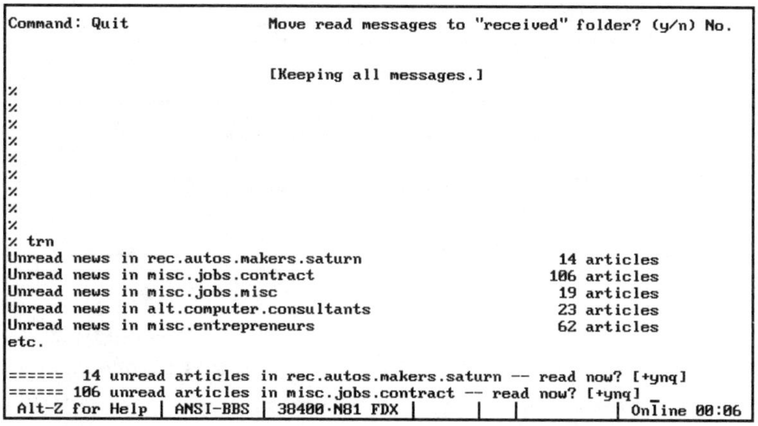

Fig. 9.1
When trn starts up, it lists the first few groups with unread articles and asks if each group should be read.

```
Command: Quit                  Move read messages to "received" folder? (y/n) No.

                           [Keeping all messages.]
%
%
%
%
%
%
%
%
% trn
Unread news in rec.autos.makers.saturn                14 articles
Unread news in misc.jobs.contract                    106 articles
Unread news in misc.jobs.misc                         19 articles
Unread news in alt.computer.consultants               23 articles
Unread news in misc.entrepreneurs                     62 articles
etc.

======  14 unread articles in rec.autos.makers.saturn -- read now? [+ynq]
====== 106 unread articles in misc.jobs.contract -- read now? [+ynq] _
 Alt-Z for Help | ANSI-BBS | 38400-N81 FDX |        |      |      | Online 00:06
```

Pressing the space bar at any prompt in trn activates the default action, which is always listed first in the square brackets following the prompt. Pressing space or + in response to the read now? prompt leads to a thread selection view for the group **misc.jobs.contract** (see fig. 9.2).

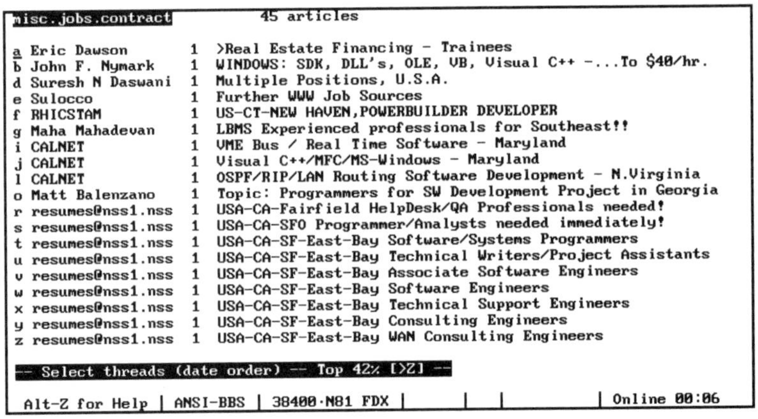

Fig. 9.2

The thread selection level in trn shows article posters and subjects, and allows you to choose which to read. The number between poster and subject is the number of articles in this thread.

```
misc.jobs.contract            45 articles
a Eric Dawson          1  >Real Estate Financing - Trainees
b John F. Nymark       1  WINDOWS: SDK, DLL's, OLE, VB, Visual C++ -...To $40/hr.
d Suresh N Daswani     1  Multiple Positions, U.S.A.
e Sulocco             1  Further WWW Job Sources
f RHICSTAM             1  US-CT-NEW HAVEN,POWERBUILDER DEVELOPER
g Maha Mahadevan       1  LBMS Experienced professionals for Southeast!!
i CALNET              1  VME Bus / Real Time Software - Maryland
j CALNET              1  Visual C++/MFC/MS-Windows - Maryland
l CALNET              1  OSPF/RIP/LAN Routing Software Development - N.Virginia
o Matt Balenzano       1  Topic: Programmers for SW Development Project in Georgia
r resumes@nss1.nss     1  USA-CA-Fairfield HelpDesk/QA Professionals needed!
s resumes@nss1.nss     1  USA-CA-SFO Programmer/Analysts needed immediately!
t resumes@nss1.nss     1  USA-CA-SF-East-Bay Software/Systems Programmers
u resumes@nss1.nss     1  USA-CA-SF-East-Bay Technical Writers/Project Assistants
v resumes@nss1.nss     1  USA-CA-SF-East-Bay Associate Software Engineers
w resumes@nss1.nss     1  USA-CA-SF-East-Bay Software Engineers
x resumes@nss1.nss     1  USA-CA-SF-East-Bay Technical Support Engineers
y resumes@nss1.nss     1  USA-CA-SF-East-Bay Consulting Engineers
z resumes@nss1.nss     1  USA-CA-SF-East-Bay WAN Consulting Engineers

-- Select threads (date order) -- Top 42% [>Z] --

Alt-Z for Help | ANSI-BBS | 38400-N81 FDX |         |    |         | Online 00:06
```

To select threads in this view, type the letter at the far left of each line and then press the space bar; this shows you another page of articles. After you have seen all the possible threads, press the space bar to display the articles. Figure 9.3 shows an article from **misc.jobs.contract**, as displayed in trn.

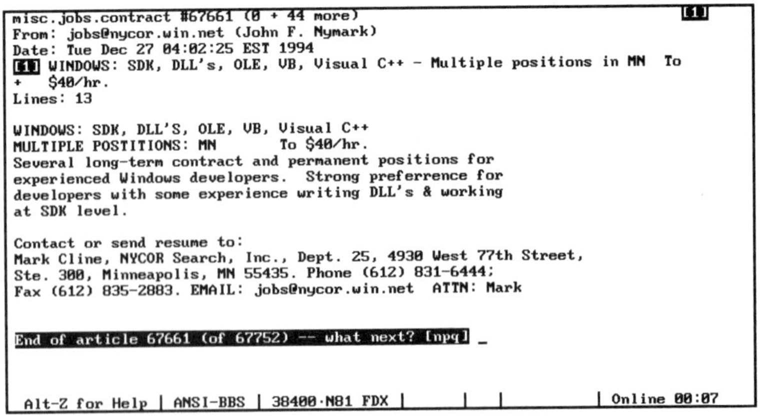

Fig. 9.3

This article from **misc.jobs.contract** includes only a tiny thread tree, shown here as [1]. Note the "what next?" prompt at the end of the article.

```
misc.jobs.contract #67661 (0 + 44 more)                              [1]
From: jobs@nycor.win.net (John F. Nymark)
Date: Tue Dec 27 04:02:25 EST 1994
[1] WINDOWS: SDK, DLL's, OLE, VB, Visual C++ - Multiple positions in MN  To
+  $40/hr.
Lines: 13

WINDOWS: SDK, DLL'S, OLE, VB, Visual C++
MULTIPLE POSITIONS: MN        To $40/hr.
Several long-term contract and permanent positions for
experienced Windows developers.  Strong preferrence for
developers with some experience writing DLL's & working
at SDK level.

Contact or send resume to:
Mark Cline, NYCOR Search, Inc., Dept. 25, 4930 West 77th Street,
Ste. 300, Minneapolis, MN 55435. Phone (612) 831-6444;
Fax (612) 835-2803. EMAIL: jobs@nycor.win.net  ATTN: Mark

End of article 67661 (of 67752) -- what next? [npq] _

Alt-Z for Help | ANSI-BBS | 38400-N81 FDX |         |    |         | Online 00:07
```

At the end of an article, trn prompts you again for your next action: n to show the next article, q to quit this group, and so on. To send an e-mail reply to the author, press r (or R if you want the posting copied into your reply). To post a follow-up article, press f (or F if you want the original posting included in your follow-up).

In the top-right corner, trn displays a thread tree. It's very simple for **misc.jobs.contract**, but as figure 9.4 shows, threads can be quite complex.

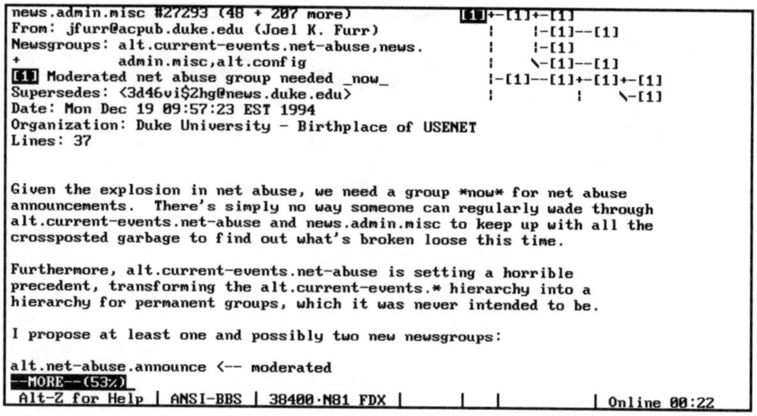

Fig. 9.4

This article from **news.admin.misc** has generated a substantial thread. Trn illustrates the pattern of follow-ups in the upper-right corner.

```
news.admin.misc #27293 (48 + 207 more)          [1]+-[1]+-[1]
From: jfurr@acpub.duke.edu (Joel K. Furr)        !  !-[1]--[1]
Newsgroups: alt.current-events.net-abuse,news.   !  !-[1]
+           admin.misc,alt.config                !  \-[1]--[1]
[1] Moderated net abuse group needed _now_       !-[1]--[1]+-[1]+-[1]
Supersedes: <3d46vi$Zhg@news.duke.edu>           !         !  \-[1]
Date: Mon Dec 19 09:57:23 EST 1994
Organization: Duke University - Birthplace of USENET
Lines: 37


Given the explosion in net abuse, we need a group *now* for net abuse
announcements.  There's simply no way someone can regularly wade through
alt.current-events.net-abuse and news.admin.misc to keep up with all the
crossposted garbage to find out what's broken loose this time.

Furthermore, alt.current-events.net-abuse is setting a horrible
precedent, transforming the alt.current-events.* hierarchy into a
hierarchy for permanent groups, which it was never intended to be.

I propose at least one and possibly two new newsgroups:

alt.net-abuse.announce <-- moderated
--MORE--(53%)
 Alt-Z for Help | ANSI-BBS | 38400·N81 FDX |      |     |      | Online 00:22
```

When reading a thread, you have a number of movement keys available to you as well as n. If you want to recheck a previous article, the [key moves you one article to the left in the tree. The] key moves you one article to the right. Pressing) moves you to the next sibling of this article, i.e., down one in the tree, which is useful if you're interested in the topic of the thread, but not in follow-ups to this particular article. If the whole thread, turns out to be uninteresting, press > to move to the next thread.

⓵ (Tip)

For more information on trn, type **man trn** at your UNIX prompt for the on-screen manual, or just start using it. At any prompt you can answer **h**, and you'll get a mini help listing.

tin

You start the newsreader by typing **tin** at the UNIX prompt. You are then presented with a list of newsgroups and the number of unread articles in each (see fig. 9.5). In addition, tin displays a short description of the newsgroup.

Fig. 9.5

When tin starts up, it lists all the groups with unread articles; select which groups to read. A three line summary of commands appears at the bottom of each screen.

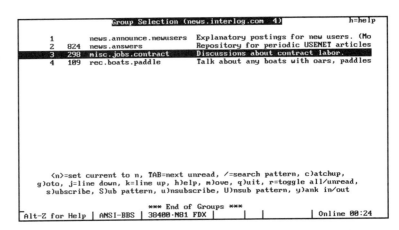

```
                    Group Selection (news.interlog.com  4)              h=help

      1              news.announce.newusers   Explanatory postings for new users. (Mo
      2    824       news.answers             Repository for periodic USENET articles
      3    298       misc.jobs.contract       Discussions about contract labor.
      4    109       rec.boats.paddle         Talk about any boats with oars, paddles









        <n>=set current to n, TAB=next unread, /=search pattern, c)atchup,
        g)oto, j=line down, k=line up, h)elp, m)ove, q)uit, r=toggle all/unread,
        s)ubscribe, S)ub pattern, u)nsubscribe, U)nsub pattern, y)ank in/out

                           *** End of Groups ***
  Alt-Z for Help | ANSI-BBS | 38400·N81 FDX |        |        |      | Online 00:24
```

Move the highlight to the group you want to read and press enter. This takes you to the group level where you can select articles or threads to read (see fig. 9.6).

Fig. 9.6

The group level in tin displays the article subject and poster and allows you to select articles or threads to read.

```
                    misc.jobs.contract (286T 296A 0K 0H R)              h=help

      209   +     US-CA-San Fran-PA-TCP/IP, UNIX BASICS        deltam@dice.com
      210   +     US-CA-San Fran-MGR-E-MAIL, LAN               deltam@dice.com
      211   +     SYBASE w/ DBA; SQR; Powerbuilder (3 open); Bo ASTON Consultant S
      212   +     Software Engineers/Network Management/Trouble Marty Lebowitz
      213   +     Sybase DBA in NY and NJ Syb 10 a plus <recrui Steven Todd Harris
      214   +     PowerBuilder with Business Object NJ <recruit Steven Todd Harris
      215   +     US-DC-Washington (metro area) NMS (Spectrum,  COMPTEL Inc.
      216   +     ne.jobs.contract                             James F. Hoell
      217   +     Real Estate Financing - Trainees             Eric Dawson
      218   +     Senior Network & Systems Administrators (Mult brianc@ddi.digital
      219   +     USA-CA-SF-East-Bay WAN Senior Systems Enginee brianc@ddi.digital
      220   +     USA-Virginia Network Engineers and Support ne brianc@ddi.digital
      221         WINDOWS: SDK, DLL's, OLE, VB, Visual C++ - Mu John F. Nymark
      222   +     Multiple Year Positions: INTERNET, WEB, GOPHE John F. Nymark
      223   +     US-CT-NEW HAVEN,POWERBUILDER DEVELOPER        RHICSTAM
      224   +     Topic: Programmers for SW Development Project Matt Balenzano

        <n>=set current to n, TAB=next unread, /=search pattern, ^K)ill/select,
        a)uthor search, c)atchup, j=line down, k=line up, K=mark read, l)ist thread,
        !=pipe, m)ail, o=print, q)uit, r=toggle all/unread, s)ave, t)ag, w=post

  Alt-Z for Help | ANSI-BBS | 38400·N81 FDX |        |        |      | Online 00:28
```

Move the highlight to the article you wish to read and press enter. This takes you to the article level (see fig. 9.7).

Tin does not display a thread tree, but indicates the number of responses to an article in the upper-right corner, along with a position indicator like "Thread 30 of 50." Figure 9.8 shows the same article in tin as figure 9.4 showed in trn. Even with the three lines of command reminders, tin actually shows one more line of the article on the first page than trn did.

Fig. 9.7

The article display in tin shows headers more compactly than trn. Note in the upper-right corner there are no responses to this article.

```
Tue, 27 Dec 1994 04:02:25      misc.jobs.contract        Thread  221 of  286
Lines 13       WINDOWS: SDK, DLL's, OLE, VB, Visual C++ - Mu No responses
jobs@nycor.win.net                                           John F. Nymark

WINDOWS: SDK, DLL'S, OLE, VB, Visual C++
MULTIPLE POSITIONS: MN        To $40/hr.
Several long-term contract and permanent positions for
experienced Windows developers.  Strong preferrence for
developers with some experience writing DLL's & working
at SDK level.

Contact or send resume to:
Mark Cline, NYCOR Search, Inc., Dept. 25, 4930 West 77th Street,
Ste. 300, Minneapolis, MN 55435. Phone (612) 831-6444;
Fax (612) 835-2883. EMAIL: jobs@nycor.win.net  ATTN: Mark




     <n>=set current to n, TAB=next unread, /=search pattern, ^K)ill/select,
          a)uthor search, B)ody search, c)atchup, f)ollowup, K=mark read,
          |=pipe, m)ail, o=print, q)uit, r)eply mail, s)ave, t)ag, w=post

                                                       -- Last response --
Alt-Z for Help | ANSI-BBS | 38400·N81 FDX |    |   |      Online 00:28
```

Fig. 9.8

This article in **news.admin.misc** has 41 responses. Notice how the Organization: header has been melded into the poster's name.

```
Mon, 19 Dec 1994 09:57:23       news.admin.misc         Thread  130 of  190
Lines 37       Moderated net abuse group needed _now      41 Responses
jfurr@acpub.duke.edu      Joel K. Furr at Duke University - Birthplace of USENET

Given the explosion in net abuse, we need a group *now* for net abuse
announcements.  There's simply no way someone can regularly wade through
alt.current-events.net-abuse and news.admin.misc to keep up with all the
crossposted garbage to find out what's broken loose lately.

Furthermore, alt.current-events.net-abuse is setting a horrible
precedent, transforming the alt.current-events.* hierarchy into a
hierarchy for permanent groups, which it was never intended to be.

I propose at least one and possibly two new newsgroups:

alt.net-abuse.announce <-- moderated
alt.net-abuse.discuss

     <n>=set current to n, TAB=next unread, /=search pattern, ^K)ill/select,
          a)uthor search, B)ody search, c)atchup, f)ollowup, K=mark read,
          |=pipe, m)ail, o=print, q)uit, r)eply mail, s)ave, t)ag, w=post

                                                   --More--(54%) [1191/2197]
Alt-Z for Help | ANSI-BBS | 38400·N81 FDX |    |   |      Online 00:30
```

To send an e-mail reply to the author, press R (or r if you want the posting copied into your reply). To post a follow-up article, press F (or f if you want the original posting included in your follow-up).

(Tip)

For more information on tin, type **man tin** at your UNIX prompt for the on-screen manual, or just start using it. At any prompt you can answer **h** and you'll get a mini help listing.

nn

In general, nn does not have a group selection level, though occasionally it will prompt you before entering a group. Usually you start nn (by typing **nn** at the UNIX prompt) and immediately are at the selection level in your first group (see fig. 9.9).

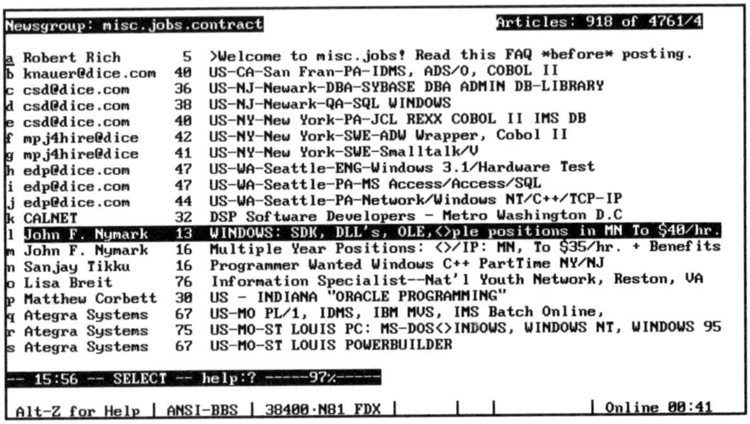

Fig. 9.9

When nn starts, you are in the selection level and can choose which articles you would like to read. The number between the poster and subject is the number of lines in the posting.

```
Newsgroup: misc.jobs.contract                         Articles: 918 of 4761/4
a Robert Rich         5  >Welcome to misc.jobs! Read this FAQ *before* posting.
b knauer@dice.com    40  US-CA-San Fran-PA-IDMS, ADS/O, COBOL II
c csd@dice.com       36  US-NJ-Newark-DBA-SYBASE DBA ADMIN DB-LIBRARY
d csd@dice.com       38  US-NJ-Newark-QA-SQL WINDOWS
e csd@dice.com       40  US-NY-New York-PA-JCL REXX COBOL II IMS DB
f mpj4hire@dice      42  US-NY-New York-SWE-ADW Wrapper, Cobol II
g mpj4hire@dice      41  US-NY-New York-SWE-Smalltalk/V
h edp@dice.com       47  US-WA-Seattle-ENG-Windows 3.1/Hardware Test
i edp@dice.com       47  US-WA-Seattle-PA-MS Access/Access/SQL
j edp@dice.com       44  US-WA-Seattle-PA-Network/Windows NT/C++/TCP-IP
k CALNET             32  DSP Software Developers - Metro Washington D.C
l John F. Nymark     13  WINDOWS: SDK, DLL's, OLE,<>ple positions in MN To $40/hr.
m John F. Nymark     16  Multiple Year Positions: <>/IP: MN, To $35/hr. + Benefits
n Sanjay Tikku       16  Programmer Wanted Windows C++ PartTime NY/NJ
o Lisa Breit         76  Information Specialist--Nat'l Youth Network, Reston, VA
p Matthew Corbett    30  US - INDIANA "ORACLE PROGRAMMING"
q Ategra Systems     67  US-MO PL/1, IDMS, IBM MVS, IMS Batch Online,
r Ategra Systems     75  US-MO-ST LOUIS PC: MS-DOS<>INDOWS, WINDOWS NT, WINDOWS 95
s Ategra Systems     67  US-MO-ST LOUIS POWERBUILDER

-- 15:56 -- SELECT -- help:? -----97%------
Alt-Z for Help | ANSI-BBS | 38400·N81 FDX |       |      |        | Online 00:41
```

To select articles in this view, type the letter at the far left of each line, and press the space bar to see another page of articles. After you have had a chance to select all the possible articles, press the space bar to display the selected articles. Figure 9.10 shows the job ad from **misc.jobs.contract** as displayed in nn.

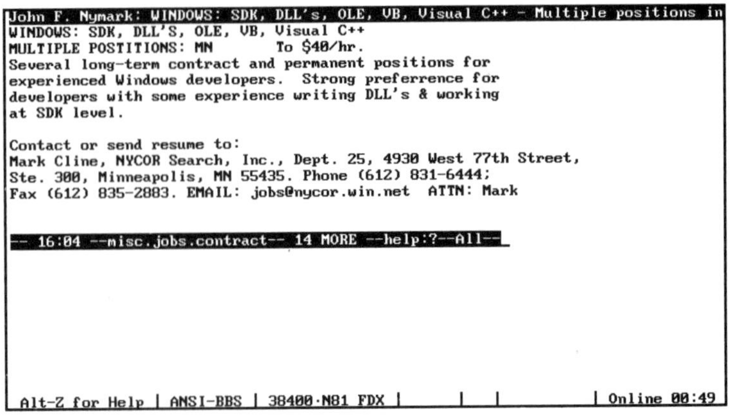

Fig. 9.10

The article display in nn shows less header information than tin or trn; and does not include any indication of follow-ups.

```
John F. Nymark: WINDOWS: SDK, DLL's, OLE, VB, Visual C++ - Multiple positions in
WINDOWS: SDK, DLL'S, OLE, VB, Visual C++
MULTIPLE POSITITIONS: MN        To $40/hr.
Several long-term contract and permanent positions for
experienced Windows developers.  Strong prefferrence for
developers with some experience writing DLL's & working
at SDK level.

Contact or send resume to:
Mark Cline, NYCOR Search, Inc., Dept. 25, 4930 West 77th Street,
Ste. 300, Minneapolis, MN 55435. Phone (612) 831-6444;
Fax (612) 835-2883. EMAIL: jobs@nycor.win.net  ATTN: Mark

-- 16:04 --misc.jobs.contract-- 14 MORE --help:?--All--




Alt-Z for Help | ANSI-BBS | 38400·N81 FDX |       |      |        | Online 00:49
```

When an article is longer than the few lines of our sample job posting, nn's lack of headers enables you to see more of the article on a single page. Figure 9.11 shows the **news.admin.misc** article as displayed in nn. Almost twice as much of the article body appears on the first page as appeared in trn and tin.

Fig. 9.11

The article displayed in nn shows more of the article body than trn or tin, but there is no indication of the many follow-ups it has generated.

```
Joel K. Furr: Moderated net abuse group needed  now          19 Dec 1994 09:57
Given the explosion in net abuse, we need a group *now* for net abuse
announcements.  There's simply no way someone can regularly wade through
alt.current-events.net-abuse and news.admin.misc to keep up with all the
crossposted garbage to find out what's broken loose this time.

Furthermore, alt.current-events.net-abuse is setting a horrible
precedent, transforming the alt.current-events.* hierarchy into a
hierarchy for permanent groups, which it was never intended to be.

I propose at least one and possibly two new newsgroups:

alt.net-abuse.announce <-- moderated
alt.net-abuse.discuss

Certain people, like Cancelmoose, would be authorized to approve their
own articles for alt.net-abuse.announce (if in fact anon.penet.fi can add
an Approved: header), but otherwise, we'd need a moderator or moderation
team.  (For fastest response, ideally we'd want everyone to just approve
their own stuff, but I don't like the alt.hackers school of thought which
tells everyone how to defeat the moderator.)

-- 16:06 --news.admin.misc-- LAST+next --help:?--Top 63%--

Alt-Z for Help | ANSI-BBS | 38400-N81 FDX |       |    |         | Online 00:50
```

To send an e-mail reply to the author, press r (nn will ask if you want the posting copied into your reply). To post a follow-up article, press f (again, nn will ask if you want the original posting included in your follow-up).

When you leave a group in nn without selecting and reading some of the articles in the group, they are marked as read. This behavior is what sets nn apart from other newsreaders. It is designed around the assumption that you only want to read a few articles from the massive flow of data that is UseNet, and it makes that winnowing as easy as possible.

⊘ (Tip)

For more information on nn, type **man nn** at your UNIX prompt for the on-screen manual, or just start using it. At any prompt you can answer **?**, and you'll get a mini help listing.

Kill files

One thing almost all the text-based readers have in common is the kill file. Originally this was used to *kill* articles that met certain criteria. This is still one of the major uses of kill files today; most readers have commands to automatically add entries to the kill file to mark articles as read.

> 66 ***Plain English, please!***
>
> **Killing** an article means marking it as read and not showing it to the user. Killing a person, in this context, means killing all articles from that person. More than one new Netter has been upset by suggestions to "just kill him and get on with your life"—it's not a death threat! 99

Typically, the criteria for killing an article would be a specific author or a specific string in the Subject: header. For example, if Joe User has been posting a lot of nasty or off-topic articles to a group you read, you might add a line to your kill file to mark all of Joe's articles as read without showing them to you. If it bothers you to read articles that quote Joe's articles, you can arrange for those to be thrown away too. Or, imagine that a group you read discusses a topic you find boring. For example, if you read **misc.kids**, you might not want to read any articles about diapers, and you can arrange to junk any article with "diapers" in the Subject: header. In trn, press Ctrl+k to edit the kill file while reading misc.kids, and add the line /diapers/j to the file. In tin and nn you are led through a series of questions that will construct the lines for you automatically. Press Ctrl+k in tin and K in nn to begin the dialog.

But kill files, at least in some newsreaders, can do far more than throw away articles. In fact, some readers call them *filters* or *memorized commands* because of the many things they can do in addition to killing articles. Based on simple criteria (who the article is from, the Subject: or a string in a header) the article can be selected for viewing, saved to a file, printed, or (for advanced users) piped through a UNIX program—all automatically.

⊗<Caution> Sometimes, if you complain about posts on a specific topic you think is inappropriate, or a user whose posts are unwelcome, you may be tersely instructed to use a kill file. If you respond "my newsreader doesn't do that," the retort may be "then buy yourself access somewhere that will let you use a decent newsreader!" It is, in general, not bad advice. You can't expect the whole Net to change because your newsreader is missing a feature.

Subject header conventions

Because of the extensive use of kill files on the net, many newsgroups have Subject: header conventions that make kill files easy to write. For example in **rec.arts.tv.soaps.abc**, each of the major ABC afternoon soap operas is assigned an abbreviation (for example, AMC for *All My Children*, and OLTL for *One Life To Live*) and posts about that soap should have a Subject: header starting with the abbreviation (for example, Subject: AMC: Erica marries again!).

Netters who want to read posts about *All My Children* set up their kill file to select articles with AMC in the Subject: header; while those who don't want to read about AMC set their kill files to throw away the articles. The subject convention started on **rec.arts.tv.soaps**, which has since been split into **rec.arts.tv.soaps.abc**, **rec.arts.tv.soaps.cbs**, and **rec.arts.tv.soaps.misc**, and has spread throughout the net.

Groups that use Subject: header conventions explain the convention and provide a list of abbreviations in their FAQ. Often a team of volunteers sends explanatory e-mail to people who post without an abbreviation in the Subject: header.

10

Other Windows and Mac News Options

If you don't have direct access to UseNet, newsgroups can often be accessed through other Internet services.

In this chapter:

- How do I get to UseNet newsgroups with other Internet tools?

- I need to access newsgroups, but I don't have access to a newsfeed or a service provider

- How to get newsgroups by CD-ROM and e-mail

Y ou want to get access to UseNet newsgroups but you don't have access to a news server? There are other alternatives, although most are somewhat limited in their access to all newsgroups. This chapter looks at how you can access newsgroups through other Internet services, such as Gopher and FTP, as well as services like Mosaic.

Newsgroups, or at least some newsgroup articles, can often be accessed through other Internet services. There are usually restrictions as to the amount of news or the scope of the newsgroups accessible through these services. Also, timeliness is not always a strong point of these services, as it may take the administrators a while to post newsgroup summaries and FAQs.

Mosaic

Mosaic is a browser developed for accessing the World Wide Web. The Mosaic software is available free of charge for practically any computer system, although most versions require a SLIP, PPP, or direct connection to the Internet to provide services. Mosaic was developed by the National Center for Supercomputing Applications (NCSA), which provides anonymous FTP access to the latest versions. Several commercial enhancements of Mosaic, such as Netscape, have been introduced as well.

World Wide Web service providers can offer newsgroup access either as a subsidiary service or in direct relation to their businesses. For example, a word processing software vendor may have a World Wide Web home page that provides access to the UseNet word processing newsgroups through a menu option. Several systems provide generic home pages that also offer newsgroup services with no limits for users who can access the system.

More common, though, is using Mosaic to directly access the UseNet newsgroups. While using Mosaic to read news is a case of considerable overkill, it can be useful when other newsreaders or access methods do not function properly. Mosaic also tends to nicely format articles on the screen, albeit at some time delay (usually a few seconds).

⊛ *{Note}* You cannot post articles to UseNet when accessing directly from Mosaic. You can only read messages from Mosaic.

When you read articles through Mosaic, they are displayed in reverse order (latest article first). This can either benefit or hinder you—it saves you from wading through days old material, even though you can't follow threads properly. To access newsgroups directly through Mosaic, you must know the name of the newsgroup you want; there is no easy method to obtain a full list from within Mosaic.

To access newsgroups from Mosaic, you must have access to a news server and the NNTP protocol. The news server address must be placed in the MOSAIC.INI configuration file under the Services section. Figure 10.1 shows the default settings that the Windows version of MOSAIC.INI uses. Macintosh versions of Mosaic use dialog boxes for these purposes, instead of having you edit the configuration file directly. Change the news server address to your provider's news server address.

①(Tip)

If you don't know the news server address, check with your service provider.

Fig. 10.1
The Services section of MOSAIC.INI must point to the NNTP news server.

Enter the name of your news server here

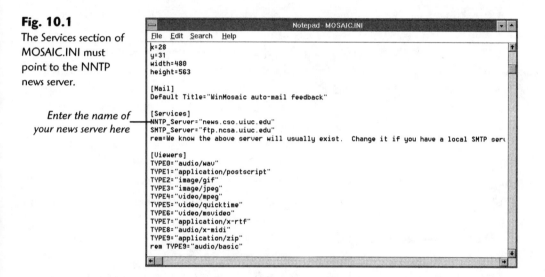

```
                          Notepad - MOSAIC.INI
 File  Edit  Search  Help
 k=28
 y=31
 width=480
 height=563

 [Mail]
 Default Title="WinMosaic auto-mail feedback"

 [Services]
 NNTP_Server="news.cso.uiuc.edu"
 SMTP_Server="ftp.ncsa.uiuc.edu"
 rem=We know the above server will usually exist.  Change it if you have a local SMTP ser

 [Viewers]
 TYPE0="audio/wav"
 TYPE1="application/postscript"
 TYPE2="image/gif"
 TYPE3="image/jpeg"
 TYPE4="video/mpeg"
 TYPE5="video/quicktime"
 TYPE6="video/msvideo"
 TYPE7="application/x-rtf"
 TYPE8="audio/x-midi"
 TYPE9="application/zip"
 rem TYPE9="audio/basic"
```

❋{Note}

Beginning with Alpha 8 of version 2.0, the latest versions of Mosaic allow you to make this change in a dialog box by choosing Options, Preferences, and then clicking the Services tab and entering the address in the NNTP Server box.

To read the contents of a newsgroup, choose File, Open URL, and enter the URL of the newsgroup you want to read preceded by the word "news:". Newer versions of Mosaic offer a more direct method, where you need only type the name of the newsgroup (preceded by "news:") at the top of the screen on the URL line. Mosaic connects to the news server and displays a list of articles available in that newsgroup. Clicking on any article title displays the contents.

Commercial Mosaic implementations

The NCSA Mosaic application has one outstanding feature: it's free. It does lack some extra capabilities that users would like, though, so commercial versions of Mosaic were bound to follow to fill the need. Among the strengths of the commercial products are simpler installation and configuration, better online help, a more stable application, and printing support.

Spry Inc.'s AIR Mosaic and Spyglass Inc.'s OEM version of Mosaic for Windows and Macintosh are two popular commercial Mosaic versions. A demonstration version of Spry's AIR Mosaic can be downloaded by FTP from **ftp.spry.com**. After running the demo version six times, users can purchase the software online using a credit card.

AIR Mosaic uses dialog boxes extensively instead of forcing users to edit the MOSAIC.INI configuration file. Other features include a drop-down list that allows you to easily jump back a few pages. Large documents and lists can be navigated more easily with a collapsible outline.

The Spyglass Mosaic version is less feature-packed than Spry's, but it is also faster (especially when viewing online images). This version of Mosaic is intended to be licensed by other vendors and then enhanced. It does have some interesting features, such as the Multiple Document Interface, which allows several documents to be opened at once. Style sheets are used, making it easier to customize the look of documents.

Commercial implementations of Mosaic are not expensive (AIR Mosaic sells for $29.95, for example), and they do offer some enhancements over the NCSA release. Whether the commercial versions are worth the money depends on how much you use Mosaic, whether you are comfortable with the NCSA version, and how much you value a slightly easier installation and configuration process.

Netscape

Netscape is a freeware (for personal use) World Wide Web browser (a commercial release, selling for $99, adds some extra functionality and technical support). Netscape is probably the fastest Web browser currently available, especially over PPP connections.

Netscape lets users post to UseNet newsgroups, making it more attractive than Mosaic for UseNet users. Netscape also allows multiple connections so that you can switch between Web pages, and it has the useful ability to download graphics separately. Several extensions to HTML (HyperText Markup Language) have been added, making the on-screen display even more attractive. Versions of Netscape are available for Windows, Macintosh, and several UNIX versions. You can download Netscape from most online service providers or through FTP from **ftp.mcom.com**.

To configure Netscape to use newsgroups, choose <u>O</u>ptions, <u>P</u>references. In the dialog box, choose the Directories, Applications and News option from the drop-down list at the top and then enter the address of your news server in the News (NNTP) Server box.

To use newsgroups in Netscape, enter **news:** followed by the name of the group and you will see a list of articles in that group like the one shown in figure 10.2. From here you can subscribe to the group, post an article, see your list of subscribed groups, or read an article.

❶ (Tip)

Earlier test releases of Netscape had an option to list all the newsgroups. This is gone in the 1.0 version, but you can still get a list of all the newsgroups by entering **news:*.*** as the URL. You can also use the * wildcard like you would with file names in DOS or Windows. For example, news:alt.* will list all the alt groups.

Fig. 10.2
A newsgroup in
Netscape. Each article
is a link you can click
to open the article.

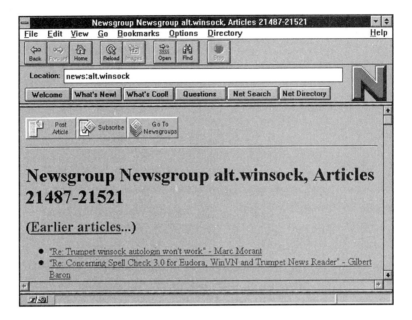

To open and read any article, just click it.

Gopher

Gopher is, to oversimplify, a menu-driven interface to different Internet
services. Most Gopher services are interconnected so that you can bounce
from one site to another through the menu selections. From the menu, you
can select the service you want to access. Gopher menu items can occasionally point to UseNet access sites or sites that offer newsgroup browsing
capabilities.

Figure 10.3 shows WSGopher, a popular Windows Gopher program, connected to a Gopher site that carries newsgroups. The window on the upper
left shows the main UseNet menu and the window on the lower right shows
the menu choices for the Alternative UseNet Hierarchies menu choice.

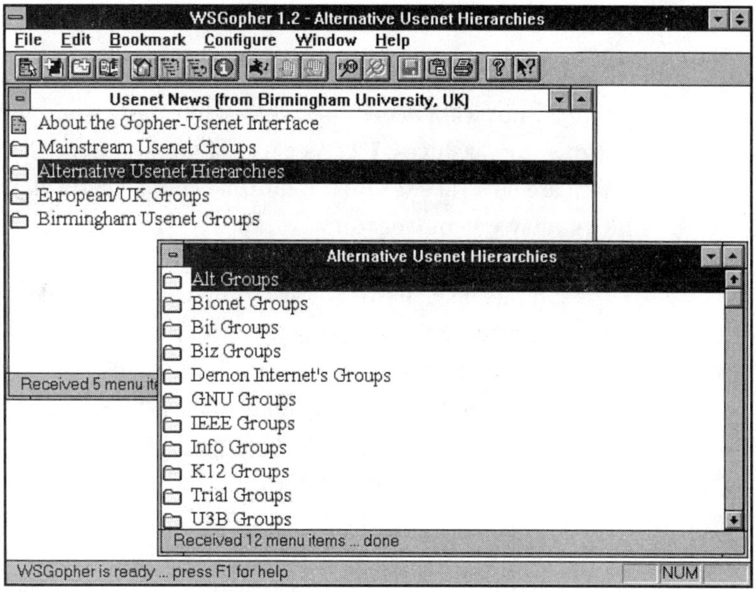

Fig. 10.3
WSGopher has several
bookmarks built in
with UseNet news
access.

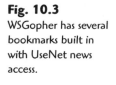

If you use Windows and want to read news via Gopher, try using the
WSGopher. Choose <u>B</u>ookmark, <u>F</u>etch to open the bookmark dialog. Then,
way down at the bottom of the category list, select UseNet news via Gopher.
Choose any of the Gopher sites from the right side.

If you are using Gopher on another system, here are a few sites to try for
news. (These do change from time to time as system administrators decide to
stop carrying news or to add news, so don't be surprised if some of these
don't work.)

Gopher Site	Menu Choice for News
gopher.bham.ac.uk	UseNet News Reader
aurora.latech.edu	USENET News
saturn.wwc.edu	USENET News via Gopher
gopher.msu.edu	News & Weather *then* USENET News

FTP

If you do not want access to UseNet on a daily basis and are more interested in FAQs and archives, **FTP** is a useful method to retrieve this information. There are several sites on the Internet that provide all the FAQs posted to the **news.answers newsgroup**.

For example, all *.answers newsgroups are archived on the system **rtfm.mit.edu**. Newsgroup postings are located in the anonymous FTP directories /pub/usenet/alt.answers, /pub/usenet/comp.answers, /pub/usenet /sci.answers, and so on. You can use anonymous FTP to connect to the system (log in as anonymous), change to the proper directory, and then issue the "get" command to retrieve a FAQ.

Some sites, usually for moderated newsgroups, offer anonymous FTP access to interesting archived threads from the newsgroup. Postings are usually made to the different newsgroups on a regular basis about the locations of these archives. The locations are often included in FAQs, too.

To use FTP access to remote systems, you must have a software implementation of FTP. Because most FTP UseNet sites deal only with FAQs or archived threads, you cannot read news on a regular basis in this manner.

Offline newsreaders

Some software packages allow you to download articles from a newsgroup to your machine for later reading, much the same way that offline e-mail packages work. In most cases, the articles in a newsgroup are simply scrolled quickly and captured by the offline reader. This allows you to read the articles later at your leisure, without chewing up connect time.

A disadvantage of the offline newsreader is that you must download many articles that you may choose to glance at or skip entirely. If you are paying for connection charges, you must weigh the advantages to reading online versus offline. Offline newsreaders are not widely used except when connections to a news server are not consistent and a download window must be used.

For the Windows user, examples of offline newsreaders are Paperboy and WRN (Windows Read News). Macintosh users can use NewsHopper, NewsFetcher, and MacSlurp for the same purpose.

Getting news by CD-ROM

All the services mentioned above require you to have Internet access in some manner. What if you don't have access? There are still a few ways to get newsgroup articles, although usually on a delayed basis.

E-mail

One access method is e-mail, which has been talked about in several other sections of this book. You can have e-mail sent to you with articles from entire newsgroups, or carefully filtered articles that match a keyword (as provided by the Stanford News Filtering Service, for example). For more information on the Stanford News Filtering Service, see chapter 6 and chapter 22, "Hot Newsgroups."

To obtain FAQs by e-mail, you may want to send a mail message to **mail-server@rtfm.mit.edu** with the words *help* and *index* in the body of the message on separate lines. This will return a message with more information about retrieving newsgroup FAQs through e-mail.

CD-ROM newsgroups

You can get newsgroup FAQs and archives on CD-ROM. Several companies regularly package FAQs and selected archives, as well as a few thousand articles in several dozen high-traffic newsgroups, and distribute them on CD-ROM through computer stores. Generally, these CD-ROMs are inexpensive since they contain public domain material.

These CD-ROMs do not contain current articles, because several months usually elapse between the date of the FAQs and the publishing of the disk. However, if you are interested in the FAQs only, this is a useful and permanent method of obtaining them.

Yet another alternative using CD-ROM is a service that mails you complete newsgroup contents on a regular basis. One such service is Common Knowledge Publishing, which issues a new CD-ROM whenever a new disk is full (usually about every week).

The service, called DiscNet, distributes via subscriptions (currently approximately $270 per 52 disks) and provides CD-ROMs in ISO 9660 format to be read on most systems (including PC, Macs, UNIX, and Amiga). By the time a disk is assembled, manufactured, and delivered, a few weeks pass, but CD-ROM does provide a useful archiving method for the vast amount of information on UseNet.

 **{Note}**_____ | For more information about DiscNet, contact Common Knowledge Publishing at (610) 433-6866, or by e-mail at **ckp@server0.cybernetics.net**. A sample of the service containing one current issue disk and a disk of general information is available for $15.

Services like DiscNet allow you to read all the newsgroup postings. Some systems even allow you to mail replies to articles through their servers, although replies are generally a waste of time because of the elapsed time.

Part III:

Using WinVN

11

Getting Started with WinVN

In this chapter:

- Where to get WinVN

- How to install WinVN

- How to start WinVN for the first time

- How to go about changing configuration information in WinVN

- The process for connecting and disconnecting from your news server

- The proper steps for exiting WinVN

With the help of WinVN, you can take out a subscription to the largest virtual newspaper in the world.

Getting started with WinVN is relatively easy. First, you need to make sure that you have established a network connection of some sort. This can be accomplished by connecting directly through a network or through a modem connection. If you have a direct network connection, contact your network administrator for instructions on the best method for using your system.

Are you connected to the Internet?

If you are going to read news by connecting via modem, you need to establish a SLIP or PPP connection through a local provider and have a TCP/IP support software package installed on your machine. You will most likely need a

Winsock-compliant TCP/IP package such as NetManage TCP/IP or PC/TCP. Once you are able to establish a network connection, you are ready to begin reading "all the news that's fit (and unfit) to print." This chapter, as well as the next few chapters, include instructions, hints, and tips on how to navigate the news using WinVN.

⊛ *{Note}*

If you need help getting a Winsock package installed, this topic is covered in *Using the Internet* and Special Edition, *Using the Internet 2nd Edition*, both published by Que.

With the help of WinVN, you can take out a subscription to the largest virtual newspaper in the world. Unlike a newspaper, though, you get to do more than just read the news. You can also be an editor, a writer, or an opinion columnist. So grab your press pass and get ready!

But is your Winsock ready?

The simple answer would be, "If you can make a connection, yes, if you can't, no." But there's a little more to it than that.

Standard Internet protocol, or TCP/IP (Transmission Control Protocol/Internet Protocol) as it's referred to, comes directly from the UNIX operating system. Because Windows users generally aren't running UNIX, connecting to the Internet using the UNIX protocol is difficult. It would be as if everybody else in the world spoke English and you spoke Russian. Without an interpreter, you couldn't talk to anyone else. Winsock is that "interpreter" that allows your Windows applications to "speak" TCP/IP. It is

highly recommended that you do use Winsock-compliant software if possible.

Every Winsock stack, whether it is NetManage TCP/IP, FTP's PC/TCP, or any of the half-dozen others out there, has a slightly different way of speaking TCP/IP. However, each stack will have settings (usually contained in an .ini file—called an init file) that bridge the gap between the stack's protocol and Winsock's. The installation software will normally set this information for you, but if you find your connection isn't working, you may have to spend some time with the manual, or worse, those dreaded tech support people.

Where to get WinVN

Because WinVN is public domain software, it is readily available on many of the anonymous FTP sites you may have encountered when downloading Windows shareware in the past. If you have a favorite FTP site, check it out—you'll probably find WinVN with other communications software packages there. Perhaps the most comprehensive collection of WinVN files and versions, including help files and FAQs (Frequently Asked Questions), is located at **ftp.ksc.nasa.gov** in the directory /pub/win3/winvn. Other sites include: **ftp.cyberspace.com**, **freebsd.cdrom.com**, and **ftp.halcyon.com**. The file name of the most current version at the .ksc site is wv16_93_11.zip. As newer versions come out, it is likely that the last number will change. For instance, the next version might be wv16_93_12.zip. Of course, you can also search for WinVN using your favorite Archie site to find more locations, but search for "wv16" to get the latest versions—a search for "winvn" will probably produce locations of old versions.

?Q&A ___ | *I've heard that there is a 32-bit version of WinVN—is this true and should I use it?*

The answers are "yes" and "probably not." Although there is currently a 32-bit version of WinVN out, it doesn't fully utilize 32-bit addressing. In fact, many users will actually take a performance hit by using the 32-bit version. Unless you're lucky enough to be running a copy of Windows 95 or are using Windows NT, it is not recommended that you use 32-bit WinVN.

Installing WinVN

Before installing WinVN, make sure that your Winsock or other TCP/IP software is working. You will also need to know the address of your news (or NNTP) server and, if you want to use e-mail in WinVN, your SMTP server. And, of course, you need to have a copy of WinVN.

66 *Plain English, please!*

SMTP stands for **Simple Mail Transfer Protocol** and is the standard method of e-mail transmission on the Internet. Other types of e-mail protocol, such as POP (Post Office Protocol) are also in use, but SMTP is the most common. Your SMTP server is the machine that acts as an electronic post office to handle your e-mail. **99**

Once you have all the pieces, you are ready to install WinVN. First, either by using the File Manager or the appropriate DOS commands, create a directory for WinVN. It might be easiest to remember if you just call the directory WinVN. You can then copy the zipped version of WinVN (or all the unzipped files) into that directory. If you haven't yet unzipped WinVN, now would be a good time to do so.

✱ *{Note}*

If you're using non-Winsock software for your connection, you will need to edit the "GENSockDLL=" line in your WinVN.INI file. Replace "GWINSOCK.DLL" with "PWKSOCK.DLL". To do this, use Notepad and open winvn.ini in your winvn directory. Then find the GENSockDLL= line and edit it appropriately.

The timezone variable

Imagine you are watching TV one evening and the announcer tells you about the world premiere of the latest blockbuster movie. You're excited as you watch vehicles exploding and lives hanging in the balance. Finally, you are told, "Tune in at 8:00 sharp!" What? You're confused—what day of the week? What time zone? How are you supposed to know when to turn on your TV?! Fortunately, you never have to deal with this nightmare situation because TV networks always make sure they tell you *exactly* when a show is going to be on.

In the same way, you need to tell UseNet what time *you* are "on." Remember, the Internet is global—to someone reading the news in Helsinki, "8:00" doesn't mean much. Setting your time zone will allow you to post in GMT (Greenwich Mean Time), the universal time standard. It is important that you provide this information to your news server. Failure to do so could cause articles you post to never show up, bounce, or bring flames into your mailbox.

Before you actually fire up WinVN, there are a couple of things you should do. First, you should set your time zone correctly. To do this, edit your AUTOEXEC.BAT file. If you are on Eastern Standard Time, you would add the line "SET TZ=EST5EDT" to AUTOEXEC.BAT. If you are unsure of your particular time zone, contact your local network administrator or refer to the WinVN user's guide—see table 11.1 for a listing of the correct time zones for the U.S. Next, create a WinVN icon in Windows and place it in a convenient Window for easy access.

Table 11.1   U.S. time zones

Hour	Time Zone	Use
5	Eastern Time	TZ=EST5EDT
6	Central Time	TZ=CST6CDT
7	Arizona (Mountain)	TZ=MST7
7	Mountain Time	TZ=MST7MDT
8	Pacific Time	TZ=PST8PDT

Each U.S. time zone requires the TZ variable to contain a different value. Time zones are based on GMT.

Starting WinVN for the first time

Once WinVN is installed, your Winsock is operating correctly, and you have established your Internet connection, you are ready to begin reading the news. From Windows, start WinVN. You will be prompted for your personal and server information before you can begin.

The following sections describe the type of information you'll need to provide (and where to get it) in order to use WinVN most effectively.

 **{Note}**

This book assumes you have located WinVN version .93.9 or later. Earlier versions may not prompt you for server and personal information on startup and may not have all the capabilities described in this book.

Server and personal information

The first screen will ask you for several things—your NNTP and SMTP server addresses, your type of mail server, and any system authorization information. The only one you are *required* to provide is the NNTP server address. To find out your local server address, you will probably need to ask your local news or site administrator. For instance, my NNTP server's address is **msuinfo.cl.msu.edu**.

If you have a mail server, you will also want to provide WinVN with your SMTP server address and indicate that your mail provider service is SMTP by clicking on the appropriate radio button.

⊗<Caution> If you do not provide SMTP server information, you will only be able to read and post news—you will not be able to send personal replies via e-mail.

There are also different options available for various types of mail servers. Figure 11.1 shows a typical configuration.

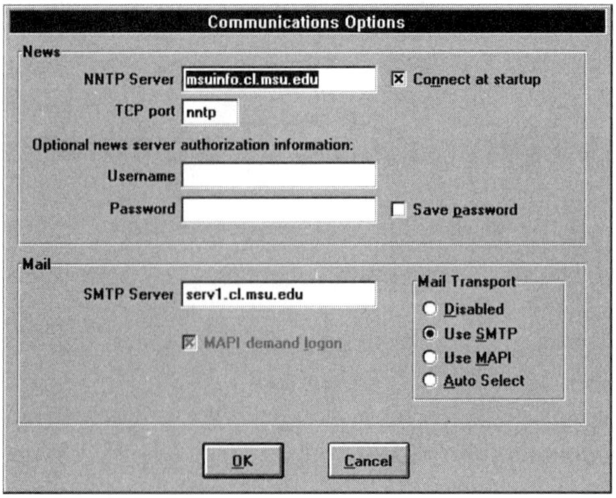

Fig. 11.1
WinVN asks you for the information most NNTP servers require. You can also provide e-mail information such as SMTP Server and your real name in the Communications Options window.

Some NNTP servers require additional user authentication in order for you to read news. If this is needed, you should provide it at this time. If you're not sure whether or not you need it, try leaving it blank for now—if you run into problems, you can always contact your system administrator later and provide the authorization.

After accepting the information, you will be prompted for your e-mail address, your Reply-to e-mail address, your real name, and your organization (see fig. 11.2). It is best that you enter the appropriate information at this time. You only need to enter information in the Reply-to e-mail address if you have more than one e-mail address and you want the additional address to be your "official" address—otherwise leave that field blank.

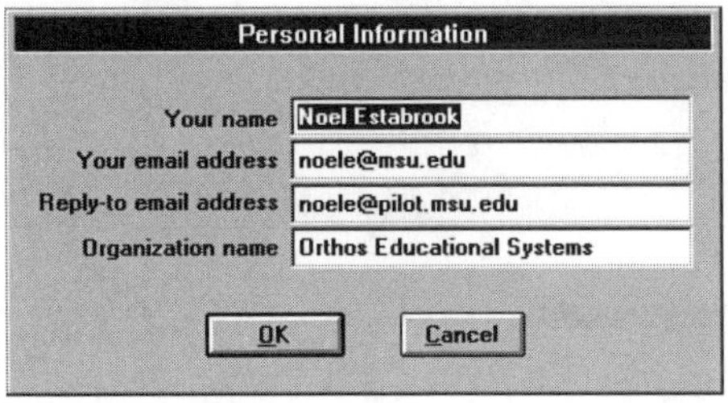

Fig. 11.2
Providing your real name, e-mail address, and organization to your NNTP server will make your postings more complete and accepted on UseNet.

Personal Information

Your name	Noel Estabrook
Your email address	noele@msu.edu
Reply-to email address	noele@pilot.msu.edu
Organization name	Orthos Educational Systems

OK   Cancel

Updating the list of groups

After telling WinVN to accept the information provided in the previous section, you will be asked whether or not WinVN should contact the NNTP server for the latest list of newsgroups. Go ahead and do it by choosing Yes; it's the only way to find out what's out there!

Good time for a cup of coffee

There are thousands of newsgroups out there. Depending upon your NNTP server, you could have access to anywhere upwards of 10,000 newsgroups! Can you imagine how long it would take a paper carrier to deliver that many newspapers to your doorstep? Right—a long time. Well, cyberspace delivers information a little faster than a 10-year-old on a mountain bike, but even with a high-speed modem connection, it can take a while. So while WinVN is looking for the news, go get a cup of coffee, say "hi" to the family, or go readjust your eyes to the light—this is going take some time.

Subscribing to some groups

When you get back, WinVN will ask you to subscribe to a few groups as you can see in figure 11.3. The process is fairly easy, as a new window will come up showing you all your options.

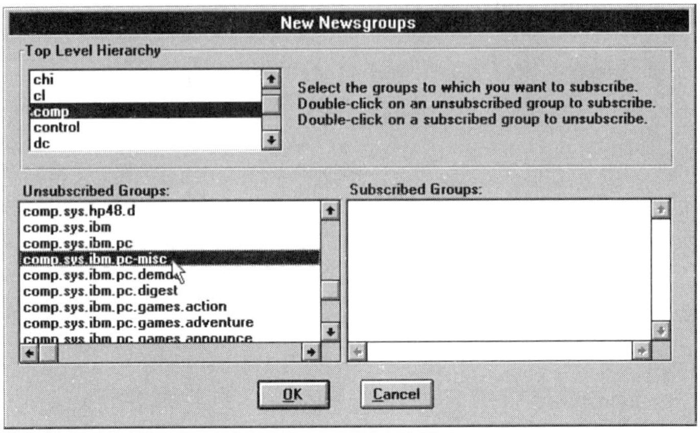

Fig. 11.3

The subscription window lets you choose groups from any of the hierarchies available at your site. Double-clicking any group will subscribe you to it.

Browse some of the hierarchies that were discussed earlier in the book, as well as some that might be unique to your server. Pick a few that catch your fancy and accept your choices. Don't worry about whether or not you picked many (or interesting!) groups—you can always change, add, or delete groups later. See figure 11.4 for a typical listing of newsgroups.

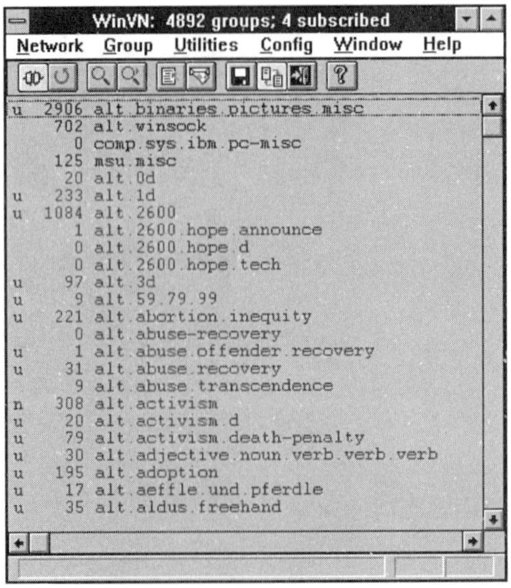

Fig. 11.4

A typical full group listing from a local NNTP server. The four groups at the top of the list have been subscribed to, the ones below are unsubscribed newsgroups. This server contains almost 5,000 newsgroups.

Authorizing yourself to the news server

So you got a message back telling you that you can't access news without authorization, huh? Well, that's easily solved—you just need to provide WinVN with the proper information to get authorized. In many cases, this is a system e-mail or access account with the accompanying password. If you already know what these are, try them first. If not, it's off to your system administrator again.

Once you have the correct information, you'll choose Config, Communications. Notice that this opens the same dialog box as you saw when you first opened WinVN. Simply press the Tab key and fill in the Username and Password fields appropriately and you will be authorized to access the news at your site.

Changing configuration information

As you become more adept at using WinVN, you will find that you will want to customize many of the settings that WinVN uses by default. Or, you may want to experiment with different settings than the ones you provided at startup. It will be helpful for you to start to familiarize yourself with some of the different settings that can be reconfigured in WinVN.

Probably the most important information you will give to WinVN is the address of your NNTP server, which we covered in the previous section. However, you might also want to alter your personal information or connection setting defaults. Even fonts and display colors are adjustable. You can change all these settings from the Config menu. The following sections go through some of the more common settings you may want to customize.

Server

It is quite likely that, in the course of reading news over a period of time, your network site might change the address of the NNTP server. Or, you might discover an NNTP server in your area that carries more groups or is more reliable. Whatever the reason, there's a good chance you may want to change the server address at some point.

The same can be said for your SMTP server. It may change address, domain name, or even its type of mail service. Therefore, it will be good if you are able to adjust to any foreseeable changes. Remember, on the Internet, the only constant is change!

To change any server information, open the Config menu and choose the Communications... option (refer back to "Authorizing yourself to the news server" earlier in this chapter for more details).

Always try to use a domain name, like **msuinfo.cl.msu.edu**, instead of the actual IP address, such as 25.8.221.6, when providing server information. The reason is two-fold. First, a server will often change its IP address but it will usually retain the same domain name. By configuring your server with the domain name instead of the IP address, you won't have to worry about changing your server address nearly as often. Second, English words are a lot easier to remember than a series of numbers.

Personal information

There will also be times when you may want to change or add to your personal information. For instance, if you start a small business and would like to change your organization name, you would probably want that change to be reflected in your correspondence on the Internet. Other reasons might be a change in e-mail address or an actual change in name due to marriage or some other circumstance.

Although it may be tempting to make your real name something catchy like Cpt. Kirk or Bill Gates, try to resist the urge. First, most people will be able to find out who you really are if they want to, anyway. Second, you may be opening yourself up to a lot of junk mail or private (even public) flaming.

To change your personal info, open the Config menu and choose Personal Info.... Simply change any information you want and accept the changes. WinVN will incorporate those changes into your very next post.

Connect at startup?

You might not have noticed, but there was a toggle setting right next to the field where you entered your NNTP server information called Connect at startup. This setting informs WinVN whether it should try to connect to the NNTP server when you start the application. This setting is defaulted to yes (indicated by an X in the box in front of the setting choice).

You will probably want to keep this on, but, then again, you might not want to. For example, if you want WinVN to be one of your startup programs in Windows, but you just want it to be available when you do want to make an actual connection, you would not want WinVN to connect at startup. It wouldn't do you any good since, without a connection in place, it wouldn't find any news for you anyway. If you do choose to turn this setting off as in figure 11.5, you will get a message that says not connected to news server when you start WinVN. To connect at that point, you need to open the Network menu and choose the Connect to Server option.

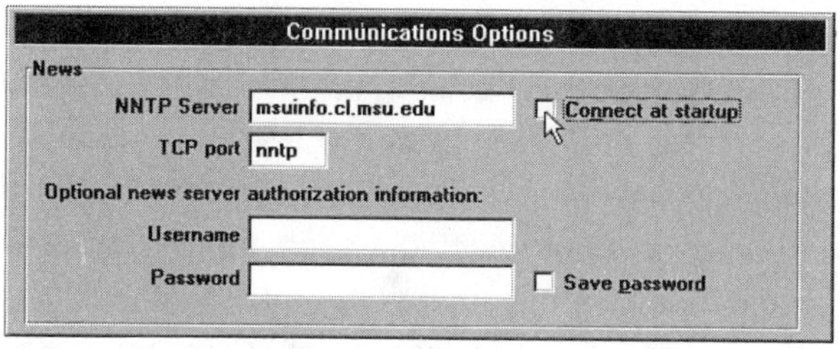

Fig. 11.5
Clicking on the box turns the Connect at startup setting off, requiring you to manually connect to your server in future sessions.

Retrieve group list on connect?

This is a setting found in the Group List... option in the Config menu. You have three choices—have WinVN check for newsgroups on your NNTP server every time you start WinVN (Yes), never automatically check for groups (No), or have WinVN ask you if you want to check for groups every time you start (Ask). Which setting you choose is really up to you, but it's good to keep in mind the pros and cons of each choice:

- Choosing Yes means that you want to always be up-to-the-minute on every new group available to you, since this option will have WinVN find all the newsgroups available when you log on, including new ones. This will certainly keep you informed. However, it will also mean extra time online whenever you use WinVN. Depending on your server and your connection, this can be an extra time-consuming step.

- Choosing No is the quickest way to begin reading news. However, you will never know what new groups are out there unless you specifically ask.

- Choosing Ask may be the best of both worlds. It does require an extra step at each startup, but it also gives you the option of deciding when you want to see new groups and when you don't.

It might be a good idea to choose Yes when you're a new user so that you can get a feel for how long your server takes to retrieve groups or whether you even find yourself ever subscribing to those new groups. As you become more experienced, you may want to choose No or Ask as you get a better idea of what you're actually using news for. It's up to you and your needs.

Fonts and screen color

This is the aesthetic setting. Do you like looking at large letters or small letters? A bright or dull background? Serif or sans serif characters? The choice is up to you. This is primarily a setting designed for your experimentation. You can use different colors for selected articles, article text, group text, article background, unselected group window background, and many others in just about any combination you want. To change the font for a given area, open the Config menu and choose the Fonts option. The dialog box for changing a font in any window is shown in figure 11.6. In order to change text or window background, open the Config menu and choose the Color option. A dialog box for changing color will appear, as seen in figure 11.7. The font and color dialog boxes are the same no matter which area you decide to change.

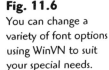

Fig. 11.6
You can change a variety of font options using WinVN to suit your special needs.

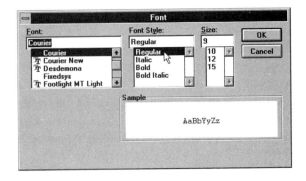

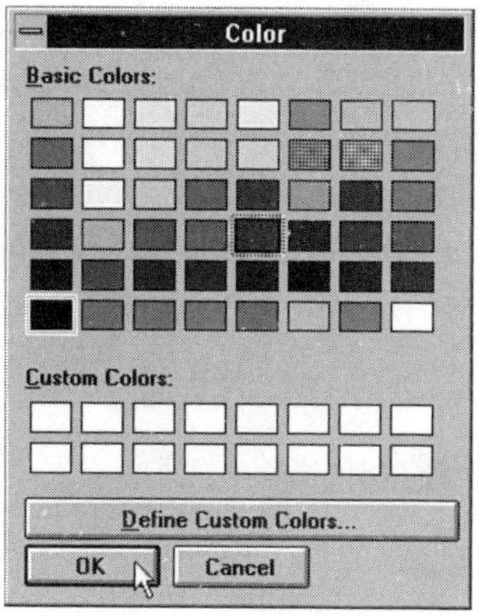

Fig. 11.7
Selecting a variety of colors for different elements is easy with WinVN.

(Tip)

You may want to set the font for Composition Text to a monospace font, such as Courier. You will discover that some Windows fonts look different when you are composing a message than when they actually show up in the group. This is because news uses standard monospacing —meaning each character takes up the same amount of space. Since many of the fonts in use today take up different space for different letters, this could throw you off when doing things like using tabs or composing simple ASCII art.

Connecting and disconnecting from the server

It's important that you connect and disconnect from your server cleanly. That is, you want to send all the right messages to the server so that no bugs or problems develop in either the server or your software. Most networking software today has this stuff built in to its code—it's just a matter of you choosing the right command so that code is sent to the server—and your machine.

In WinVN, this "code" is located in the Connect to Server and Disconnect from Server options in the Network menu. Unless you turned the Connect at startup option off, you will probably never have to use the Connect to Server option—WinVN will automatically execute that command when you start it up.

It is always a good idea to choose the Disconnect from Server before exiting WinVN, however (see fig. 11.8). If you *don't*, your machine probably won't explode and the Net police won't come knocking on your door. In fact, you may never notice anything unusual. But one day, you may try to connect and get some strange unrecognizable error that tells you that you can't. Finally, making a clean break, in the words of Captain Hook, is just "good form"! So take a little advice and do this one extra step before you turn off the news.

Fig. 11.8
Choosing to actively disconnect from the server can save you some trouble later on.

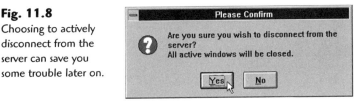

Exiting WinVN

The last step you need to perform is exiting WinVN. This is accomplished in the usual Windows way—by double-clicking on the Close box or choosing to Exit from the Network menu.

Before exiting, though, there's one more thing you might want to do. Under the Config menu, there is another option called Confirmations.... There is one other setting in there that you may want to pay attention to—the Confirm Save on exit setting. If you are as forgetful as I am, it is strongly recommend that you turn this setting on (its default setting is off). That way, if you make changes to windows, configurations, or anything else during your news session, you will always be given a reminder that those changes need to be permanently saved. Turning this setting off could cause you to repeat unnecessary steps in the future.

12 Newsgroups in WinVN

In this chapter:

- How to start up WinVN after configuration
- How to subscribe and unsubscribe to newsgroups
- How to search for, select, and move subscribed groups
- How to open groups to read
- The basic elements of groups
- How to update your article list

The biggest difference between UseNet and the newspaper that's delivered to your doorstep on Sunday is the size— UseNet is a lot bigger.

The newsgroup structure is the heart and soul of UseNet. You can choose from hundreds, if not thousands of topics. Find information on where to find a rare breed of dog, download a picture of a space shuttle launch, or find out the latest news in your local community. It's all there, ready for you to read.

Perhaps it would be helpful to think of UseNet the same way you think of your local newspaper—there are sections for sports, national events, arts, and a myriad of other topics. The biggest difference between UseNet and the newspaper that's delivered to your doorstep on Sunday is the size—UseNet is a lot bigger—and the delivery is more dependable, too!

The structure of UseNet newsgroups is surprisingly parallel to a newspaper, too. Your newspaper has an Arts & Entertainment section—UseNet has a section of rec. newsgroups (see chapter 2 for more information on newsgroup structure). Your newspaper has a Local section, and so do most NNTP servers. Each section of UseNet, then, has a related subset of groups within that section. The comp. section, for instance, contains newsgroups related to computers and computing. The trick is in narrowing down all those choices to the newsgroups that interest you most. This chapter gives you the tools you need to do just that.

Starting WinVN again

Once you've established a connection to an NNTP server and configured WinVN properly, running WinVN is as easy as a couple of mouse clicks. It is assumed that, at this stage anyway, you've provided accurate NNTP server information and have configured WinVN to retrieve new newsgroups at startup. Remember, retrieving newsgroups at startup is a fairly time-consuming process, so you have a few minutes to scan ahead as they're retrieved. Once WinVN has all the information it needs, the Main window will appear similar to figure 12.1.

> If you don't want to view unsubscribed newsgroups, open the Config menu and choose Group List. Click the box next to Show Unsubscribed Groups to deselect that option. A button on the Main Window menu bar allows you to do the same thing with the click of the mouse.

Fig. 12.1
WinVN displays the newsgroups that were obtained from your NNTP server. Sub-scribed groups appear at the top and unsubscribed groups are listed below subscribed groups.

```
┌─┬──────────── WinVN: 4882 groups; 4 subscribed ──── ▼ ▲ ┐
│ — │ Network  Group   Utilities   Config   Window   Help      │
│   ├──────────────────────────────────────────────────────┤
│   │ ⊂⊃ ↻ │ ⊕ ⊖ │ E ⊠ │ ⊟ ⊡ ⊠ │ ?                        │
│   ├──────────────────────────────────────────────────── ▲┤
│   │ n    640 alt.winsock                                  ▐│
│   │ n   2670 alt.binaries.pictures.misc                  ░│
│   │ u    126 msu.misc                                    ░│
│   │ n    836 rec.pets.dogs                               ░│
│   │ u      7 alt.0d                                      ░│
│   │ u    194 alt.1d                                      ░│
│   │ n   1018 alt.2600                                    ░│
│   │ u      3 alt.2600.hope.announce                     ░│
│   │        0 alt.2600.hope.d                            ░│
│   │ u      1 alt.2600.hope.tech                         ░│
│   │ n     93 alt.3d                                     ░│
│   │ u      6 alt.59.79.99                               ░│
│   │ n    220 alt.abortion.inequity                      ░│
│   │        0 alt.abuse-recovery                         ░│
│   │ u      2 alt.abuse.offender.recovery                ░│
│   │ n     31 alt.abuse.recovery                         ░│
│   │ u     27 alt.abuse.transcendence                    ░│
│   │ n    283 alt.activism                               ░│
│   │ u     17 alt.activism.d                             ░│
│   │ u     76 alt.activism.death-penalty                 ░│
│   │ u     45 alt.adjective.noun.verb.verb.verb          ░│
│   │ n    198 alt.adoption                               ░│
│   │ u     18 alt.aeffle.und.pferdle                     ░│
│   │ u     20 alt.aldus.freehand                         ▼│
│   ├──────────────────────────────────────────────────────┤
│   │ ← │                                            │   → │
└───┴──────────────────────────────────────────────────────┘
```

Familiarizing yourself with the WinVN Main window

Search for newsgroups by text using these two buttons.

WinVN tells you how many groups are on your server and how many you've subscribed to.

This button toggles the display of unsubscribed newsgroups.

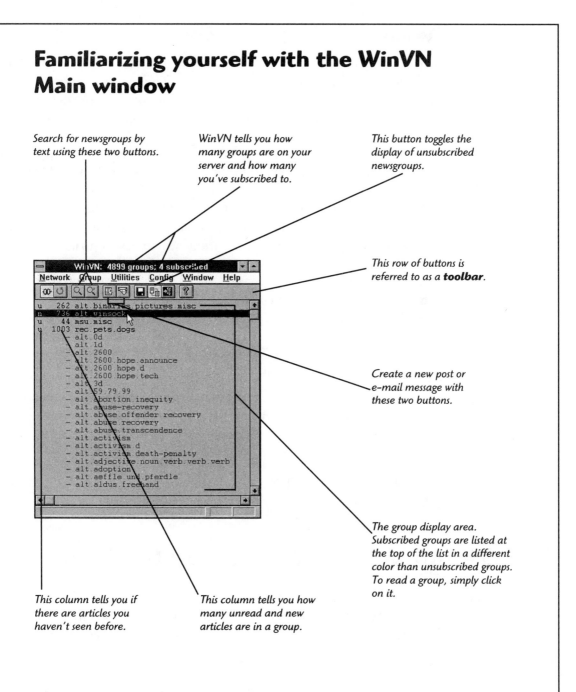

This row of buttons is referred to as a **toolbar**.

Create a new post or e-mail message with these two buttons.

The group display area. Subscribed groups are listed at the top of the list in a different color than unsubscribed groups. To read a group, simply click on it.

This column tells you if there are articles you haven't seen before.

This column tells you how many unread and new articles are in a group.

What's in the Main window

The Main window is WinVN's "Control Center," so to speak. You can change configurations, change connection status, select groups, and perform many other operations from the Main window. The preceding page gives you a quick overview of the Main window.

In addition to the standard pull-down menus, WinVN has added some helpful buttons at the top of the window to allow you to perform often-used functions with a click of the mouse. The buttons are self-explanatory—simply click and hold down your mouse button on each one and a short description of each is displayed at the bottom of the window. Before releasing your mouse button, move the pointer away from the button so as to not select it.

The second key area of the Main window is the actual newsgroup information, which you need to be familiar with to navigate UseNet. There are several things you need to pay attention to:

- *The newsgroup names:* The newsgroups you have subscribed to appear at the top of the list.

- *Article number:* Each group has a number displayed next to it representing the number of articles in that group. If no articles are retrieved, a "-" appears rather than a number.

- *Group status:* An "n" displayed in front of a group indicates that new articles have been found since you last read the group. A "u" indicates that unread (though not new) articles are in the group.

Subscribing and unsubscribing to groups

With WinVN, subscribing and unsubscribing to newsgroups is a snap. You can subscribe to one, two, a dozen, or as many groups as you want. You can browse through the list of groups to find something of interest or search for a specific work to find something to subscribe to. Once you are done with a group, you can unsubscribe to it just as easily.

Searching for groups

Searching for newsgroups in WinVN has become much easier with newer versions. This is a good thing, as a typical user is frequently on the look-out for new or different groups. For instance, a coworker might ask you a question that you don't have the answer to. In past times, you'd simply shrug your shoulders and offer a sheepish, "I don't know." With WinVN, though, you can wink, smile, and say, "Let me find out."

Let's say that somebody asked you if you knew anything about hypnosis. What would you do? Well, perhaps the following steps will help you out.

1 First, open the Group menu and choose the Find option. Clicking on the magnifying glass button will do the same thing.

2 WinVN will prompt you for a string to search for. Type in the string of characters you're looking for (for instance, **hypnosis**).

3 Click OK and WinVN will highlight the first group that has the requested string of characters, as in figure 12.2.

4 If you'd like to find another group with the same string of text, open the Group menu and choose the Find Next option (or click on the button with the magnifying glass and the red arrow). Repeat step 2 and the next group with the desired text will be highlighted.

5 If you want to take a look at the group as soon as it's found, simply double-click the group—WinVN retrieves any articles in the group for you to browse and read.

6 If you'd like to subscribe to the group, click the group to highlight it, open the Group menu, and then choose Subscribe Selected Groups.

Fig. 12.2

When WinVN finds a desired group, it automatically displays the group and shows a "**>**" next to it. When you ask for a group about hypnosis, **alt.hypnosis** should be the first group WinVN finds if your NNTP server carries that group.

```
━                WinVN: 4882 groups; 4 subscribed        ▼ ▲
 Network   Group   Utilities   Config   Window   Help
 ┌◐─┐ ○  Q Q⃗  ▤ ▽   ▤ ▣ ▨   ?
 u      1 alt.hurricane.andrew                            ▲
 u     57 alt.hypertext
 u      5 alt.icelandic.waif.bjork.bjork.bjork
 u     45 alt.illuminati
 n     16 alt.image.medical
        0 alt.imploding.kibo
 u      2 alt.india.progressive
        0 alt.indian.superior
 n    169 alt.individualism
 u     46 alt.industrial
 u      3 alt.industrial.computing
        0 alt.inet92
 u    103 alt.infertility
        0 alt.info-fest.in.tuebingen
 u      4 alt.info-science
 u      2 alt.info-theory
 u      1 alt.internet.access
        0 alt.internet.access-wanted
 n    245 alt.internet.access.wanted
 u     77 alt.internet.media-coverage
        0 alt.internet.networks
 u    399 alt.internet.services
 u     10 alt.internet.talk-radio                         ▼
 ◆ ◄                                                    ► │
```

Q&A

> **Why would I want to read a group without subscribing to it?**
>
> Have you ever gotten one of those magazine trial subscriptions in the mail? Think of reading an unsubscribed group as being the same thing (except without the cost!). Shocking as it may seem, newsgroup names (just like magazine titles) don't always tell the whole story about the contents of a newsgroup. Reading some articles before you subscribe can save you from subscribing to a newsgroup that you're really not interested in and can also let you lurk on the group for a while to get a feel for it.

Selecting multiple groups

What happens if you find several groups that you'd like to subscribe to? Do you have to go through the process of subscribing to each one individually? Fortunately, the answer is "no." WinVN allows you to select and subscribe to many groups at once.

Let's say that you find several groups located next to each other that you'd like to select, how would you do it? WinVN makes it simple—just position your pointer on the first group, click your mouse button (and hold it down) while dragging down to the last group you want to select. Release your button, and voila!, they're all selected. Although you can still only choose to read one group at a time, you can subscribe, unsubscribe, or move the selected groups to the top as if they were a single group.

Sometimes, though, the groups you want to select aren't conveniently next to each other. What to do, what to do? Easy—click the first group to select it then move your pointer to the next group and, while holding down the Control key, click again. You'll notice that both groups are now selected (see fig. 12.3). As before, these groups can be manipulated as a set rather than individually.

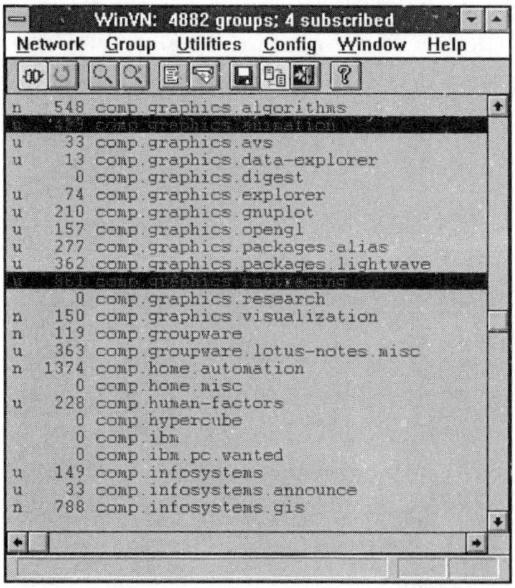

Fig. 12.3

Using the Ctrl+click method, you can select two noncontiguous newsgroups.

Moving subscribed groups to the top of the list

Once you have subscribed to a number of newsgroups you'd like to read on a regular basis, you may want to change the order in which you read them. Perhaps you'd like to have the groups listed in order of most to least traffic, or in order of importance to you so that you can ignore the lower-most groups on occasion. Arranging groups the way you want them arranged is accomplished by using the Moving Subscribed Groups to Top of List function.

To move a group to the top of your list, first select the desired group by clicking it. Then, under the Groups menu, choose Move Selected Groups to Top. The group (or groups) now appear at the top of your group list and at the top of your Newsrc file.

Unsubscribing from a newsgroup

There will often be occasions when you will want to unsubscribe from a newsgroup. Maybe you subscribed to it for a short time to get some specific information, you got it and you're ready to leave. Perhaps you're simply tired of reading it or don't have the time. Once you are ready to unsubscribe, simply click on the group to highlight it, open the Group menu, and choose the Unsubscribe Selected Groups option. Once unsubscribed, the group will return to its former place in the unsubscribed group list.

The Newsrc file

You've seen the phrase before, and you know it has something to do with UseNet news, but what? In a nutshell, the Newsrc file is where your particular newsgroup information is stored—which groups have you subscribed to? How many articles have you read? Not read? All of this information is stored in the Newsrc file.

The .newsrc file (as it's called by UNIX) is really a UNIX convention and is still the standard for UNIX newsreaders, which comprise a majority of newsreaders in use today. As a result, most PC and Macintosh-based newsreaders have kept this convention to maintain compatibility with UNIX— only they've taken the dot off the beginning of the file name. In fact, if you happen to already have a .newsrc file from a UNIX account, you can simply copy that file to your WinVN directory, rename it "Newsrc" and you're ready to go!

Opening a group to read

Now that you have a better understanding of how to find and arrange groups, it's time to actually look at a group to see what one looks like in WinVN. Remember, just double-click the group to retrieve all its articles into WinVN.

In addition, the same techniques you used to select groups in the Main window apply to selecting articles in the Group window. The click, click-and-drag, and Ctrl+click methods of selecting groups will remain the same for selecting articles.

⊗<Caution> Know your limits and subscribe to groups intelligently. Don't subscribe to a lot of groups with heavy traffic if you know you're only going to read news once a week. Doing so will require a lot of time and effort on your part just to find articles that interest you. As a general rule, it's a good idea to check the news on a regular basis—every day is ideal, but at least several times a week is recommended.

Configuring the number of articles to retrieve

As discussed briefly earlier, the number of articles available for your viewing largely determines how much time you will spend browsing and reading newsgroups. Obviously, the fewer articles you tell WinVN to retrieve, the quicker you can read. Retrieving fewer articles, however, may also cause you to miss important ones. Although you can always retrieve additional articles later, people often forget to do so. How you balance these considerations is up to you.

When deciding how many articles you'd like to deal with, it is very important that you take into consideration how often you read news, how long you have to read articles, when you can read them, and how fast, dependable, and expensive your connection is. Once you have weighed these factors and made a decision, it's time to tell WinVN how many articles you'd like to see.

What's in the Group window?

These two buttons let you search for articles with particular text in the subject line.

The title bar gives you the name of the newsgroup and how many articles are currently unread.

The menu bar gives you a number of options to choose from.

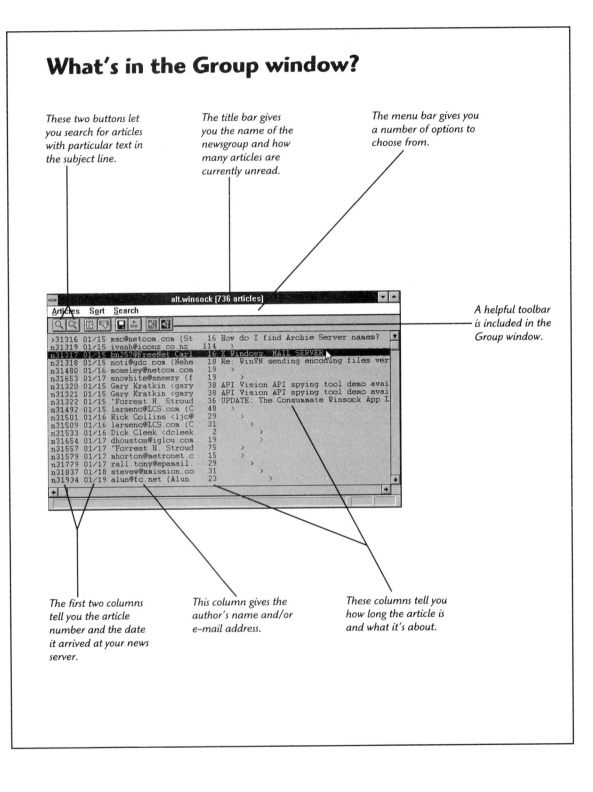

A helpful toolbar is included in the Group window.

The first two columns tell you the article number and the date it arrived at your news server.

This column gives the author's name and/or e-mail address.

These columns tell you how long the article is and what it's about.

①(Tip)

The first few times you try WinVN, you may want to see how the default settings fit your needs. You may find that it is already configured to your tastes. As the saying goes, "If it ain't broke, don't fix it!"

You can bring up the Article List configuration window one of two ways.

1 From the Main window, open Config menu and choose Article List.

Or

From the Group window, open the Articles menu and choose Preferences.

2 A dialog box appears that allows you to set up how WinVN retrieves news articles (see fig. 12.4).

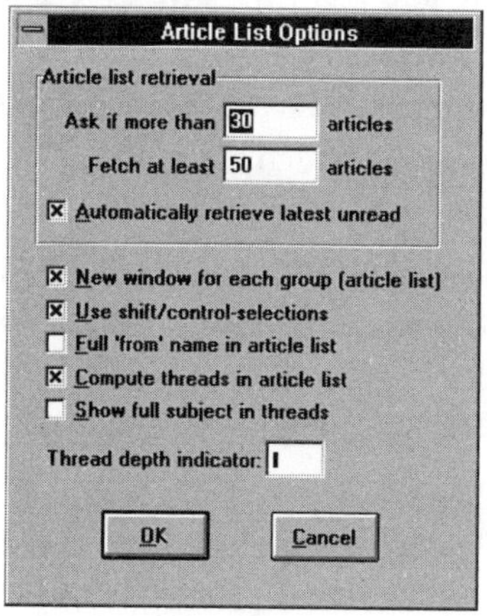

Fig. 12.4
The Article List Options window lets you choose how you want WinVN to retrieve articles from your NNTP server. Two data entry fields and one toggle box are available in the Article list retrieval area.

The three settings in the Article list retrieval area can be set as follows:

- If you want WinVN to always retrieve all unread articles, select the Automatically retrieve latest unread box. If this choice is marked, it doesn't matter what the other two settings are—WinVN will always retrieve and display all unseen articles.

- If you do not want to always view all of the unread articles, but instead decide for whatever reason that you'd like to limit how many articles

WinVN retrieves, you need to make sure the <u>A</u>utomatically retrieve latest unread box is empty and enter the desired information in the other two areas.

- The Ask if more than x articles option tells WinVN how many articles it can retrieve without asking your "permission" to retrieve more. Remember, even if you tell WinVN to retrieve a low number of articles, WinVN will still give you the option of retrieving more if it encounters a group with more than that number of articles. In other words, if you configure WinVN to ask you if a group has more than 25 articles, and you try to retrieve a group with 140 articles in it, WinVN will present you with a dialog box allowing you to override the configuration and retrieve all 140 articles. So if you are in a situation where you can't always retrieve all articles, you know that you at least have the option to retrieve all of them.

- The second field, Fetch at least x articles, tells WinVN how many articles you want retrieved, even if there aren't that many unread articles. For instance, if you set this to 50 and try to retrieve a group with 100 articles, 20 of which are unread, WinVN will retrieve the 20 unread articles plus the most recent 30 articles before those. Although not often used, this setting can come in handy, especially in newsgroups that have long ongoing discussions that you keep up with. With this setting defined, you can maintain access to the most recently posted articles for reference, even if you've already read them.

①(Tip)

Never set the Fetch option to 0—always set it to at least 1. A setting of 0 retrieves all messages, regardless of other settings, due to WinVN's retrieval protocol.

Article status

You may have noticed some symbols in front of some of the articles WinVN retrieved. If you haven't, you'll certainly see them appear after you've spent some time reading, finding, and saving articles. An article can be marked in several ways.

Symbol	Description
s	If an "s" appears in front of an article, this tells you that the article has been seen, saved, or otherwise viewed. This letter appears only after you've accessed the contents of an article.
n	An "n" indicates an article that has shown up on your NNTP server since you last read mail. It tells you that the article is brand new.
SPACE	A space in front of an article indicates that either WinVN has no information on the status of the article, or you have not yet viewed or otherwise looked at the article.
>	A ">" in front of an article indicates that WinVN found an article with a subject header that you requested by opening the Search menu and choosing Find.

⊗<Caution> Be aware that if you do not exit each group individually, the Article Status information may not be saved. Consequently, the next time you use WinVN, you have to reread or sort through articles that you've already seen. For convenience and efficiency, exit each Group window when you are done with it.

Updating the article list

There will be occasion when you will want to update the articles in a group without wanting to exit the group and select it again. For instance, if you post a question to a high-traffic local newsgroup and suspect that an answer might be posted relatively quickly, you might want to retrieve articles a couple times to see if someone has responded.

If you want to retrieve the most current articles in a group without exiting the Group window, open the Articles menu and choose Update from Server (or Ctrl+U). WinVN then contacts the NNTP server and retrieves any articles that have shown up since you last retrieved them.

Sorting Articles

WinVN can sort articles in a particular group in several ways. The options available are under the Sort menu in the Group window. The different ways of sorting articles are as follows:

- *By Date*—This sorts a group from the earliest date to most recent date a particular article is received at the NNTP server. All articles from January 1st are at the top, all articles from January 2nd are below those, and so on.

- *By Subject*—Choosing this option groups articles together according to topic. To allow you to see all responses to a particular post, the Re: (regarding) prefix to the subject line is ignored (see fig 12.5).

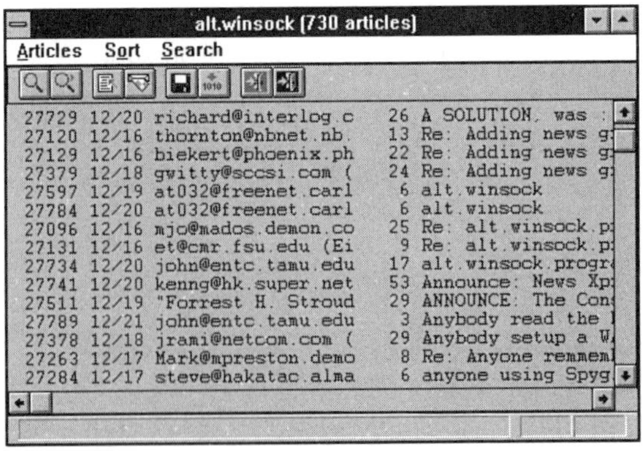

Fig. 12.5
When a newsgroup is sorted by Subject, all articles relating to a particular subject are grouped together for reading ease.

- *By # lines*: This sorts articles by the number of lines. Articles with the fewest number of lines in the message are at the top and messages with the most lines are at the bottom. This is a quick way to determine who is concise and who "talks" a lot.

- *By Threads*: This option is similar to the by Subject option. The only difference is that threading actually shows you to which article a particular post is responding.

66 *Plain English, please!*

Although chapter 6 covers threads in detail, it might be helpful at this point to remind you what a thread is. A **thread** is nothing more than a conversation that (hopefully) deals with one topic. Any given newsgroup has any number of threads, or topics, going at any one time. When someone posts an article beginning with "Re:," they are either beginning or continuing a thread; the newsgroup readership knows this because the subject line of the original article is included. Just as different individual threads weave in and out to make a whole piece of cloth, so do many threads of conversation make a whole newsgroup. 99

- *By Article Number:* This is the default setting for WinVN. This displays each article in the order it was received by your local NNTP server.

- *By Author:* Viewing articles by author allows you to look at one poster's articles all at once. An author can be indicated by a real name or by an e-mail address, depending upon the mail server of the poster. Authors are listed in alphabetical order with this option.

Although each option has its own unique advantages and disadvantages, some are more useful than others. Hardly anyone sorts articles by number of lines. On the other hand, one of the most popular methods of sorting is by threads. Because we tend to think in a linear fashion, dealing with chunks of information at a time is often useful. How you choose to sort the articles is an individual decision that you can make best according to your own needs and desires.

13

Reading Articles in WinVN

Now it's time to learn some of the shortcuts, some of the "tricks of the trade," that will allow you to read faster and more effectively.

So this is what you've been waiting for. You finally get to read some news. Hey, who's kidding whom? We both know that you've already peeked at some articles on your way to this chapter. But now it's time to learn some of the shortcuts that will allow you to read news faster and more effectively. WinVN makes the basics of reading news very easy. Fortunately for you, WinVN also offers some advanced features to further your newsreading skills. In this chapter, you learn how to utilize some of those capabilities.

Opening articles

Ever tried to read your morning newspaper by looking at it folded up with a rubber band around it? It's pretty difficult. Well, it's time to take the rubber band off WinVN and start reading. As with the Main window and the Group window, the Article window offers a toolbar that provides shortcuts for frequently used tasks. Take a few minutes to familiarize yourself with these buttons now.

✳ *{Note}* _____ | The alt.winsock newsgroup is useful for learning more about Winsock applications such as WinVN. There are a lot of knowledgeable people on the group who use Winsock applications of all sorts. Be warned though, there are typically lots of articles posted every day—what is called a "heavy traffic" newsgroup.

WinVN opens multiple windows

Have you ever seen one of those Picture-in-Picture (PIP) televisions? You know the ones—you have the main channel on the big screen and a couple others that you might be interested in inset in the corners of your TV picture. WinVN lets you do basically the same thing with the news.

You're probably already familiar with how Windows works, so this is probably not a radically new concept. However, the operation of multiple windows has some pretty nice benefits to newsreading. What if you want to quote one article while responding to another one? With two windows open, it's a snap. What if you'll be looking at several groups over an extended period of time during one newsreading session and don't want to bother opening and closing groups every five minutes? Again, WinVN makes this easy. One piece of advice to take with you—if you're in the habit of always closing windows when you leave them, you might want to temporarily get out of that habit to use WinVN most effectively.

Just double-click and read

This section probably contains the shortest instruction you'll ever find— double-click. That's it. Just use the scroll bar in the Group window to find the article you want and double-click on the article. A new window will open with the contents of the article displayed.

Q&A

I subscribed to a newsgroup full of pictures and somebody posted a series of auto photographs from Hot Rod magazine. Is this legal?

No. The same copyright laws that apply everywhere else apply to cyberspace, too. You cannot reproduce, distribute, or otherwise use copyrighted material of any type—doing so is both illegal and unethical. Also, you cannot use a post of any sort in any material you produce without the author's permission.

Searching for articles

Having the capability to search for particular articles within a group often comes in handy when reading newsgroups. Especially in high traffic groups, where you can be confronted with several hundred articles a day, searching for particular articles can save you a lot of time.

Let's say, for example, that you subscribe to **alt.winsock** to find out a little more about upcoming versions of WinVN. After returning from a three-day week-end, you fire up WinVN only to discover that there are almost 700 new articles to read. Because it will take too long to read through hundreds of articles to find the few that might talk about WinVN, you can either forget about it—or you can use WinVN's search function.

To search for relevant articles, you would choose Find under the Search menu in the Group window (or you could press Ctrl+F). This will search all subject headers for what you're looking for. You also can use the search button on the toolbar.

{Note}

WinVN's search command is case insensitive. In other words, it doesn't matter whether or not you capitalize letters—searching for articles containing "winvn" will still yield articles that contain "WinVN."

After you tell WinVN to search for the desired articles, the first one found (called a **hit**) will be highlighted and preceded by a **>** (see fig. 13.1). If the article doesn't appear to be what you were looking for, you can choose the Find <u>N</u>ext option in the <u>S</u>earch menu (or press F3). You can continue to search until you have found what you want or until all the relevant articles have been located.

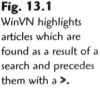

Fig. 13.1
WinVN highlights articles which are found as a result of a search and precedes them with a **>**.

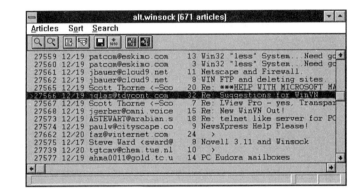

Following a thread

The concept of a thread was introduced in the last chapter. A thread is simply a series of posts pertaining to the same topic or subject line. Most newsgroups, with the exception of a few like the *.forsale newsgroups, are comprised primarily of threads. WinVN allows you to automatically "thread" newsgroups on retrieval. It is highly recommended that you leave this setting on (it's default setting)—doing so makes reading more efficient and effective (see fig. 13.2).

⊗<Caution> After telling you how efficient and wonderful threads are, it's time to burst the bubble a little bit. Just because a number of posts contain the same subject line doesn't necessarily mean they all deal with the same topic. Usually, by the time a thread has been responded to several times, the articles no longer reflect the original subject line—they become "off-topic." In a perfect world, when the content of a post becomes significantly different than the subject line, the person changing the subject should change the subject line. However, this isn't a perfect world and people are lazy, so be prepared—you can't always judge a book by its cover.

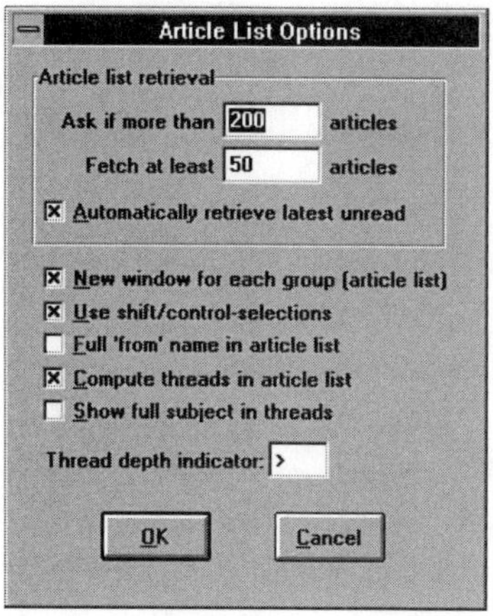

Fig. 13.2
WinVN offers several
different threading
options. Here,
threading is enabled
and a **>** has been
chosen as the
threading symbol.

```
┌─────────────────────────────────────┐
│  ─        Article List Options       │
│ ┌─Article list retrieval───────────┐ │
│ │  Ask if more than │200│  articles │ │
│ │  Fetch at least │50│   articles   │ │
│ │  ☒ Automatically retrieve latest unread │ │
│ └──────────────────────────────────┘ │
│  ☒ New window for each group (article list) │
│  ☒ Use shift/control-selections      │
│  ☐ Full 'from' name in article list  │
│  ☒ Compute threads in article list   │
│  ☐ Show full subject in threads      │
│  Thread depth indicator: │>│         │
│                                       │
│      ┌────────┐    ┌────────┐         │
│      │   OK   │    │ Cancel │         │
│      └────────┘    └────────┘         │
└─────────────────────────────────────┘
```

Going to the Next Article

If you are like lots of other news readers out there, you may want to quickly go from article to article without having to close the one you're reading and double-clicking the next one. WinVN offers several one-step options to accomplish this. All the options can be found under the View menu in the Article Window.

- **Next Article (Ctrl+N).** If you wish to go directly to the next article in the group you're reading, you need to choose the Next Article option. Choosing this option closes the current article window and opens a window for the next article in the group. You also can go to the next article by clicking the Right Arrow button on the Article Window toolbar.

- **Next Unseen (F2).** If you have been skipping around some and would like to look at the next article, but don't want to bother seeing the next article if it's one you've already read, you need to pick the Next Unseen option under the View menu. Clicking the Eyeglasses button on the toolbar accomplishes the same thing.

- **Next with same subject (F3).** Also called "Poor man's threading." If you are involved in reading a thread and want to quickly go to the next article in a thread, choosing the Next with same Subject option will accomplish this. This is particularly helpful if you chose not to display articles by threads on start-up. Clicking the Curving Arrow button next to the Eyeglass button on the toolbar also takes you to the next article with the same subject line.

Thread options

The Article List... option under the Config menu enables you to determine how you are going to thread (or not thread) articles. The fourth option, Compute threads in article list, lets you decide if you want to thread newsgroups. WinVN's default setting is On, so you need to click on the box if you don't want to thread. As was discussed in the last chapter, threading is very useful and it is recommended that you take advantage of this WinVN function.

The next two options let you determine exactly how the threading will look. If you turn Show Full Subject in Threads off, only the thread symbol will appear in the subject line of every threaded

article after the first (see fig. 13.3). If you leave it turned on, the entire subject line of each article will appear (see fig. 13.4). Also, the indentation of the symbol will indicate to which article a post is replying, sometimes called a thread layer. If a thread symbol is tabbed three times, that article is posted in response to an article with a double-tabbed thread symbol.

Lastly, you get to determine what symbol WinVN will use to indicate threaded articles. The standard symbol is the **>**, WinVN sets the threading symbol to a **|**, but feel free to choose any character you like.

When the user chooses not to show the full subject lines of threaded articles, only the threading symbol is used. Here, there are six layers to the thread.

When the user chooses to show the full subject lines of threaded articles, the entire subject line is displayed. Notice that the articles are still layered.

Marking articles as read

To avoid the hassle of having to decide what you have read and haven't read, most newsreaders will "mark" articles for you. WinVN is no exception. Anytime you view an article, WinVN marks the article as read by placing an "s" next to it and highlights it in a different color. Also, with an article highlighted while in the Group window, a click of the right mouse button will also mark an article as read.

You also can manually mark an article as read. To mark an article yourself, click (or Ctrl+click when marking more than one article) on the article(s) you would like to mark as read, and then choose the <u>M</u>ark Selected Articles as Seen option under the Articles menu, and you're done. This option is best used when you need to stop reading news, but would like to come back to the group later without wading through articles you're uninterested in.

(Tip)

> The quickest way to mark articles as read is by "catching up" the group. When you "catch up," you're telling WinVN that you don't want to see any of the current articles the next time you read news—only new ones. To catch up, simply choose the Catch-up and Exit option under the Articles menu when you are finished reading a group.

Reading ROT13 encrypted articles

(X)<Caution>

> Do not confuse encryption with encoding. This section deals with the encryption of information, which is the process of converting what text really says into a secret code. In other words, you're translating one type of text into another type of text. However, encoding, which will be covered in chapter 15, deals with converting non-ASCII, or non-text, information (such as binary files) into text that can be transported through ASCII-based media—such as e-mail and news.

To brighten up your day, you decide to read some jokes on **rec.humor.funny**. As you go from joke to joke, you encounter a post that looks like it's been written in Japanese or Greek instead of English (see fig. 13.5). What happened? Is there something wrong with your machine? Did you do something wrong? Probably not. Instead, you've likely encountered an article encrypted in ROT13. A ROT13 article generally contains offensive material or information that a casual reader may not want to see, such as the revelation of a much-awaited movie's ending (sometimes called a spoiler). The subject line of a ROT13 post will appear normally, but the text of an article, once selected, will be encrypted. To decrypt such an article, simply select the ROT13 option under the View menu while in the Article Window (or Ctrl+R).

What is PGP?

As you've probably guessed, ROT13 is not very secure—anybody can read it. But suppose you want to transfer information securely over insecure electronic channels, such as through NNTP or SMTP servers? For that, you would need a good encrypter. As luck would have it, one exists—PGP.

PGP stands for "Pretty Good Privacy" and was developed by Phil Zimmerman of Pretty Good Software. Basically, PGP works on the concept of keys—or modes of encryption. With PGP, every user has two keys—both a public and a private one. For example, Bob can reveal his public key, which Sue will then use to encrypt a message to Bob. However, Bob then uses his additional private key to decrypt the message that Sue sent using his public key. In this way, only Bob will be able to read that message, because he's the only one with his own private key. Because the private key is required to decrypt the public one, no one else can decrypt his public key.

This multi-level method of encryption provides both security and authentication of information over public channels. To get the latest on freeware versions of PGP, FTP to **bitsy.mit.edu /pub/PGP**.

Plain English, please!

ROT13 (which stands for "**ROT**ate **13** characters") is a simple encryption scheme designed to hide the contents of a particular article. There's no huge secret to how ROT13 works—every letter in a post is "rotated" 13 letters forward. As an example, the letter "A" would be switched with the letter "N" and the word "but" would appear as "ohg" when encrypted using ROT13.

Fig. 13.5
An article encrypted with ROT13 may look rather strange.

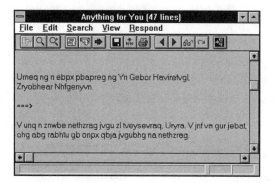

Saving articles

WinVN is capable of saving any article you choose, anywhere you'd like. You can either save individual articles from the Article window or multiple articles from the Group window.

Why save articles?

There are many reasons you might want to save articles. Reading news is much more than just glancing at a group, reading a few articles, and then moving on. Newsgroups contain a wealth of information and pointers that you may want to save. The following are a few reasons why you might want to save articles:

- *For posterity.* In the course of reading the news, you run across an attractive quote or a compelling article you want to keep for reference.

- *For information.* An article may point you to a particularly useful FTP site. Or, the monthly FAQ might be posted on your favorite newsgroup and you want to keep it as reference. In any event, having useful information on-hand at times when you're not connected to news can be very helpful.

- *For later use.* You may find yourself reading an interesting thread that you'd like to read later and just don't have time at the moment—maybe you'd like to save it on a disk and read it at home where you don't have a modem. In addition, most news servers delete messages after they're a few days old, so if you miss them, they may be gone forever. Whatever the reason, saving articles let's you read news when you're ready.

You will have other reasons to save articles. It's good to know that, when you do find yourself wanting to save an article, a group of unrelated articles or a whole thread, WinVN offers you this capability.

Saving an individual article

Many times, you will simply want to save a single article. The most common method for saving an individual article is to save it while in the Article window. To save an article while reading it, first choose the Save option under the File menu in the Article window. Clicking on the Floppy Disk button on the toolbar does the same thing. Next WinVN will ask you to name the file you want to save the article as (see fig. 13.6). Once you have done so, the article is saved in the appropriate location.

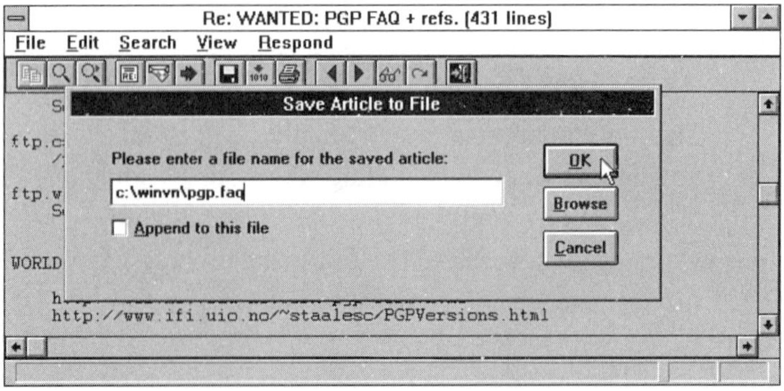

Fig. 13.6
When you choose to save an article, WinVN asks you to select a location and file name. Once the proper information has been entered, WinVN saves a copy of the article.

⚙ *{Note}* It is a good idea to save files in standard "8.3" DOS format and with a name that's easy to reference. For example, if you are in the habit of saving jokes off of **rec.humor.funny**, you could save the files as *filename.rhf*.

Saving multiple articles

There may be occasion when you'll want to save more than one article. For instance, it was mentioned earlier that you might want to save a whole thread for later reading, this would be a good time to save more than one article. Saving multiple articles requires two steps.

First, you must select the articles you wish to save. There are several ways you can do this (some you already know):

- *Click and drag.* Click at the beginning of the number of articles you'd like to save and drag your mouse while holding down the button.

- *Ctrl+Click.* Click on the first article you'd like to save. Then, while holding down the Ctrl key, click on any other article you'd like to save.

- *Select Articles Containing String.* Suppose you want to save all articles containing a certain word—for instance, "WinVN." WinVN offers an option under the Articles menu in the Group Window called Select Articles Containing String. When you choose this option, you can tell WinVN to automatically select all articles that contain "WinVN" in the subject line.

Once the articles are selected using any of the methods above, you can choose the Save Selected Articles... option under the Articles menu, give the file a name, and you have successfully saved all the desired articles (see fig. 13.7).

Fig. 13.7
After selecting a group
of articles to save, you
can choose to save
those articles under a
single file name.

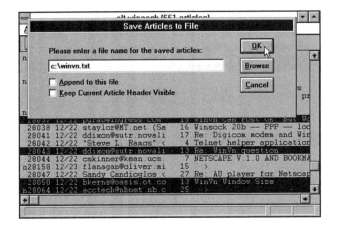

Searching for content in an article

There will be times when you are looking for specific information within a
long article. For example, you may be reading a particular newsgroup's FAQ
and wish to find a section dealing with a particular topic. Just as you can
search for newsgroups from the Main window and search for articles from
the Group window, you also can search for article content and key words
from the Article window.

Appending saved articles

Now that you know you can save many articles
under the same file name, you must be wonder-
ing if you can save related articles in the future
under that same file name without destroying the
original file's contents. You can, and WinVN calls
the process "appending files."

Figure 13.8 shows that there is an additional
option available, called Append To This File. If
you select this option before clicking OK, WinVN
saves the selected articles to the end of the file
you choose.

For example, suppose you want to gather all the
articles about WinVN for an entire week. Obviously, you couldn't stay connected to your NNTP
server all week, nor would you want to wait a
whole week to read news. Instead, you could save
all the WinVN articles on day one. Then, on day
two (or three, or four), you could again select all
the WinVN articles, save them, and append them
to the original file containing the WinVN articles.
In this way, you can collect multiple articles over
time (or over newsgroups) in one place.

First, you must select the article to read. Once the Article Window is open, you can choose the Find option under the Search menu or click the appropriate button on the toolbar. WinVN then prompts you for a word or phrase that you would like to search for (see fig. 13.8). If it appears anywhere in the article, WinVN scrolls down to the portion of the message which contains the word or phrase. You also can use the Find Next command to locate multiple instances of the desired text.

Fig. 13.8
WinVN gives you the capability of quickly searching an article for particular text.

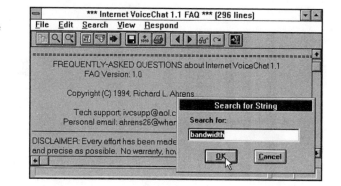

Printing articles

There will be occasions when you would like a hard-copy of a particular article. Perhaps you want to share some information with a colleague who can't receive the article electronically or maybe you'd like to take the information with you on the road where you won't have access to a computer. Situations like these make it necessary to use WinVN's Print function.

In order to print an article, you must be reading it. After selecting the article, choose the Print option under the File menu or click the Print button on the toolbar. A new dialogue box appears asking you to customize your hard copy. You can change the quality of the printout, print only a selected portion of an article or even print to a file. WinVN uses your standard printer settings, so you probably won't have to change these, but you can if you want. Once you have selected the appropriate options, click OK and watch the article print on your printer!

X<Caution> Although WinVN automatically assesses your printer setup from the Windows printer control panel, it is always a good idea to check this information in any new application before using it. Choose Pint Setup... under the File menu to view your printer information. If any of the settings are incorrect, you can correct them now so that all future printing will go smoothly.

14
Writing Articles and Responses

As luck would have it, you know the answer to the question that was posted on your favorite newsgroup! But how do you let everyone in cyberspace know you know (and do you even want to)?

In this chapter:

- How to create and use a signature
- How to reply to articles publicly and via e-mail
- What "quoting" is and how to use it in your posts
- How to create and post your own articles
- How to log your posts
- How to Batch Send your posts
- How to encrypt your posts

U p to now, your experience has probably been limited to reading newsgroups. Now it's time to move on. You've been reading newsgroups a while and somebody just posted to your favorite newsgroup, **bionet.genome.arabidopsis**, that they'd like to know what factors influence chlorophyll deficiency in viney, fleshy-fruited Arabidopsis (what most of us call watermelons). As luck would have it, you know the answer to the question! But how do you let everyone in cyberspace know you know (and do you even want to)? That's what you discover in this chapter.

⊛ *{Note}*___ | You know those people who always have an opinion on everything and are all too willing to share it at the drop of the hat—whether they have all the facts or not? It's quite likely that you've run into many of these people—and you probably don't like them much, either. Unfortunately, that's probably how you'll end up coming across on the Internet if you begin posting and replying to articles your first day. Instead, read some newsgroups for awhile before contributing. Get a feel for who posts, what is acceptable, and what has just recently been covered. If you do, you'll be able to make a quality contribution to UseNet and might very well save yourself a lot of grief.

Using a signature

Everybody has their own special identity—something that sets them apart from everyone else. Unfortunately, when you are represented by nothing more than a collection of pixels on a computer screen, it's hard to set yourself apart.

Furthermore, with the dynamic nature of the Internet, the only way you could possibly expect to identify yourself to everyone would be to write a little information about yourself into every post—a daunting and time-consuming task for anyone.

However, there's no need for despair—WinVN has a way of making it possible for you to express yourself without typing in those extra lines in every post. WinVN gives you the option of creating a **signature file**, which can include just about anything you want —your name, your address, a witty saying—and can automatically be attached to the end of any correspondence you send.

Creating a signature file

Creating an identity by using a signature file is easy and fun. You can be creative or business-like, tell about yourself, or tell a joke—how you want to come across on UseNet is up to you. Whatever you decide, it is probably a good idea to use a signature (often called a "sig" on the Internet). It's standard practice for most people to use a signature on the Net.

✱ {Note}

If you have been using e-mail, you may already have a signature file. If you do, and you know the name of the file your signature is stored in, you can probably proceed immediately to the next section. However, you may want to browse this section in case you'd like to create a new one in WinVN to use or change your current one.

Creating a signature file is as easy as using your favorite editor. There is really no need to use a professional word processing application to create a signature file, as any formatting or special characters would be lost anyway. Instead, using **Notepad** in Windows should be sufficient.

1 Open Notepad to edit your signature file.

2 When creating your sig, make sure that you include your name and your e-mail address. If you like, you also can include other personal information, such as your phone number, address, alternate e-mail addresses, and any other information you desire. It's also a good idea to keep your signature to under 75 characters per line. Finally, many people like to include a clever saying or some ASCII art in their signature.

3 Once you have edited your signature file, save the file under an appropriate name (something like myname.sig will do) in the WinVN directory. Once this is done, you can return to WinVN.

ASCII art

Looking for a way to let out that Rembrandt in you? Then maybe ASCII art is the way to do it. Many people on the Internet have become quite adept at drawing little pictures using nothing more than the standard ASCII characters available on your standard keyboard. In fact, there is even a newsgroup dedicated to ASCII artists and mavens alike called **alt.ascii-art**.

It is quite a challenge to come up with a little picture that helps identify yourself and your tastes. There are even computer programs out there that will turn a standard picture into ASCII art. Usually ASCII art is not copyrighted and can be copied and used. However, before using someone's ASCII art, it is good netiquette to e-mail the artist expressing your appreciation for the work and informing them of your intent to use their art.

It is considered bad form to have an extremely long signature like the one in the figure (4–5 lines is considered standard), so keep this in mind if you would like to use ASCII art in your signature. In addition, it is equally important that you use a monospace font like Courier so that any art or formatting is maintained when you post.

An example of ASCII art. This work would be too long to include in a signature.

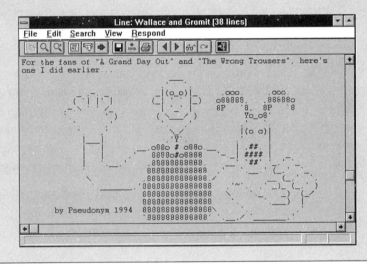

Configuring WinVN to use your signature

After you have created your signature, it's time to tell WinVN to use it. This option can be set by opening the Config menu and choosing the Compositions... option. At the bottom of this new window, there is an option allowing you to enable your signature file. To enable your signature, click this box.

Next, you need to tell WinVN the name of your signature file. I called mine noel.sig and saved it in my WinVN directory (see fig. 14.1). If you don't know where yours is, use the Browse option to find it. Once you have found it, click OK and proceed.

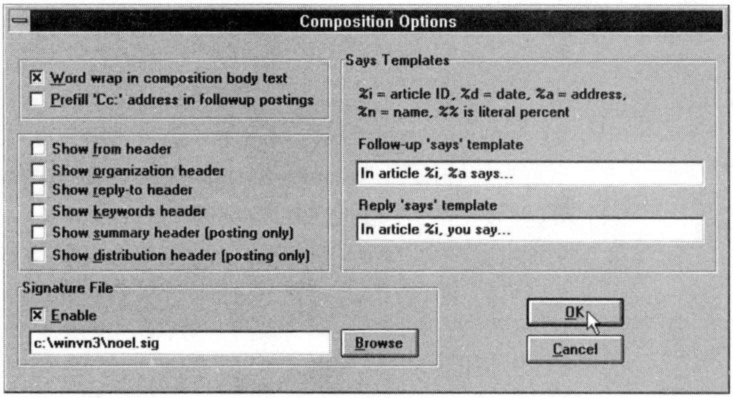

Fig. 14.1
Once you have told WinVN how to use your personal signature by setting and enabling your signature file, you are ready to go.

One other note: It would probably be a good idea to post a test message to UseNet to make sure your signature file is being appended appropriately and appears as you'd like it to.

⊛ *{Note}*

Do not just pick any newsgroup to post test messages to, as you will be flamed without mercy. There are special newsgroups that have been created specifically for this purpose. Whenever you need to post a test message—whether it's to test a signature or for any other reason—post to one of these newsgroups. **alt.test** is probably the most often used of these special test newsgroups. Whenever you send a message to these newsgroups, auto-responders will send you e-mail confirmations that your test message has been received.

Replying to an article

Next to reading messages, you will spend a majority of your time on UseNet responding to messages. Once you have made the decision to respond to an article, commonly referred to as "posting a reply," you still have one more decision to make—do you post your reply to the newsgroup where everyone can read it or do you respond only to the original author. Some things to consider in your decision:

- *Relevance.* If your reply is in keeping with the thread or question asked, you'll probably post it to the group. A reply that may be off-topic but still of interest to the group may want to be posted under a different subject line. A totally off-topic offering should probably be e-mailed or posted under a new subject line.

- *Appropriateness.* This is related to relevance. Ask yourself if your reply is appropriate for this newsgroup. For example, extolling the virtues of Windows on **comp.sys.macintosh** is probably not a good idea. In such cases, sending e-mail to an individual requesting such information might be better. In addition, it might also not be appropriate to post a reply if 20 other people have already answered it—this will only succeed in increasing useless traffic.

- *Politeness.* Make *sure* that your post is in keeping with netiquette. If someone requests that you reply via e-mail, do so. If your post is controversial but on topic, post it to the group; if it's nothing more than a personal attack, save it for e-mail—or don't send it at all.

Remember to **RAP** before you reply.

⊗<Caution> After years of reading and posting news, I have developed what I call the "24-hour rule." The rule is simple—if you find yourself emotionally reacting to a post, wait 24 hours before posting a reply. If you follow this rule, you will often find that the post wasn't even worth replying to at all. By spending some time cooling off, you can avoid posting things you will later regret and will be able to produce a more thoughtful, even-tempered reply.

Replying by e-mail

There will be occasions when you want to reply directly to someone instead of posting a reply to the entire group (see fig. 14.2). Perhaps you're replying to someone who requested e-mail responses or maybe you want to say something off-topic. When you do want to send a personal reply, WinVN makes it simple:

1 While reading the article, open the Respond menu and choose the Followup Mail option (or press Ctrl+O).

2 Notice that WinVN automatically fills in the subject line and recipient's address for you. If you want to change these (or any other) header fields, simply click in the appropriate field and type in the correct information. For instance, if you wanted to Forward the article to someone else, you would click in the To: line and enter the appropriate e-mail address.

3 Edit the original article and write your reply. For further help on this procedure, see the sections on quoting and replying later in this chapter.

4 Open the Mail menu and choose the Send option.

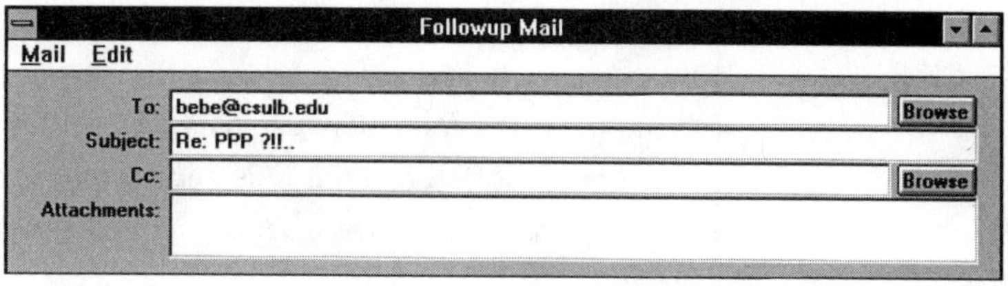

Fig. 14.2
Replying with
Followup Mail sends
a private reply to a
newsgroup poster.

Posting a follow-up message

Posting a follow-up message to a newsgroup is similar to sending a private reply. However, instead of using the Followup Mail option while reading the message, use the Followup Article option after opening the Respond menu (or press Ctrl+L) to send your reply to the group instead of the poster (see fig. 14.3).

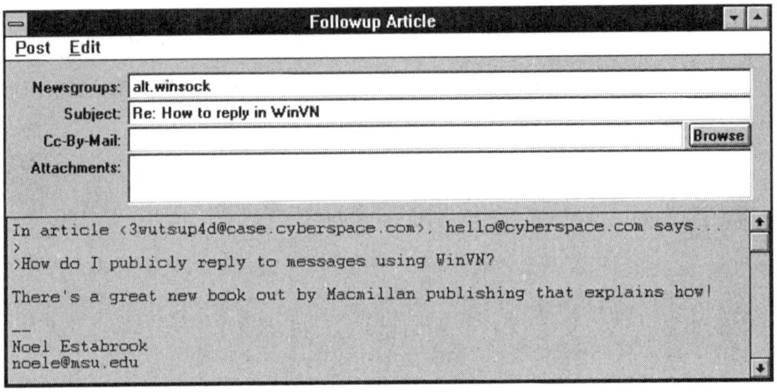

Fig. 14.3

Replying with
Followup Article sends
a public reply to a
newsgroup.

The first difference you'll notice when sending a public reply is in the field that indicates who the message will be sent to. When composing follow-up mail, the message was sent To: an individual, as indicated by their e-mail address. Composing a follow-up article, however, causes WinVN to send the message to a Newsgroup:. In other words, the newsgroup is the recipient. All other basic header information is the same as in a personal reply. You may then edit and write your reply (using the techniques outlined in the following sections). When you're finished, open the Post menu and choose the Send option.

⊗<Caution> When posting a reply, try to avoid the "me, too!" syndrome. A lot of newcomers on the Net will see an offer they'd like to take advantage of or a sentiment they agree with and will post a reply that says nothing more than, "I agree," or "Send me that information too, please." To be brutally honest—nobody cares, and most people consider it rude and a waste of bandwidth to post such a message. This type of message is best saved for e-mail and kept out of newsgroups.

WinVN also offers another neat feature. What if you have a text file that contains an answer to someone's question? It would take a long time to re-type the entire file into your response, and it would probably even take too long to open the file, cut the text, and paste it into your article. WinVN allows you to read a file into any article or reply. To include the text from a file into your response, open the Mail (or Post) menu and choose the Read File... option. After locating the file you'd like to include, double-click it and, voila! it is now in your article.

Quoting

What would your reaction be if someone came up to you and said, "You know, I think you're right, I agree with you 100 percent"? After deciding that they should probably be in a mental institution, you'd scratch your head and wonder what they could possibly be talking about.

Unfortunately, the same thing can happen on the Internet. Many times people post a reply, either personally or publicly, that includes only their reply and none of the text of the original post. In what they believe to be an attempt to save space, they delete the original message and simply type in their reply. When this happens, a lot of people simply skip the message while scratching their head in confusion.

To avoid this problem, it is always a good idea to **quote** the message you are replying to. You'll notice that, when you send a reply, the text of the message you're replying to is included in the message body, with every line preceded by a **>**. This is called quoted text and it is what gives your reply context and allows everyone else (especially those who may not have read the post you're replying to) to know what you're talking about. Deleting all the quoted material in a post eliminates that context for future readers.

There is another way to quote text in a reply, and that is by pasting the text from another post into your message. To do this, open the message you want to quote from, select and copy the text, and then paste it in your reply. When you do this, always make sure you reference the person you're quoting—using both their name and e-mail address. This information is generally found at the beginning of the body of a message and also can be copied and pasted.

⊛ *{Note}* — If you open the Config menu and choose the Compositions... option, you will see a section entitled **Says Templates**. These configurations determine how a person or article is referenced for private and public replying and posting. The default for a private reply is "in article x, you say" and the default setting for a public reply is "in article x, johndoe says". Most people leave these defaults as they are. However, feel free to experiment with them as you wish.

Fig. 14.4
Even though the original post was much longer, the person replying included only the text being answer as quoted text.

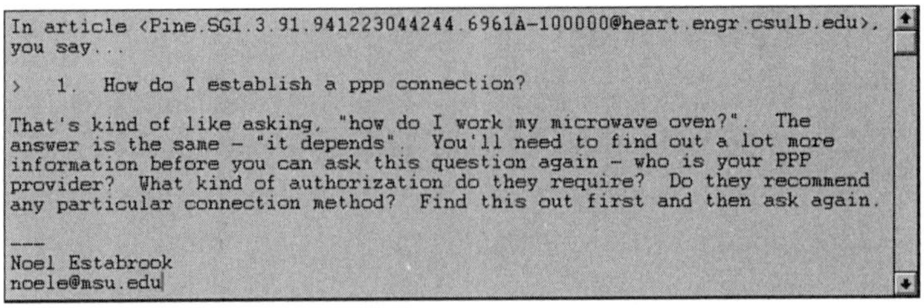

```
In article <Pine.SGI.3.91.941223044244.6961A-100000@heart.engr.csulb.edu>,
you say...

>   1.  How do I establish a ppp connection?

That's kind of like asking, "how do I work my microwave oven?".  The
answer is the same — "it depends".  You'll need to find out a lot more
information before you can ask this question again — who is your PPP
provider?  What kind of authorization do they require?  Do they recommend
any particular connection method?  Find this out first and then ask again.

——
Noel Estabrook
noele@msu.edu
```

You can edit your reply, including the quoted text, by using the standard Windows cut and paste methods. Keep in mind that it isn't necessary to include all the text from the original post—delete text that you aren't replying to or that is irrelevant. Also, keep your reply as succinct as possible. When posting a reply, especially when posting to a group, it is important to use bandwidth wisely.

For instance, a two-page message takes up more bandwidth than a one-page message, so the more concise you are, the less bandwidth you use. For a practical example, imagine trying to drive several sports cars through a two-lane tunnel—it'd be pretty easy, right? Now, imagine trying to push 100 semi-trucks through that same tunnel in the same amount of time. You couldn't do it—you would simply have to take more time to get all the trucks through the tunnel. Remember that the UseNet "tunnel" can only take so much traffic, so try to drive a sports car if you can.

66 *Plain English, please!*

Bandwidth is a term that you will probably see popping up quite often on UseNet. Basically, bandwidth is the amount of space a particular transmission uses. On newsgroups, this translates into the size of messages sent. 99

Sending the reply

After you have decided how and where to reply, edited your message, and checked your quoting, you are ready to send, or post, the reply. The process for sending private and public replies is almost identical.

To send a private reply, choose the Send option under the Mail menu (or press Ctrl+S) and WinVN will e-mail your reply for you. To post a public reply, choose the Send option under the Post menu (or press Ctrl+S). Also, before you send your message, take an extra moment to make sure you want to send it—remember hundreds, if not thousands, of people will be reading it.

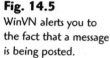

Fig. 14.5
WinVN alerts you to the fact that a message is being posted.

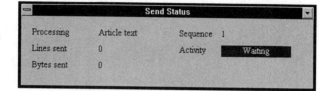

Posting your own articles

As you become more familiar with the news, you'll begin to participate more fully. One of the things you'll want to do is to make original contributions to groups. Maybe you have a question that you'd like to ask, or you might like to start a discussion about a topic you're curious about. To do this, you need to post a new article to a newsgroup. WinVN allows you to do this in several different ways. Also, keep in mind that there is always a corresponding command available for sending private e-mail messages.

Starting a new article from the Main window

It's quite easy to post a new article from the Main window:

1 Under the Utilities menu, there is a New Article option. To start a new article, choose this option or click the corresponding toolbar button.

2 Next, you see a window that is identical to the one you saw when posting a reply (refer to fig. 14.3). The contents of this window are different in several ways. First, you must fill in the name of the newsgroup(s) you want to post to. However, if you select a newsgroup by clicking it before choosing to post, WinVN will fill in the newsgroup's name for you.

3 You will need to provide a subject line because you aren't replying to an already existing thread.

4 Finally, you'll notice that there is no text in the message body, so you won't be able to quote material, unless, of course, you paste quoted material in from another article. So you'll need to type, paste, or read in material to comprise the contents of the article.

5 Once the article is done, you can send it as explained in the previous section on replying to messages.

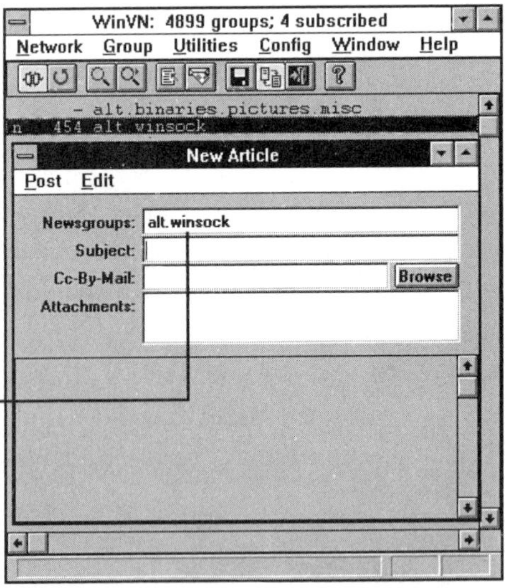

Fig. 14.6
By selecting a newsgroup before posting a message from the Main window, WinVN automatically fills in the newsgroup's name for you.

Selected newsgroup

①(Tip)___

Subject lines can often determine whether or not your post is read and/or responded to. There are a few ways you can help. To begin with, try keeping the subject line to under 30 characters—longer subject lines may not fit in some newsreaders and your article will be ignored. Second, make the subject line relevant and specific. Don't make a subject line like "For Sale" in the **misc.forsale** newsgroup. Instead, you might want to make your subject line something like, "FS—Port. CD Player". Lastly, don't use all capital letters in the hope of drawing attention to your post. A post that says, "I NEED HELP PLEASE!!!" is less likely to recruit help than "Help establishing PPP please?" and is more likely to upset people.

Starting a new article from the Group window

Perhaps the most common place you'll post a new article from will be the Group window. Usually, the idea for a new post or reply comes while already reading a newsgroup or article. Starting a new article from the Group window is similar to starting one from the Main window.

From the Group window, the New Article option (Ctrl+L) is under the Articles menu, even though the New Article button on the toolbar remains the same. To compose a new article, choose this option or click the corresponding toolbar button.

When the Composition window appears, you'll notice that the name of the newsgroup is automatically provided. Unless you wish to crosspost and add some newsgroup names to this field, you only have to fill in the subject line and the article text.

⊗<Caution> Avoid mass crossposting to too many groups. Doing so consumes a lot of bandwidth, makes follow-ups more difficult, and could lead to trouble with your system administrator. Crossposting was discussed in detail in chapter 4.

Writing the article

What an article says is the most important part of any post. It can invoke discussion, sympathy, answers, flames, or it can simply be ignored, depending on the content. As previously mentioned, try to be concise when composing your post. Keep your post as simple and focused as possible. Try to use a little humor or other "personalizing" elements, such as emoticons, if appropriate.

You also will want to make sure that WinVN's word wrap is on. Word wrap is on by default in WinVN, so you shouldn't need to do anything to change it. Basically, word wrap places a carriage return (sometimes called a line-feed) at the end of each line and makes sure that a word that may go off the end of a line is placed at the beginning of the following. This makes your posts easier for most newsreaders to handle and facilitates ease of reading and replying.

To make sure word wrap is on, look in the Compositions... option under the Config menu from the Main Window or in the Preferences option under the Post menu from the Composition window. Turn word wrap off at your own risk, as your post may appear as one long sentence in some newsreaders and will be hard to quote in replies.

Headers everywhere

When you enabled your signature and checked on the word wrap status in WinVN, you did so in the Composition Options window. If you noticed, however, there were a lot more options to choose from—these are the Header options. You may have already caught on that every post you read has information at the top of the article that you likely don't pay attention to. This information makes up a message's **header**.

Whether you realize it or not, every time you post, WinVN includes header information about you and your post. Each header item of your post can be viewed by you if you want. Clicking each

item in Composition Options window will cause that header to be displayed in your Composition window.

Most people leave a majority of these headers hidden. However, with some exploration and experimentation, you may want to have some of them displayed. The Newsgroups:, From:, Organization:, and Reply To: fields are automatically filled in by WinVN. You must provide information for the Subject:, CC-by-Mail:, Keywords:, Summary:, Distribution:, and Attachments: fields. Most users usually leave the Distribution: and Attachments: fields empty.

An article editing window with all header items displayed. The poster has filled in all the desired header information.

New Article
Post   **Edit**
Newsgroups:	alt.winsock
Subject:	When is new v. of WinVN due?
From:	noele@msu.edu (Noel Estabrook)
Organization:	Orthos Educational Systems
Reply-To:	noele@pilot.msu.edu
Cc-By-Mail:	21504zr@ibm.ead.msu.edu [Browse]
Keywords:	WinVN
Summary:	Asking for new version
Distribution:	
Attachments:	

```
I have just gotten WinVN .93.9.  Does anybody know when
the new 1.0 version will be coming out and if it will have
any additional features that haven't been talked about in
the FAQ?

Noel Estabrook
```

Posting the article

Your message headers are correct, you've written a relevant and succinct message, it's word-wrapped and ready to go. The last step, sending the message, is the easy part. From the <u>P</u>ost menu, choose the <u>S</u>end option (or press Ctrl+S).

After you have posted your article, update the newsgroup and read your newly posted message. If it hasn't shown up on the newsgroup yet, just wait a few minutes (some news servers are faster than others). Pay special attention to the header information to see what your header looks like. To further experiment, make sure to post to the **alt.test** newsgroup.

! *(Tip)*

> The Distribution: header is one header that you may want WinVN to display at all times. Although not used often, it can be useful. For example, what if you want to try to sell your car over the Internet and so you post a "want ad" to **misc.forsale**? It won't do much good to find a buyer in New York if you live in California. In this case, set your distribution field to local so that your ad won't appear to the world (the distribution field's default). Be warned, though, that not every system administrator defines distribution locations the same way. Your sysadmin might think the United States is "local," so be careful!

Take a deep breath—thousands of people may be reading your article right now.

? *Q&A*

> ### I posted my article, but it's been five minutes and it still hasn't shown up—did I do something wrong?
>
> No, you may just have a news server that updates slowly or sporadically. Or, there may just be a problem somewhere along your newsfeed. Just be patient. On some rare occasions, a wait of as long as 24 hours might be encountered. If it hasn't shown up within a day, *then* you can worry!

Logging your posts

We all know people who keep everything—you know, pack-rats. Usually, a pack-rat is someone who likes to keep lots of useless stuff just for the sake of having it. On the Internet, however, saving every little thing that comes our way is quite helpful.

What if someone misquotes you in a follow-up? Or challenges something you said two months ago? Or wants you to re-send or e-mail that brilliant post from last July? WinVN's post logging capability prepares you for such contingencies.

WinVN logs posts by default, so if you don't want your posts logged, you need to manually turn the setting off. Logging settings are found in the Logging... option under the Config menu. Notice that the logging of both news posts and e-mail is already enabled and default names for the log files are provided—mail.log for e-mail messages and post.log for posts. If you would like to change the default names, you may do so.

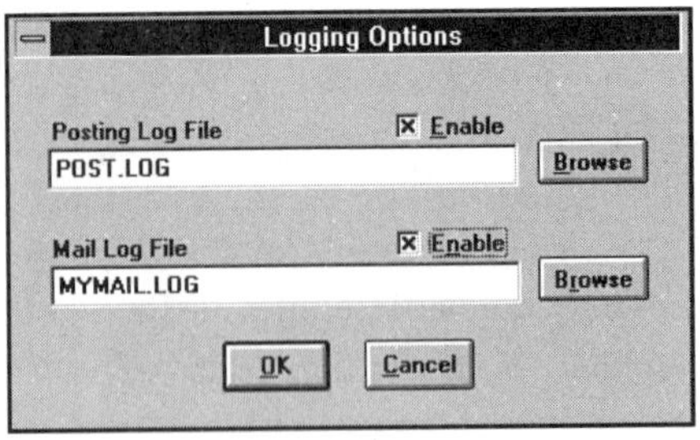

Fig. 14.7
WinVN automatically logs your e-mail messages and posts for you and provides default file names that you can modify if you wish. Some people save their log files on a floppy disk for permanent archiving purposes.

Every post and e-mail you send while using WinVN will now be saved—including the header information and signature from each post. You use this file just like any other text file—send it as an attachment, open it in your favorite word processor, use portions of it in other documents, or in any other way you might use a text document.

❋ *{Note}* It is a good idea to "clean up" your log files every so often—especially if you post and send e-mail often. Failure to do so may result in much-needed disk space being consumed or in not being able to open the file in a simple text editor like Notepad. To reduce the text in your log files, simply open them in your favorite word processor and cut the unneeded text. You also can delete the whole file and create a new, empty one at any time.

Batch sending posts and e-mail

What do you do if your Internet provider charges an arm and a leg for online time? As you've seen, news can take quite a bit of connect time. Is there any way that you can reduce these costs? Yes, there is—WinVN calls the process **batch sending**. Although batch sending is useful primarily for composing articles offline, it also can be used by those who simply want to send all of their posts or e-mail at the same time. Batch sending with WinVN is easy and requires no special configurations. The Batch Send sub-menu is located under the Utilities menu in the Main Window. The Batch Send sub-menu allows you to send either posts or e-mail messages.

Preparing to batch send offline

If you are using the Batch Send function to post and e-mail offline, there are several things you need to do. First, connect to your NNTP server as you normally would, reading and marking articles in the standard manner. When you see an article you'd like to reply to or have an idea for an article you would like to post, open a new Composition window with the recipient name (whether newsgroup or individual) and subject line filled in. Then leave the Composition window and move on to the next message.

Once you have read all the news you want and have created composition windows for your posts, replies, and e-mail messages, disconnect your server from WinVN and then follow the necessary procedure for disconnecting from your Internet provider. You do not want to actually exit your Winsock Client—sending the disconnect command for your particular Winsock will usually do. You are now offline, however, all your Composition windows remain open so that you can proceed with your messages as if you were still connected. Though you can not start new articles while disconnected, you can start and compose new e-mail messages offline. In order for batch sending to work, these composition windows *must* remain open—do not close them.

Composing and batch sending

Whether you are batch sending while online or offline, composing articles and e-mail messages is the same as if you were still online. Simply select each Composition window, write and edit each message, and then move on to the next one. If having many windows open at a time is confusing to you, you can minimize each composition window when you are finished with it.

After you have composed all messages and posts, you are now ready to batch send. Of course, if you have composed your articles offline, you must first re-establish a connection to your Internet provide and connect WinVN to your NNTP server. When you have done this, open the Batch Send option under the Utilities menu. To send posts, choose the Posts option; to send mail, choose the Mails option.

Encrypting a message with ROT13

In the section "Reading ROT13 Encrypted Articles" in chapter 13, you learned about decrypting messages in ROT13. In addition to being able to read ROT13 encrypted messages, you can also send them. In fact, encrypting messages using WinVN is a simple process.

To encrypt an article or e-mail message:

1 Compose it as you normally would. When it is written, you are ready to encrypt it.

2 Highlight the text that you want to encrypt (you can encrypt any portion of a message). If you would like to encrypt the entire message, open the Edit menu and choose the Select All option or press Ctrl+A.

3 Once all the desired text is highlighted, open the Edit menu and select the ROT13 option or press Ctrl+R. Your message appears as ROT13 text.

4 You can now send the message normally.

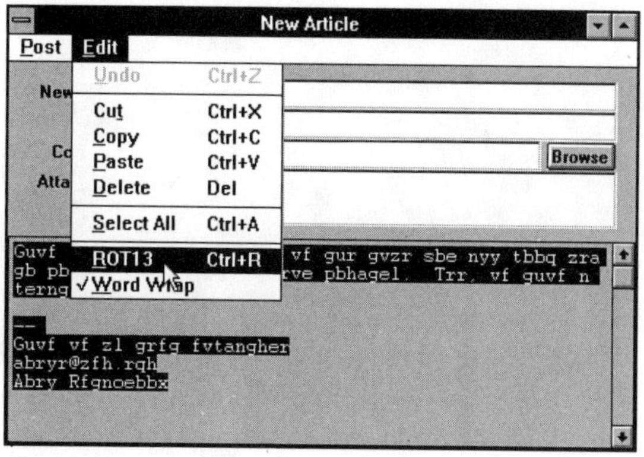

Fig. 14.8

Encrypting a message using ROT13 can only occur after first highlighting the text to be encrypted. Many people don't encrypt their signatures, but this person did.

15

File Attachments

In some groups you can find software posted to transfer and use. In others, you can find pictures of famous (and not so famous) people, audio clips from songs, multimedia movies, and more.

Most of the time, the messages you read in UseNet newsgroups are text. You might read an article reviewing the latest Star Trek movie, a recipe for tuna casserole, or even find an answer to a question about your favorite newsreader software.

Not all UseNet newsgroup articles are just text, however. In some groups, you can find programs, shareware, freeware, and public domain software posted that you can transfer and use. In others you can find pictures of famous (and not so famous) people, audio clips from songs, multimedia movies, and more.

Posting and using programs or graphics on UseNet requires a few extra steps. This chapter covers these steps in detail.

What are file attachments?

When an article is posted to a newsgroup, the body of the article usually contains the whole message. However, sometimes you want to send a file with your message (or have the file be your message). In this case, you can attach the file you want to send to your message, much as you might attach a large document to a cover letter. The message and file (called a **file attachment**) are treated as one entity by UseNet and the Internet. Unlike e-mail, which allows a separate physical entity called an **attachment**, most newsgroup attachments are part of a message, simply appended to the end of the text.

The use of file attachments is controlled not by the Internet, but by your newsgroup package. Not all software supports file attachments. The file attachment must be handled in a special manner; there is no easy way to attach a file if your software can't perform the task. Fortunately, WinVN handles this whole process easily.

File attachments raise a problem, though. Files used on most computers are 8-bits long and contain valid ASCII characters and control codes that are decoded by the machine to have special meaning. Binary files for a PC, for example, are composed of 8-bit characters with ASCII values from 0 to 255, although the first 26 characters are control-codes, meaning they consist of the Ctrl key and another character.

UseNet, though, can't handle the non-ASCII characters from ASCII value 0 through 25. If you try to send characters below ASCII 25 through to a UseNet newsgroup, they will be converted or lost, as they are interpreted by the software controlling access to the Internet in different ways. If a character does manage to be converted and transmitted, when it is received at the other end, it is not converted back to its original value, and hence the meaning of the character is destroyed.

⊗<Caution> Simply put, you can't send binary files over UseNet without changing their character values to something UseNet can handle. If you send binary files over UseNet, the original file is corrupted.

Binary conversion

Now you know why we can't send binary files to UseNet. Logically, though, there must be some way to convert the non-ASCII characters to a transmittable character, then reconvert back when the character is received. Not surprisingly, the process for converting these non-ASCII values was developed early in the history of UseNet and the Internet.

There are actually several ways to convert the characters to transmittable ASCII values. One of the most widely used is a process called **uuencode**. The "UU" part of the name stands for "UNIX to UNIX," as uuencode was originally part of a UNIX-based utility suite called **UUCP** (UNIX to UNIX Copy). To convert a uuencoded file back to binary, a companion program called **uudecode** is used. Uuencode is the most widely used conversion program on the Internet, although some different conversion schemes are occasionally used.

What does a uuencoded file look like?

Try displaying a binary file so you can see what it looks like. In a DOS window or at the DOS prompt enter the command:

```
type c:\command.com
```

You will see a few lines displayed on-screen with a bunch of strange codes including smiley faces, Greek symbols, and blocks of graphics. In all, the file doesn't look like much. You actually only see those characters within the larger file that can be displayed on-screen: there are lots of characters (most of them, in fact) that you can't see as they can't be displayed. All the strange codes are non-ASCII characters, which cannot be sent over the Internet.

We can uuencode the COMMAND.COM file so that it can be sent over the Internet (which we wouldn't do, of course, because it is copyrighted). Part of a uuencoded version of COMMAND.COM looks like this:

```
M9"!#3TU-04Y$+D--/30T*(4EN<V5R="!D:7-K('=I=&&@)3$$:6X@9')I=F4@
M)3(-"B&%0<F5S<R!A;;GD@:V5Y('10(&-0;G1I;G5E("X@+B!N&#H<#&I497)M
M:6YA=&&@8&9%T8V@@:F]B("A9+TX+Q/-#86YN;;;W@97AE8W5T92 E,0T*$T5R
M<F]R(&EN($$5812!:&QE#8QHHHB&D')O9W)A;2@;69I;&&9S&%I;;;E&I:&+M
M96U0<&0--"A8L-"DDYO964@99FEL92!H86YD;;&5S&D&H5!#A9"!!#;;;;VUM86YD4[R
```

```
M(&9I;&4@;F%M90T*#D%C8V5S<R!D96YI960@&0T*365M;W)Y(&%L;&]C871I
M;VX@97)R;W(#F#0I#86YN;W0@;&]A9"!#3TU-04Y$+"!S>7-T96T@:&%L=&5D
M#0HA#0I#86YN;W0@<W1A<G0@0T] ]-34%.1""P97AAI=&EN9P!T*+&@E
M=F5L('!R;V-E<W,@,86))O<G1E9"!P@8V%N;F]T(&-O;G1I;G5E#0H"#0J,# $
M. H! (P, 0        B0$ !-7<FET92!P<F]T96-T(&5R<F]R#0H%=%:60@;
M=6YI=.E;W0@<F5A9"F0@:7N9V%E*&1879191804@<F5Q=65S=I$$871A(&5R
M<F]R(4EN=F%L:60@9$5V:6-E(')E<75E<W0@<&%R=P13965K(&5R
M<F]R$DEN=F%L:60@;65D:6$@='EPP='H$D'EP91!396<T:W;(@:FYVD&ER:YT
M97(@6U=5T(&1F('!$A<&F<&5R<F]R$5=297#9A)R$E(&%A6QT(&15R<F%%E860@
M9F%%U;'0@'0@97R)R<W(W(/1V55N97A)A"!F86EL=7)E)E$5$ -H87]I;F<@
M.DQ08TTL@=F%L:60@9$55N$S#E:(C(.%9N9V4V4/1D:!%5CE<%9<N9V4V4/1D:
M:6QA8FQE(&1F("'09E8C=V55'S'R&AAA,&15<DU0A9$5C:!%3%$;!%6BA
M<VUA8F%-H$]U="#'09<&F H9YU;@;L&17(6#%S<W@;%;@&<%9<%C?99$
MI0^R!:[P'TP???!P ("9P@>";\(2@A<"<%T$T&$CTA"2D=<T0B<(`G"(@"(I"
```

You can see that although the file doesn't make any sense to us, all the characters are ASCII and hence can be transmitted on the Internet.

⊛ *{Note}* | To be accurate, uuencode converts a file of 8-bit characters into 6-bit printable ASCII characters. All Internet sites pass 6-bit printable characters without modification, so no alterations to the contents are performed at all.

A uuencoded file has every character with a legal ASCII value, even though it may represent a non-ASCII code when it is converted back to binary. Keep in mind this warning with uuencoded binary files: any change in the text, even as small as one character, can render the conversion back to binary inaccurate and the binary file may not function properly.

⊗ *<Caution>* | Changing a character in a uuencoded graphics file may not alter the displayed picture, as a single character may be a very small part of the total image. Binary executables, on the other had, may behave unpredictably if a single uuencoded character is modified. As a general rule, don't modify any character in a uuencoded file.

At the top of every uuencoded file is an identifier. The exact layout depends on the version of the uuencode software, but a typical line looks like this:

```
begin 444 command.com
```

The line is used by uudecode to indicate where it should start converting characters. It keys on the word begin at the start of the line. Converted material includes anything following that line through an end line preceded by a blank line:

```
end
```

The numbers following the keyword begin are the file permissions, used by UNIX and carried over to other operating systems for compatibility. The file name following the file permissions is the name of the file when it is uudecoded. When the sender uuencodes the file, they can specify the decode file name (although most people leave it the same as the original file name). The receiver can edit the file name, if necessary.

⊛ {Note}

Since some systems, like Macs and UNIX computers, can have file names with many more characters than Windows and DOS computers, you may find uuencoded posts that have illegal DOS file names. We'll show you how to fix this later in the chapter.

Incidentally, uuencoding a file typically increases its size (due to the need to convert nonprintable characters to printable ones as well as to indicate that a conversion has taken place). Typically, a binary file expands by 35 percent when uuencoded.

Uuencoding a file

If you want to send your favorite graphic image to a newsgroup, you must encode it for transmission. The process depends on the newsreader, news poster, or e-mail package you use. In general, many graphically based software packages have an option to uuencode a file that is included in a posting. Most command-line software packages do not have this option; you must rely on a separate utility to perform the encoding.

> **⊗<Caution>** Do not post uuencoded files to newsgroups without making sure they are welcome! There are usually dedicated newsgroups for binaries, pictures, sound files, and other large files. Sending a uuencoded file to a discussion-based newsgroup is considered a major breach of etiquette because of the amount of time it takes to download the message.
>
> If you are not sure your uuencoded file will be welcome, don't post it! Instead, post a message that asks if anyone would like it. If enough people want it, you may be asked to post it anyway. Don't assume that everyone will want your file!

What is MIME?

MIME is the Multipurpose Internet Mail Extension. MIME was developed to allow binary files easy passage through the Internet. Some newer protocols (like X.400) can handle encapsulated data like a binary file, but most of the protocols in common use cannot handle anything out of the printable ASCII character range.

MIME is slowly being supported by popular packages, but many e-mail systems and newsgroup readers still lack support for it. Before sending a MIME attachment, check that the receiver of your message can properly handle MIME. If not, the recipient has no easy method of accessing the attachment.

MIME has a newsgroup on UseNet. Check the group comp.mail.mime for discussions. If you would like more information about MIME, FTP to **ftp.netcom.com** and get the file /pub/mdg /mime.txt. Written by Mark Grand, this document contains a useful overview of the subject. For some sample MIME messages, FTP to **thumper.bellcore.com** and check the directory /pub/nsd/samples.

Uudecoding a file with WinVN

So you've just read a newsgroup article with a file attachment that you want to get.

The first thing you need to be able to do is recognize that the message contains a uuencoded file. Typically, a uuencoded file is sent with some text preceding the encoded characters. This practice identifies the contents and helps the recipient keep together messages sent separately. The start of a full message may look like this:

```
From: tpci!tparker (Tim Parker)
Subject: Spreadsheet for room reflections
Date: Tue, 20 Dec 1994 18:55:29 -0500
X-MAILER: MKS Internet Anywhere - Compose 1.0A0
X-MKSIA-ATTACHMENT: U-roomref.exl

This is a UUEncoded Excel spreadsheet that calculates room
reflections and standing waves based on your input of room
sizes.  It can be used to alter boundary effects from your
speakers.

Tim

begin 777 roomref.exl
MZ5T58'@5   "W#P  =0X  (42
M          #H9  >#B[_+@0!^^A9 !X.+O\N" '[Z$X '@XN_RX, ?0H0P >
M#B[_+A !Z#D '@XN_RX4 >@O !X.+O\N& 'H)0 >#B[_+AP!Z!L '@XN_RX@
M >@1 !X.+O\N) 'H!P >#B[_+B@!G"Z /C0! '0(Z P <P/H&@@"="=P^H"U 0
M4U"T!R[__'R"'E !"!O@/U&Z#B_X"M .QP!A[j_1P:y#/DD_'y1[_y1[y/[_y"a[//y[a_[y8
M=0-8^</HM #H%*0  &)L8&!!08  !^@# %CXPS+__'HH..Y87@/d8S2$R_QZ*CL&
M'[@6,TPS&n L;B;CHj4z/jHcL2Z.p.@< '4#Z$0  )J    #Q := R,P"8#!@, 0(-  Z^0y'
M6,'-0)H,^ 0 (=2(FH@@  /4A)=1DFH0H  /4S$=1 Fo2a_.0=PCgy_@o/2 @
M6,''FQP8!      N" @)J,( ":C"@ Fo22 )j,. ,-6y'@:T4gy2gJ&, #W__W0#
M^.L!@0<?7L.X EC-(0K =0BX UB[ 0#-(<y/gy-(?gy,gy%[P#!0L.'YSH&_^=Z9[^
M @  <@"00(    +/ @              +A @/O @/M @
```

To decode a file in a message that you have open, follow these steps:

1 Choose <u>F</u>ile, <u>D</u>ecode Article. This opens the decode dialog box shown in figure 15.1.

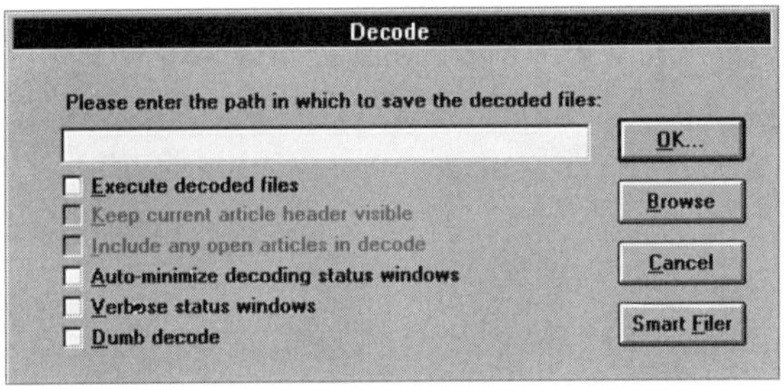

Fig. 15.1
WinVN decodes
uuencoded articles
quickly using this
dialog box.

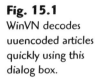

2 Enter the path to save the decoded file to (or click the Browse button to open a dialog box to choose a path).

3 If you have other windows open with articles that you want to decode, select the Include any open articles in decode option.

4 Click OK to begin decoding the file.

If all goes well, two message boxes will open showing you the progress of the file decoding. When done, your file will be ready to use in the directory you told WinVN to put it in.

Q&A | **I got an error message that said** `Decode Missing Parts` **and when I tried to use the decoded file, I couldn't. What's wrong?**

Sometimes a file is too big to fit in one message. When this happens, the file is split into several messages. If you had only one of the messages open, WinVN can't decode the entire file. Find the messages with the other parts and open them too and try again. Or see the next section for an even easier way.

?Q&A ┌─── *The file started to decode then a new dialog box popped up with an Invalid file name message (like the one shown in this figure). What next?*

```
─ Invalid file name c:\temp\metallica-blackened.med. Select new name
  File Name:                    Directories:              ┌─────────┐
  ▓▓                            c:\temp                   │   OK    │
                                                          └─────────┘
  10fig09.pcx        ▲          🗀 c:\            ▲        ┌─────────┐
  addresse.dir                  📂 temp                   │ Cancel  │
  anthem1.mid                   🗀 macros                 └─────────┘
  anthem1.wrk                   🗀 mghill                 ┌─────────┐
  blues5.mid                    🗀 mtable                 │ Network...│
  cat.htm                       🗀 win32ole               └─────────┘
  cd-lists.xls
  cgiparse.c         ▼                         ▼
  List Files of Type:           Drives:
  ┌─────────────┬─┐             ┌──────────────────┬─┐
  │ All Files   │▼│             │ 🖫 c: jim'        │▼│
  └─────────────┴─┘             └──────────────────┴─┘
```

What's happened is that the file you are trying to decode came from another system, like UNIX or a Mac, that allows different characters or longer file names. The first thing you need to do is decide if you even want the file. If it's a program, you won't be able to run it. If it's a graphic, movie, or sound clip, you should be able to use it if you have the right program.

To save the file, enter a legal file name in the File Name box in the dialog box. Then click OK and the decoding will proceed.

DON'T press Cancel in this dialog box. That can cause WinVN to crash!

Decoding multiple files in WinVN

Sometimes a file is too big to fit into one message. When this happens, you'll find several messages with similar subjects that end with part 1 of 3, part 2 of 3, etc. In this case, you'll want an easy way to decode the file in the messages.

Another reason to decode several messages at once would be that you see several different messages you want to get different files from. You can choose to decode as many files at once as you want.

The best way to decode multiple files is to:

1 Select all the messages you want to decode in the group window. (See "Selecting multiples articles to save" in chapter 13. Even though you won't be saving the article, you'll still use the Control and Shift keys in the same way to select multiple articles.)

2 Choose <u>F</u>ile, <u>D</u>ecode Selected Articles. This opens a decode dialog box like the one shown in figure 15.1.

3 Enter the path to save the decoded file to (or click the <u>B</u>rowse button to open a dialog box to choose a path).

❶ (Tip)

> If you check the <u>K</u>eep current article header visible option, WinVN will automatically scroll the group window to show the header of the article being decoded. If you like to track the progress of the decode and you have a lot of files selected in a large group, this can be useful.

4 Click <u>O</u>K to begin decoding the files.

You'll see the same message boxes updating the status that you do when you decode a single file. The only differences will be that you'll see more status messages because you are decoding multiple files.

Smart Filer

Smart Filer is WinVN's automatic decoding utility, which allows you to quickly decode files without worrying about too many dialogs popping up asking for destination file names. It's also a file management utility that transparently renames files and extensions, particularly illegal extensions, as files are pulled down from UseNet. For example, it renames a simple post with a 15-character name so it conforms with the DOS 8.3 format.

To open and configure Smart Filer, choose <u>C</u>onfig, <u>S</u>mart Filer. This opens the dialog box shown in figure 15.2.

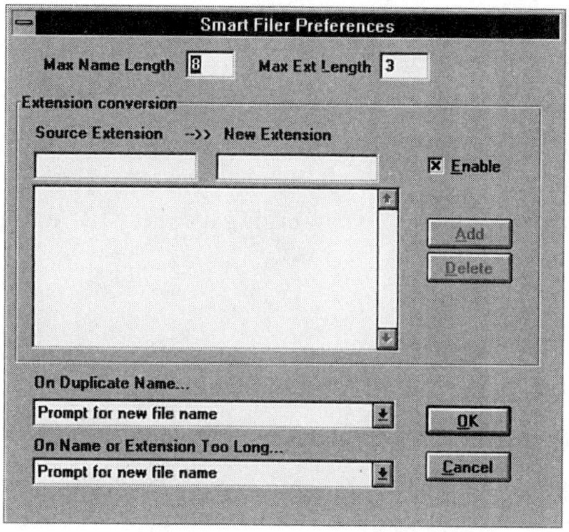

Fig. 15.2
WinVN's Smart Filer
lets you automatically
convert files without
worrying about
renaming and
directories' paths.

The Smart Filer dialog box lets you set the way incoming files are handled. The top of the dialog lets you set the file length, normally 8 characters for DOS file names and 3 characters for DOS file extensions.

At the bottom of the dialog are two scroll lists that indicate how you want WinVN to handle problems. There are two different actions to instruct WinVN about: duplicate file names and illegal file names.

The default setting for duplicate file names is to prompt you if problems occur, but you can set the system to automatically overwrite existing files or to change the file name by adding a number to the beginning or end of the file name or replacing the extension with a number. Overwriting files should not be set on unless you are very confident that you won't destroy files by accident.

The default setting for file names that are too long is to prompt you for a new name. But you can choose automatic truncation of file names to make it fit or you can choose to skip all vowels and punctuation to try to make it fit.

The middle section of the Smart Filer dialog lets you build a list of conversions for file extensions. For example, if an incoming file has the extension .uue.Z (which is legal in UNIX), you can set Smart Filer to convert it to .UU (or any other extension) automatically. A handy conversion is when there is no file extension at all and you want to tag a ".txt" so that you can browse the file easily in Windows. You can create as many file extension conversions as you want.

Saving articles to decode later

In chapter 13, we discussed saving articles. You can also save articles that have uuencoded attachments, following the same methods you used to save a normal text article.

Why would you want to do this? There are a couple of reasons. First, if your online time is expensive, you can save a little bit of time by saving all the files and decoding them later when you aren't online. This won't save much time, but every little bit helps.

Another reason is that sometimes WinVN may have trouble decoding a file. This could happen if a part of the file is missing or if the encoding wasn't done perfectly. If you try to decode a file using the procedures in the last two sections and this happens, you'll have to download it again when the rest of the parts are available or use another decoder. If you save it first, you can always come back and get the other part to

decode later either with WinVN or another product like WinCode (discussed later in this chapter).

To use WinVN to decode a file in a saved article, follow these steps:

1 Go to the main WinVN screen and choose Utilities, Decode a File. You'll see the same basic decode dialog box that was shown earlier.

2 Choose a directory to save the decode file in, and then choose OK. This opens a file dialog box.

3 Pick the file to decode and choose OK.

That's it. You'll see the same message boxes as before.

Attaching a file to an article with WinVN

With WinVN, it's a snap to encode a file and attach it to your article. Everything is handled by dialog boxes and menus. To attach a file, follow these steps:

1 Create a new message to attach the file to. (See chapter 14, "Writing Articles and Responses," if you need a refresher on this.)

①(Tip)

> You can enter the subject and text of the message before or after you attach the file. It doesn't matter.

2 Choose <u>P</u>ost, <u>A</u>ttach. This opens the Attach dialog box.

3 Enter the complete path and file name of the file to attach in the top text box in the dialog.

or

Click the <u>B</u>rowse button. This will open a standard Windows Open File dialog box that you can use to pick from by choosing the right drive, directory, and file.

❂{Note}

> If WinVN recognizes the type of file you are attaching by the extension, such as GIF or MPEG, it will automatically set the Content Type box to match this. You can also select this yourself if you want to. It isn't essential to do this. Some newsreaders can take advantage of this additional information but your post will be fine without it.

4 Choose the Encoding type from the drop-down list. Unless the FAQ for a group tells you otherwise, ALWAYS choose UU. It's a good idea to go ahead and select Make Default after you choose this. Then you won't have to set this each time you post.

The dialog box should now look something like figure 15.3.

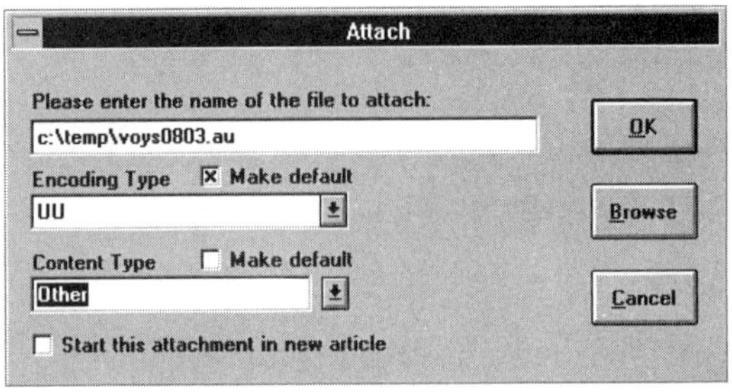

Fig. 15.3
The Attach dialog box
with the complete
path and file name
filled in and the
Encoding type UU
selected.

> **①(Tip)**
>
> In some groups, netiquette requires you to post a description of the file first
> and then the file. Like a cover page on a long fax, this allows readers to
> read your description first, which may only be a few lines long, before
> deciding if they want to spend the time downloading the file, which may be
> several hundred lines long. To do this, select Start this attachment in new
> article. This way the article you create with the description will be the first
> message and the file will begin as a new message.

5 When you are finished, click OK. After you do this, you'll return to the
New Article window. Your attachment will be shown in the attachment
text box as shown in figure 15.4.

What's a uue file?

One convention used with some operating
systems is to attach the file extension ".uu" or
".uue" to a uuencoded file; this extension is
added to label the encoded files. This practice is
not widely used; if you see the extension ".uue,"
at least you will know what it is.

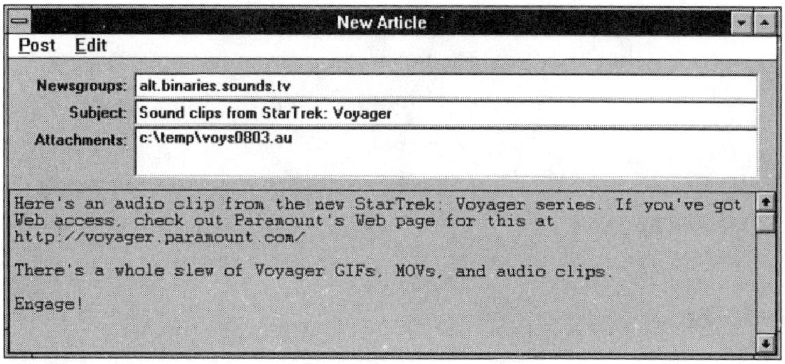

Fig. 15.4
The New Article
window. The file
c:\temp\voys0803.au
will be attached to this
file after the end of
the description in the
body of the article.

6 Once you are satisfied with the message and the attachment, choose
Post, Send to post the article with the attachment.

That's it! You've successfully posted a message with a file attachment.

Breaking large files into parts

At times you will need to send a really large file to a newsgroup. Some
newsreader software cannot handle large files. The exact limits depend on
your software (either in your news package or the gateway to the Internet),
but few systems can handle multi-megabyte files without truncation. You
have to split large files into several smaller files. WinVN also does this
automatically. In fact, you can post big files without any extra work!

When you attach a large file to an article in WinVN, just use the same procedure that you did to attach any other file. WinVN will break it into the necessary number of parts and number the parts so that readers can tell they are
all part of the same file.

There are two options you may be interested in for handling large files. First,
if you post files and someone complains that the parts are too big (since
some newsreader software and UseNet systems can only handle smaller
files) you can break your posts into smaller pieces. To do this, follow these
steps:

1 Choose Config, Attachments in the main WinVN window (or choose Post, Preferences, Attachments in a New Article window). This opens the Attachment Preferences dialog box shown in figure 15.5.

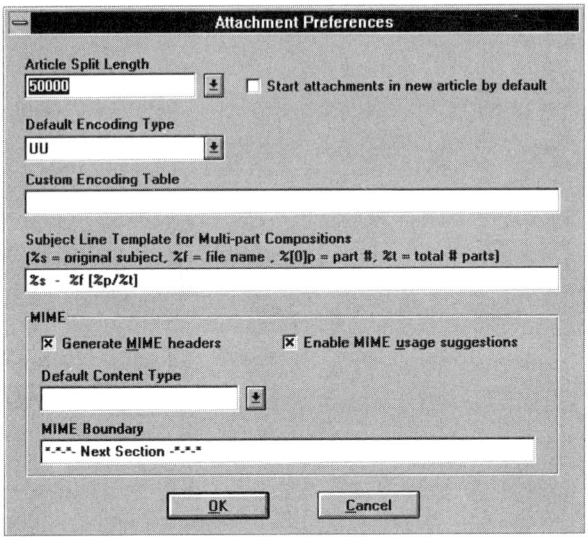

Fig. 15.5
The only options we'll be interested in here are the Article Split Length and Subject Line Template.

2 Change the number in the Article Split Length to a smaller number. Remember the smaller the number is, the more pieces your post will be broken into, so don't make it too small. Most systems can handle the default value of 50000. You'll probably never find a system that can't handle 25000, so that should be the lowest value you use.

3 Click OK when you are done.

⊛ {Note}⎯⎯⎯ If you've been reading along in this chapter and followed the advice to make uu the default code type in the previous section, you'll be asked here if you want to deactivate MIME header generation. Don't worry about what it means, just choose Yes.

Making useful subject lines for multiple part posts

The other option related to large files here is how WinVN names the subject of each part for large posts. By default, when you post an article in WinVN with a large file that gets broken into parts, the subject for each part will be:

- the subject you gave the article when you created it, followed by

- the file name of the file you attached, followed by

- some numbers that indicate how many parts there are and which part it is

This usually looks something like this:

```
Testing Binary - screen40.pcx [0/4]
Testing Binary - screen40.pcx [1/4]
Testing Binary - screen40.pcx [2/4]
Testing Binary - screen40.pcx [3/4]
Testing Binary - screen40.pcx [4/4]
```

In this case, Testing Binary is the subject I gave to the article. screen40.pcx is the name of the file I attached. The 4 at the end of each set of numbers means the files were broken into four parts, the first number shows what part it is. The part numbered 0 is the description of the file in the article. If you choose Start This Attachment in New Article in the dialog box when you attach the file (as described earlier in the chapter), the part with the description is numbered 0 and the next part that starts the file is numbered 1.

So now you understand what all of this means. For most people, the default subject template is just perfect. If you need to customize this though, open the Attachment Preferences dialog as shown in step 1 in the previous set of steps.

⊗<Caution> If you make a mistake here and post obviously bad subjects, you are likely to be flamed for all eternity. Stick with the defaults for a few months until you have a good feel for the program. And make your first post after you make the change to a test group.

The box to enter the template for the subject line is under the text that begins "Subject Line Template." You can enter any of the following in this box:

- To include the subject that you gave the main article as part of the subject line of each of its parts (which is a very good idea), enter %s.

- To include the file name with each part, which is a good idea but not necessarily required, enter %f.

- To include the part number for each part, enter %p.

- To include the total number of parts, enter %t.

{Note}

It's important to include this part number information so that someone reading your posts knows which part goes first when they decode it!

You can include any other text in the box if there is something you want included in the subject of every multiple part post. In the default setup, the - [/] characters are repeated in every article.

(Tip)

It's not a good idea to include a cute or long piece of text as part of every subject. This will often get you flamed and identify you as a newbie.

WinCode: Another useful uuencode utility

For Windows users, a few utilities are devoted to simplify the manual encoding and decoding process. One of them is WinCode, a utility that supports both uuencode and uudecode as well as the MIME base64 coding system (see the sidebar "What is MIME?" earlier in this chapter). WinCode includes the capability to compress files and assemble libraries.

(Tip)

Look for WinCode to support BinHex, a popular Macintosh file encoding scheme, in a future version.

Why would you want to use a utility like WinCode? Even if your newsreader supports uuencoding and decoding (like WinVN does), the built-in utilities are sometimes limited. WinCode does a better job of prompting you when it finds a file name that isn't legal in DOS, and it performs both encoding and decoding faster that WinVN's routines. WinCode also provides better capabilities for handling larger files that must be split into smaller parts and then rejoined when decoding.

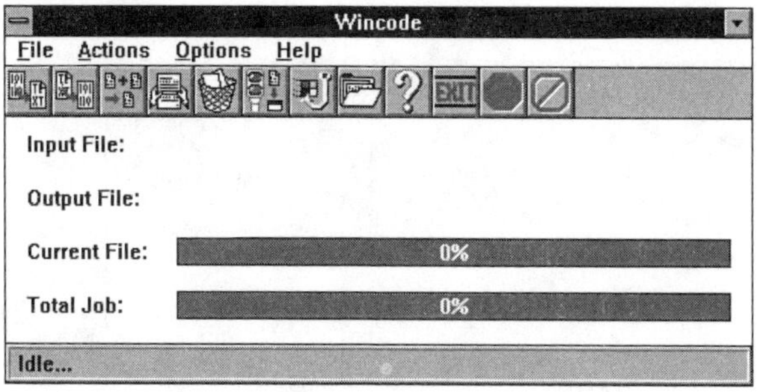

Fig. 15.6
WinCode is a useful freeware utility that provides uuencode and uudecode capabilities for Windows users.

To install WinCode, unzip the file you downloaded in a temporary directory and run the install.exe program. Then just follow the directions on-screen.

To use WinCode to encode a file, choose File, Encode. Then choose a file from the dialog box shown in figure 15.7.

To decode a file, choose File, Decode. Select the file to decode from the dialog box. All the files encoded in the file will be decoded.

WinCode has some powerful options that let you select the specific behavior of WinCode, including automatic compression to a ZIP file. To open the options dialog shown in figure 15.8, choose Options, Encode.

Getting WinCode

You can usually find WinCode by FTP at the CICA FTP site or one of its archives. The FTP address is **ftp.cica.indiana.edu**. WinCode will be in the /pub/pc/win3/util directory with the name wcode26.zip. (This number and name may change slightly with new versions.) Or look for this same file at the Macmillan FTP site at **ftp.mcp.com** in the /pub/que/netcdwin directory.

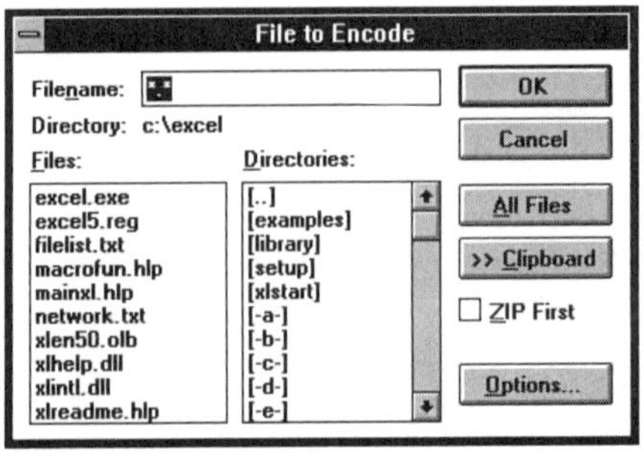

Fig. 15.7
When you select
Encode from the
WinCode menu, you
choose the file to
encode in this dialog
box.

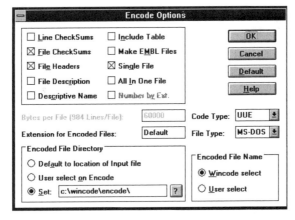

Fig. 15.8
The WinCode Options
lets you select the
behavior of WinVN's
encoding routine.

Other useful programs for handling file attachments

If you find yourself transferring a lot of pictures, sound files, movies, and programs on UseNet, you will need several other utilities.

First, you may find that a lot of the files posted on UseNet are compressed. The most common compression technique you'll see is called **ZIP**. The next section discusses a good Windows program to use to zip and unzip files.

If you transfer a lot of graphics, you need some kind of viewer to look at them (or play the movies or listen to the sounds, depending on exactly what you download). See the section "Graphics viewers" later in this chapter.

WinZip

When a file is converted to ASCII characters by a program like uuencode, it can grow in size depending on the number of non-ASCII characters that must be converted. A binary file can be quite large. For example, a full-screen SVGA graphic file can be 500 KB. Sound files can be even larger, with a two-minute sound sample for Windows running up to 4 MB, depending on its complexity.

WinZip for Windows, for example, developed by Niko Mak Computing, is a full Windows-based system that uses a user-friendly interface rather than a complex DOS command line. Figure 15.9 shows WinZip with a library of bitmap files open.

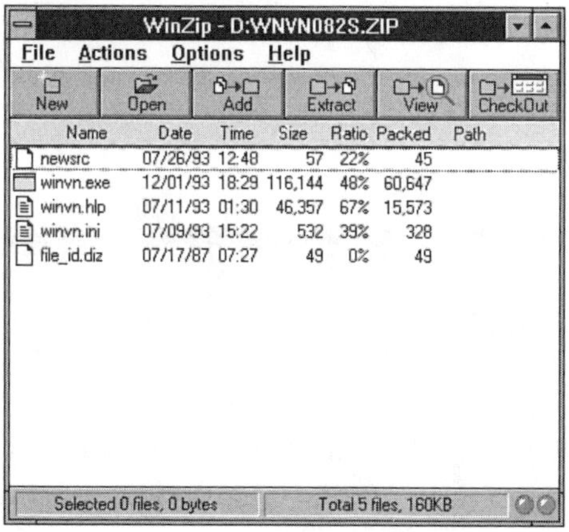

Fig. 15.9

WinZip with a library of bitmap files.

Automatic compression and decompression

Some mail packages can automatically compress a file for you when you attach it to a message. Some systems automatically decompress files when received. America Online, for example, lets your system automatically decompress received files; it doesn't have to save the compressed file and run a utility.

Graphics viewers

If you plan to browse a lot of online graphics files, you may want to look for a small, fast viewer that won't slow you down when scanning for an image you like. Be sure that you find a utility that can handle the image type you are after (PCX, BMP, GIF, and so on).

For viewing GIF or JPEG images, there are many great choices. Two of the most popular are Lview and WinJPEG. If you want to make the graphics detach into Windows screen savers, VuSav is a good screensaver module to display GIF and JPEG images. (VuSav is part of a larger package called VUPrint, which also is good for viewing and printing graphics.)

For MPEG movies, a good movie player is MPEGPLAY. The Media Player that comes with Windows will play Video for Windows (AVI) files. And with QuickTime add-ins, you can use Media Player to play QuickTime movies too.

Viewers in online services

Many utilities are available for seeing the contents of compressed graphics files while online. When you are using an online service such as CompuServe, America Online, or Delphi, you might not want to download a graphics file until you have seen its contents. A utility can display the file's contents before you start the download process, saving you from wasting time on unwanted files (assuming you can see the contents, of course). CompuServe's Windows-based WINCIM, for example, has a built-in GIF viewer that lets you see GIF files while online. Prodigy, on the other hand, has a real-time display utility that works within the service.

Table 15.1 Viewer files names and where to get them

Program	FTP Location	File Name
Lview 3.1	ftp.cica.indiana.edu /pub/pc/win3/desktop	lview31.zip
WinJPEG	ftp.cica.indiana.edu /pub/pc/win3/desktop	winjp251.zip
VuSav	ftp.primenet.com /users/h/hamrick/	vuepri33.zip
MPEGPLAY	ftp.NCSA.uiuc.edu /Web/Mosaic/Windows/Viewers	mpegw32h.zip
QuickTime	ftp.NCSA.uiuc.edu /Web/Mosaic/Windows/Viewers	qtw11.zip

If you're really into graphics, look for Que's new book, *Graphics on the Net*, for expert advice on finding and using the best graphics and graphic tools on the Internet.

Part IV:

Using NewsWatcher

16

Getting Started with NewsWatcher

If everything is properly set up and tested, NewsWatcher makes the connection to your news server and you're ready to participate in the wonderful world of Internet news.

ow's a good time to review and perhaps to make a list of things you need to check:

- Have you correctly configured MacTCP? This is a good time to check and double-check that all your IP numbers are in the right places. See chapter 8, "Choosing a Macintosh TCP Newsreader," for a more complete explanation.

- Have you correctly configured InterSLIP or your PPP software? This is a good time to check and double-check that you have the correct baud rate, telephone number, and IP numbers carried over to the InterSLIP or PPP software. See chapter 8 to review.

- Is your modem connected? Remember the first rule of troubleshooting: Always check the plug.

- Have you tested everything to make sure your SLIP connection is working properly?

⊗<Caution>   This example is pretty simple and a very common method of handling dial-in users. But, some service providers assign the addresses of their dial-in users dynamically, which means you may have a different series of settings.

The best thing to do is to ask your service provider for the name of another Mac user, or contact your local user group to see if you can get a screen shot of the proper settings.

If you're still confused by MacTCP, you might want to get a copy of *The Internet Starter Kit,* Second Edition, published by Hayden Books, for a more complete explanation.

Where to get NewsWatcher

NewsWatcher is a free program available from Northwestern University. It's important to note that NewsWatcher is described as "beta" software and is subject to constant updates as the authors work their way through a to-do list. This chapter and the next three chapters are based upon a version of the NewsWatcher 2.0b release. You can use FTP to get NewsWatcher directly from Northwestern, or you can use MacTCP programs such as Anarchie or Fetch. If you haven't obtained either of these programs, see chapter 8 for details on how and where to obtain them.

Using either of these programs offers you another chance to make sure that your SLIP or PPP connection is working properly and that you have the most recent version of both NewsWatcher and **helper programs**. Helper programs are almost as important as NewsWatcher itself because they allow you to download graphics and software, or as your skills increase, to use NewsWatcher to surf the Internet.

Getting MacTCP ready

Setting up MacTCP and your SLIP or PPP connectivity program may be easy or complicated depending upon your individual situation and the needs of your service provider. Chapter 8 provides a more detailed explanation, and there are a number of excellent books on the subject including *The Internet Starter Kit* from Hayden Books. The most important thing is to have the proper information from your service provider. Don't worry, once you get it set up, you should never have to change it.

Let's walk through setting up MacTCP. The figures are screen shots from my setup, which is

not very complicated. Remember, the IP address, modem settings, and telephone numbers will be different for your configuration:

1 Select MacTCP from your Control Panels.

2 On MacTCP's first window, select how you'll connect, and fill in the IP address assigned to your machine. In this example, we chose InterSLIP. Your choice will vary depending upon how you're connecting and the software you're using.

This is the first screen in the MacTCP Control Panel. You need to know the IP number assigned your computer and how you'll connect.

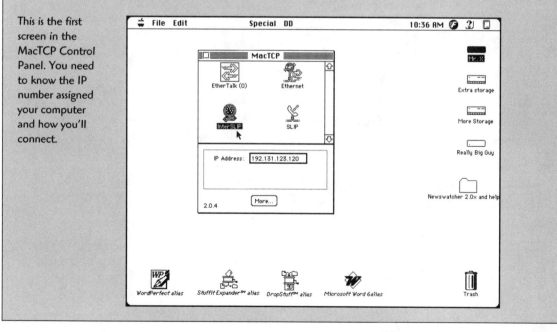

continues

3 Click the More button. On MacTCP's next window, fill in how your IP address is assigned, the gateway address for your service provider,and the Class license of your service provider. You can ignore the information about subnetting, unless your service provider tells you that they usesubnetting. Finally, provide both the name and IP address for your service provider's domain. Make sure you click the default radio button next to the domain name server information selection. You should get this information from your service provider.

MacTCP's second screen is more involved; you may need to get help from your system provider.

```
┌─Obtain Address:────┐   ┌─────── IP Address:───────────┐
│ ● Manually         │   Class: [ C ]  Address: 192.131.123.120
│ ○ Server           │   Subnet Mask: 255.255.255.0
│ ○ Dynamically      │   ▓▓▓▓▓▓▓▓▓▓▓▓▓▓▓▓▓▓▓▓▓▓▓▓▓▓▓▓▓
│                    │          Net | Subnet | Node
│        +           │   Bits:  24      0       8
│                    │   Net:    [12616571]    □ Lock
└─Routing Information:┘  Subnet: [0]           □ Lock
  Gateway Address:       Node:   [120]         □ Lock
  [192.131.123.1]       ┌─Domain Name Server Information:─┐
                        Domain          IP Address  Default
                        college.antioch.edu 192.131.123.11  ●
  ( OK )  (Cancel)                       192.131.123.11  ○
                                         192.131.123.11  ○
```

4 If you're using InterSLIP and you ran its installer program, open the Apple menu andselect InterSLIP setup (or locate InterSLIP setupon your hard drive).

5 Tell InterSLIP how you'll connect and at what speed, the type of modem you have (Hayes-compatible is a good first choice), the SLIP dial-up number, your IP number, and the IP number of yourservice provider.

6 Restart your computer.

After you create a new service in InterSLIP, you need to tell it how you'll connect, the IP addresses of your computer, and your service provider's news server.

```
┌══════════════ college ══════════════┐
  Serial Port: [ Modem Port ▼]    Gateway: [ Direct Connection ▼]
  Baud Rate: [ 9600 ▼]
  Data Bits: [ 8 ▼]
  Stop Bits: [ 1 ▼]
  Parity: [ None ▼]
  □ Hardware Handshaking          IP Address: [192.131.123.7]
  ☒ Speaker on while dialing      Nameserver: [192.131.123.11]
  Dial Script: [Hayes®-Compatible Mod...▼]  □ RFC 1144 TCP Header Compression
  Dial: [ Tone ▼]                 MTU Size: [1006]
  Phone No.: [7676455]
  Modem Init: [at&f]              (Cancel)   ( OK )
```

Here's a simple, step-by-step procedure to use Anarchie:

1 Open your Apple menu, locate InterSLIP Setup, and connect to your service provider.

2 Locate Anarchie, launch the program, and wait until the list of "bookmarks" is on your desktop.

3 Either scroll through the list (or type the letter **n**) until you locate the folder for NewsWatcher (see fig. 16.1).

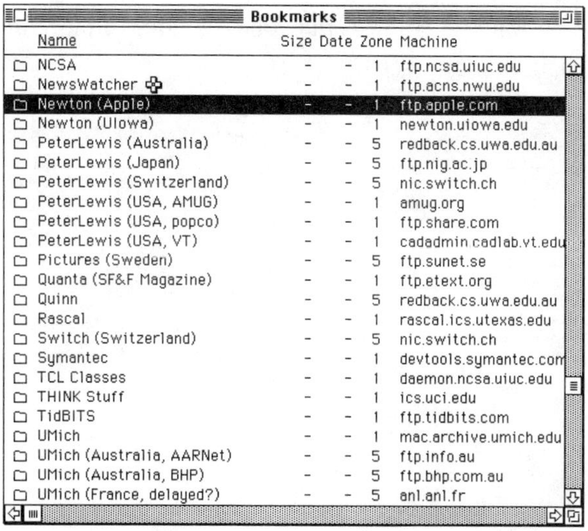

Fig. 16.1

You'll find NewsWatcher and its Helper programs in the NewsWatcher folder on Anarchie's bookmark window.

Name	Size	Date	Zone	Machine
☐ NCSA	–	–	1	ftp.ncsa.uiuc.edu
☐ NewsWatcher ✿	–	–	1	ftp.acns.nwu.edu
☐ Newton (Apple)	–	–	1	ftp.apple.com
☐ Newton (UIowa)	–	–	1	newton.uiowa.edu
☐ PeterLewis (Australia)	–	–	5	redback.cs.uwa.edu.au
☐ PeterLewis (Japan)	–	–	5	ftp.nig.ac.jp
☐ PeterLewis (Switzerland)	–	–	5	nic.switch.ch
☐ PeterLewis (USA, AMUG)	–	–	1	amug.org
☐ PeterLewis (USA, popco)	–	–	1	ftp.share.com
☐ PeterLewis (USA, VT)	–	–	1	cadadmin.cadlab.vt.edu
☐ Pictures (Sweden)	–	–	5	ftp.sunet.se
☐ Quanta (SF&F Magazine)	–	–	1	ftp.etext.org
☐ Quinn	–	–	5	redback.cs.uwa.edu.au
☐ Rascal	–	–	1	rascal.ics.utexas.edu
☐ Switch (Switzerland)	–	–	5	nic.switch.ch
☐ Symantec	–	–	1	devtools.symantec.com
☐ TCL Classes	–	–	1	daemon.ncsa.uiuc.edu
☐ THINK Stuff	–	–	1	ics.uci.edu
☐ TidBITS	–	–	1	ftp.tidbits.com
☐ UMich	–	–	1	mac.archive.umich.edu
☐ UMich (Australia, AARNet)	–	–	5	ftp.info.au
☐ UMich (Australia, BHP)	–	–	5	ftp.bhp.com.au
☐ UMich (France, delayed?)	–	–	5	anl.anl.fr

4 Double-click on the NewsWatcher folder to open it. You'll see files for NewsWatcher, its user manual, and another folder labeled "Helpers." In this folder you'll find anarchie, dropstuff-with-ee, fetch, finger, internet-config, macwais, macweb, ncsa-mosaic, ncsa-telnet, netscape, ph-12, stuffit-expander, tn3270, turbogopher, and uuundo. (Note that the names will be lowercased, and will reflect the most current version of the program.)

5 To bring these files from Northwestern to your desktop, simply select the files you want and double-click.

⊛ *{Note}* _____

Northwestern's site is often busy, so you might want to try to get these files from another major FTP site like **Info-Mac** (or its mirrors), **UMich**, or the **WU Archive** at Washington University.

As interest in the Internet increases, and Internet traffic grows, these sites may also be busy, so be patient.

Anarchie will do the rest. You might as well relax or read ahead while Anarchie is working. If you chose to download all the Helpers in the same session, this process may take an hour or more depending on the speed of your modem (see fig. 16.2).

Fig. 16.2

After you're done downloading NewsWatcher and its Helpers, you should have everything you need in one folder on your desktop.

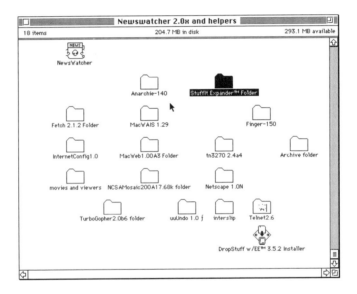

Another option is to use Fetch (see fig. 16.3). Fetch works very much like Anarchie, with one major difference. With Fetch, you need to know the address of the FTP site you're going to—in this case **ftp.acns.nwu.edu**. You'll want to give your user ID as "anonymous," your password as your e-mail address, and look in the directory /pub/newswatcher/helpers.

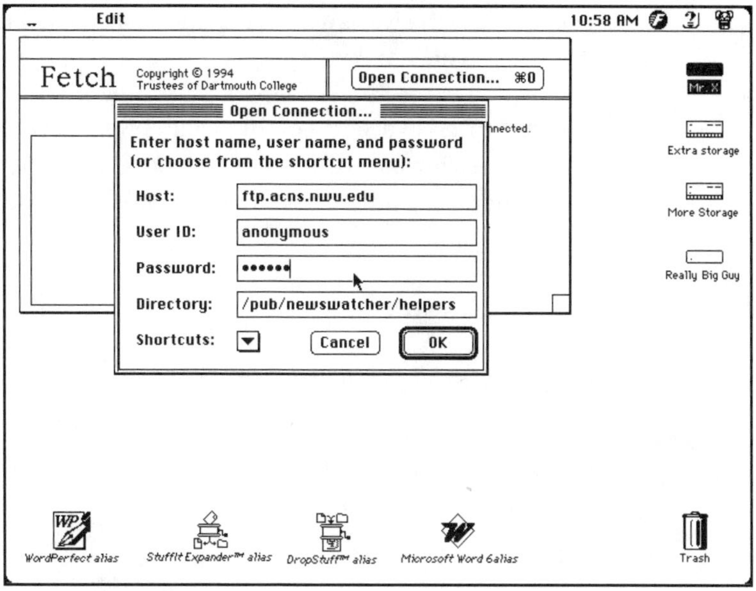

Fig. 16.3
Fetch is another FTP
program you can
use to download
NewsWatcher.

Which program is better? It's really six of one and half a dozen of another.
Anarchie makes it easy to download files, Fetch has the additional capability
to upload files. It doesn't hurt to have copies of both.

Once you've downloaded NewsWatcher and its Helpers, create a folder for
them and keep them all together. You'll see the value of this later as you
begin to use the Helpers.

(Tip) — Download StuffitExpander first and open it. It can work in conjunction with
Anarchie or Fetch to automatically unhex and unstuff programs as they arrive
on your desktop.

Installing NewsWatcher

If you've mastered the three basic Macintosh skills—point, click, and drag—
and have checked and double-checked your list, you should be able to set up
NewsWatcher and read the news in about 10 minutes.

To begin, locate the NewsWatcher application, click once to select it, and double-click to open it.

You open the first in a series of three windows. Provide the information requested in each window. When you're done, press Return and NewsWatcher will gather a list of newsgroups available from your news server.

Here's a "quick start":

1 Tell NewsWatcher how you'll use the program: in a Lab, Shared, or Private.

2 Tell NewsWatcher the name of the machine (or machines) where you get your news and mail.

3 Tell NewsWatcher your name and your e-mail address.

4 Press Return.

Starting NewsWatcher the first time

NewsWatcher is going to need some information about where you get your news and who you are before it can begin. If you've properly configured MacTCP and tested the SLIP or PPP connection to your service provider, you should have all the information NewsWatcher needs.

Selecting where or how you use NewsWatcher

NewsWatcher is designed for use by students in a Mac lab, by persons who may share their Mac, or by individual users (see fig. 16.4).

If you're working from a Mac in a lab at school, you should select the Lab button. NewsWatcher will prompt you to insert your personal floppy disk where you will complete the setup. Notice that if you use NewsWatcher in a school lab environment, the person who administers the lab may have configured NewsWatcher so that you must use a personal floppy disk.

If you plan to share your Mac and NewsWatcher with another family member or officemate, you should select the Shared button. NewsWatcher will prompt you for the Personal NW folder name of the first user and create your preferences there. The next time you use NewsWatcher, you can start from your personal preferences file in your personal NewsWatcher folder. If you want to add additional NewsWatcher users, start from the NewsWatcher application and you can repeat the process to create preferences including unique names and e-mail addresses for additional users.

We'll assume that the answer to the first question NewsWatcher asks you is Private. If this is true for your situation, just click the Private button.

Fig. 16.4
NewsWatcher's first dialog box needs to know how you'll use the program.

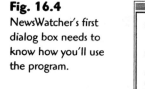

Welcome to NewsWatcher

Welcome to NewsWatcher! We need to get some information from you before you use the program for the first time.

How do you plan to use NewsWatcher?

Click the "Private" button if you are using a private Mac.
Click the "Shared" button if you are using a shared Mac.
Click the "Lab" button if you are using a lab Mac.

[Quit] [Lab] [Shared] [Private]

News and mail information

NewsWatcher needs to know where to look for the news, and where you get your e-mail so that it can gather a list of the newsgroups available to you, and later, when you get involved with reading news, know where to send your mail.

What NewsWatcher needs here is either the names or IP numbers of your news server and mail server. Figure 16.5 uses the IP addresses (192.131.123.11) for a server "named" **college.antioch.edu**. You'll have to take your setups from the information provided by your own service provider.

Note that the names or numbers may not be the same. Some systems put news on one machine and mail on another.

Domain names are easier to remember than IP numbers, so make sure to ask your service provider for the domain name. There is no magic to whether you use the IP address numbers or spell out the names, although experienced users will tell you that computers tend to react somewhat faster to IP numbers because they have less work to do.

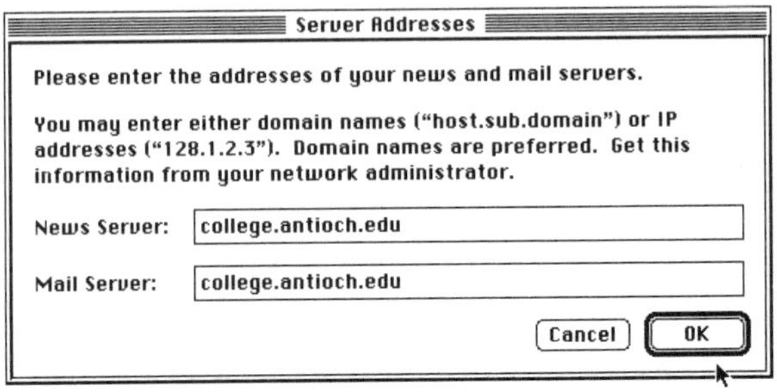

Fig. 16.5
You need to tell NewsWatcher where to go to get your news, and where to send your mail.

```
┌──────────────── Server Addresses ────────────────┐
│                                                   │
│  Please enter the addresses of your news and mail servers. │
│                                                   │
│  You may enter either domain names ("host.sub.domain") or IP │
│  addresses ("128.1.2.3"). Domain names are preferred. Get this │
│  information from your network administrator.      │
│                                                   │
│  News Server:  │college.antioch.edu            │  │
│                                                   │
│  Mail Server:  │college.antioch.edu            │  │
│                                                   │
│                           ( Cancel )  ╔═══════╗   │
│                                        ║  OK   ║   │
│                                        ╚═══════╝   │
└───────────────────────────────────────────────────┘
```

Personal and account information

NewsWatcher also needs your personal information. You don't have to provide all the information NewsWatcher asks for; it will run if you only provide your e-mail address. It's good netiquette, however, to provide other readers with your personal information. Figure 16.6 is filled in as a professional. If you're using NewsWatcher and the Net solely for personal entertainment, you need only give your real name.

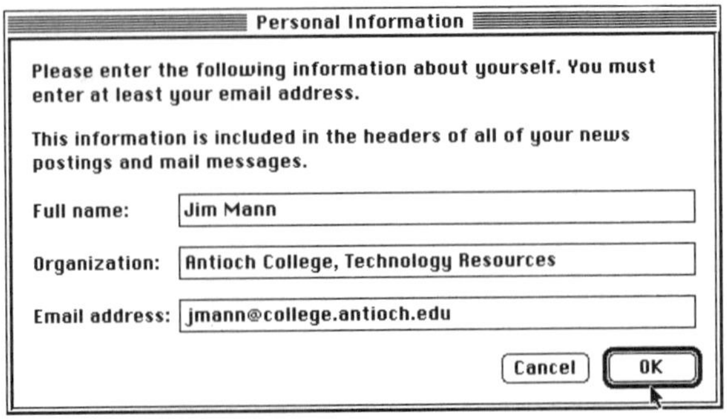

Fig. 16.6
Before you can run NewsWatcher, you need to tell it your name, organization, and e-mail address. You must provide at least your e-mail address. Fill in this information and click OK; NewsWatcher will connect with your news server.

```
┌──────────────── Personal Information ────────────────┐
│                                                      │
│  Please enter the following information about yourself. You must │
│  enter at least your email address.                  │
│                                                      │
│  This information is included in the headers of all of your news │
│  postings and mail messages.                         │
│                                                      │
│  Full name:     │Jim Mann                         │  │
│                                                      │
│  Organization:  │Antioch College, Technology Resources│ │
│                                                      │
│  Email address: │jmann@college.antioch.edu        │  │
│                                                      │
│                           ( Cancel )  ╔═══════╗      │
│                                        ║  OK   ║      │
│                                        ╚═══════╝      │
└──────────────────────────────────────────────────────┘
```

NewsWatcher is configured and ready to go.

When you click OK or press Return (remember that buttons surrounded by double marquees mean you can use Return rather than click with your mouse), NewsWatcher activates your SLIP program and dials up your service provider.

If everything is properly set up (and tested), NewsWatcher will make the connection to your news server and you'll be ready to start participating in the wonderful world of Internet news.

⊛ {Note}

Although it might seem tempting, this isn't the time to call yourself "picard@enterprize.starfleet.fed." First, it's pretty stupid and has been done by just about every hack on the Net.

Second, and probably more important, many systems run authentication programs. What this means is that if you don't provide your real name and e-mail address, there is a good chance that your local system will not allow you to post messages.

If you really want a double-blind, anonymous account, you may want to spend some time investigating anonymous services.

❶ (Tip)

Because the initial setup takes about a minute and a half even if you're a slow typist, you might want to use your SLIP program to connect to your host before you begin the initial setup.

Some systems have a limited number of SLIP connections available. It's a good idea to ensure that you're actually connected before you have NewsWatcher try to gather the news.

Updating the list of groups

Once NewsWatcher connects with your news server, it will gather a list of all the newsgroups available to you. Be patient—this may take some time depending on the number of groups you have and the speed at which you can connect. NewsWatcher only does this the first time you run the program. You won't have to wait so long the next time the program runs.

If you're lucky and your system offers most or all the 10,000 newsgroups available, it could take some time for NewsWatcher to gather the complete group list (see fig. 16.7). Relax, pat yourself on the back, reintroduce yourself to the family, go to the fridge and get a drink.

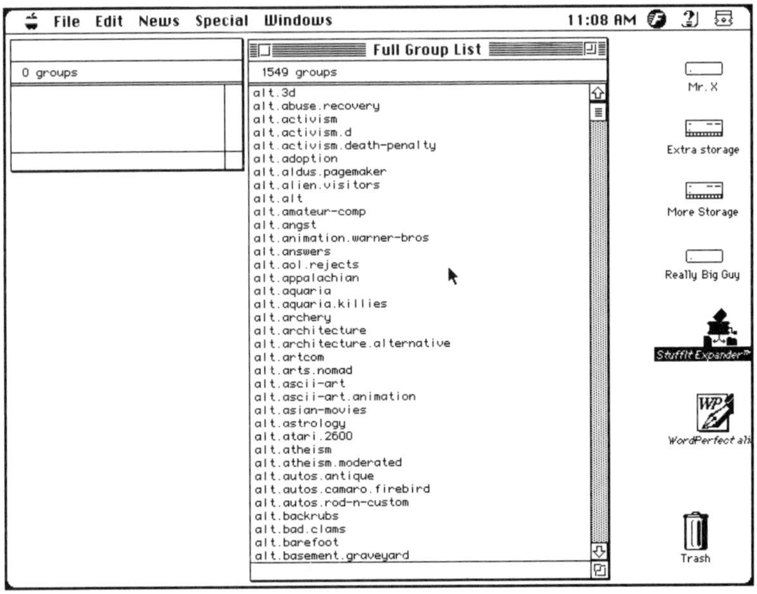

Fig. 16.7
It may take a while for NewsWatcher to gather your Full Group List for the first time. Don't despair—once NewsWatcher has the list in memory, the process will be faster the next time you run the program.

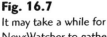

At this point, you're ready to begin reading the news.

If you are new to UseNet news, you should start by using the Full Group List window to browse in any of the groups that look interesting. Click the Full Group List window to bring it to the front. To open a group, double-click its name. This opens a window listing the subjects and authors of all the current articles in the group. To open an article, double-click its line in the Subject window.

Most people like to select a small number of groups to which they subscribe. These are the groups that you decide you're most interested in reading.

You can always reopen the Full Group List window; in the future you will probably want to subscribe to additional groups.

Setting up your group list

After getting the full group list, NewsWatcher opens an untitled window. This window is where you subscribe to groups and eventually create your own personal newsgroup list.

To subscribe to a group, simply point at it with your mouse, click once to select it, and while holding down the mouse button, drag it from the Full Group List window to the untitled window. The result should look something like figure 16.8.

You can also add more than one group at a time. You can Shift+click to select a contiguous part of the list and then drag, or you can ⌘+click to select several non-adjacent groups and then drag to subscribe. Or you can select a group and choose Subscribe from the Special menu.

Fig. 16.8
You create your personal group list by dragging newsgroups from the Full Group List window to the Untitled group window and saving the result.

Once you've dragged several groups to the untitled window and set up a first pass at your personal group window, open the File menu and choose Save to save your personal group list. You can use any name you like: "Jim's Groups," "Mac Groups," or whatever. For future examples, we'll name our personal group list "Your Group List."

✳ *{Note}* You may also want to create an alias of this list and put it in your Apple menu or in some other convenient place. This will save you time the next time you start NewsWatcher.

To subscribe to additional groups, follow these steps:

1 Reposition the two windows on-screen so that both of them are visible. If you have a small screen, it's okay if the Your Groups window is partially obscured by the Full Group List window.

2 Click the Full Group List window to bring it to the front.

3 Select the groups to which you want to subscribe in your Full Group List window.

4 Drag them into the Your Group List window.

5 After subscribing to additional groups (if any), close the Full Group List window.

Now the only window on-screen is the Your Groups window. This is the window you use to read the news most of the time. (Don't worry about closing the Full Group List window. You can always get it back quickly later, when and if you need it, by opening the Windows menu and selecting Show Full Group List.)

Moving around the Full Group List window

You can navigate through the Full Group List window by opening the Edit menu and by choosing Find. (The Keyboard shortcut is ⌘+F.) Type the first two initials of a group.

For example, type **co.sy.ma** (comp.sys.mac) and you'll jump to the newsgroups that discuss Macintosh topics.

Go ahead, guess, you can't hurt anything.

Type **re.ar.tv** to go to groups about your favorite TV shows and **ne.ne** to go to the news new user group.

Changing configuration information

By now you've probably looked through several newsgroups, read some articles, and have become a fledgling Net news hound. Before you get too far away from your initial setups, take some time to explore NewsWatcher's menus and commands and touch up some of your settings.

Setting preferences

The good news about NewsWatcher is that if you never change any of its default settings, and if you have all the necessary Helper programs, you'll be able to jump right into the news. Even better is that NewsWatcher is a very deep and elegant program that gives you a tremendous amount of control over how the program works. To tweak the program to your liking, the most important command is the Preferences command in the File menu.

NewsWatcher has many preferences and settings. They are all set using the Preferences command in the File menu. This command opens a dialog box. A pop-up menu at the top of the window is used to select different topics (see fig. 16.9). The two most important topics are Newsreading Options and Signature. You'll want to explore the other topics as your experience grows.

Fig. 16.9
This list of topics is available in the NewsWatcher Preferences menu item. If you do nothing, News-Watcher's defaults will let you read and post to newsgroups. Tweaking these options is part of making the program your own.

Newsreading options

This dialog box allows you to control the way you view the news (see fig. 16.10). At this point, it's okay to just leave the default settings as they are. NewsWatcher should work just fine, but as your experience grows, you'll probably want to come back and tweak the program to better suit your personal needs.

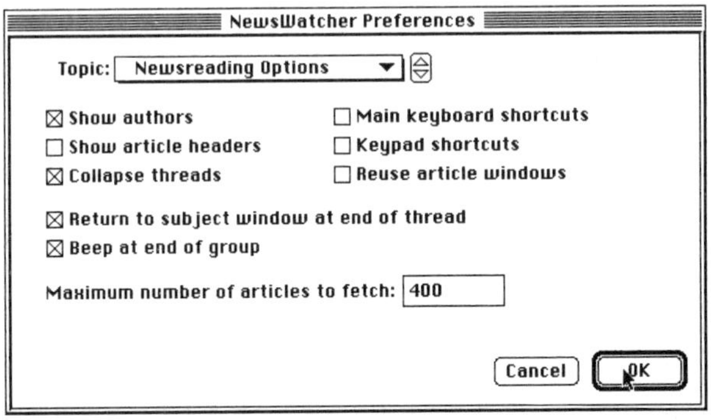

Fig. 16.10
The Newsreading Options topic. The default options are shown.

NewsWatcher Preferences

Topic: Newsreading Options ▼ ⊕

☒ Show authors   ☐ Main keyboard shortcuts
☐ Show article headers ☐ Keypad shortcuts
☒ Collapse threads   ☐ Reuse article windows

☒ Return to subject window at end of thread
☒ Beep at end of group

Maximum number of articles to fetch: 400

[Cancel] [OK]

Here's a brief description of what each option does:

- *Show authors (default on).* By default, NewsWatcher displays both authors and subjects in subject windows. Turn this option off if you want to display only subjects, not authors. This makes Subject windows open faster, especially over slow dialup connections.

- *Show article headers (default off).* By default, NewsWatcher does not show the full article header when it opens article windows. It only shows the most important header information in the panel area of the article window. If you prefer to have full article headers displayed by default, turn this option on.

- *Collapse threads (default on).* By default, NewsWatcher shows threads collapsed in subject windows. If you prefer to have threads expanded by default, turn this option on.

- *Main keyboard shortcuts (default off).* The main keyboard shortcuts are described in detail in the section titled *Keyboard and Keypad Shortcuts.* The keyboard shortcuts are off by default. You must turn them on if you want to use them.

- *Keypad shortcuts (default off).* The keypad shortcuts are off by default. You must turn them on if you want to use them.

- *Reuse article windows (default off).* By default, the Next Article and Next Thread commands close the current article window and open a new article window for the next article or next thread. Some people prefer to reuse the existing open article window. This causes less window redrawing on the screen, which some people find distracting, especially on slower Macs. When you turn this option on, NewsWatcher makes reused article windows bigger if necessary, but it never makes them smaller.

- *Return to subject window at end of thread (default on).* By default, when you reach the end of a thread, the Next Article command returns to the subject window so that you can select the next interesting article and open it. Some people prefer to have NewsWatcher open the next unread thread automatically. You should turn this option off if you use the newsreading style where you preselect all the interesting articles in a subject window.

- *Beep at end of group (default on).* By default, when you reach the end of a group, the Next Article and Next Thread commands return to the subject window and beep. You must use the Next Group command when you want to mark all the articles in the current group read and advance to the next group. Some people prefer to have NewsWatcher automatically close the current subject window in this situation and open the subject window for the next group with unread articles. You will probably want to turn this option off if you use the newsreading style where you preselect all the interesting articles in a subject window.

- *Maximum number of articles to fetch (default 400).* By default, when you open a group, NewsWatcher fetches and displays only the most recent 400 unread articles in the group. This helps improve the perfor- mance of the program, especially over slow dial-up connections. You can override this preference by holding down the Option key while you open a group. A dialog box appears asking you to enter the most recent number of articles to fetch. NewsWatcher resets the unread list for the group to the most recent number of articles you specify, fetches the authors and subjects for those articles, and opens a subject window displaying just those articles.

Signature

This preferences topic is where you type your signature (see fig. 16.11). What you enter is automatically included at the end of all messages you post.

People like to use a standard signature at the bottom of all their postings and mail messages. A signature, for example, would typically give your name, organization, and e-mail address.

Some people also like to include pithy little sayings, jokes, and so on. Other people find this stupid. A good rule of thumb is to keep your signature block to four lines and avoid including things like your picture or artwork created with X's and O's. For some examples of clever signatures, and signature files using ASCII art, see chapter 4.

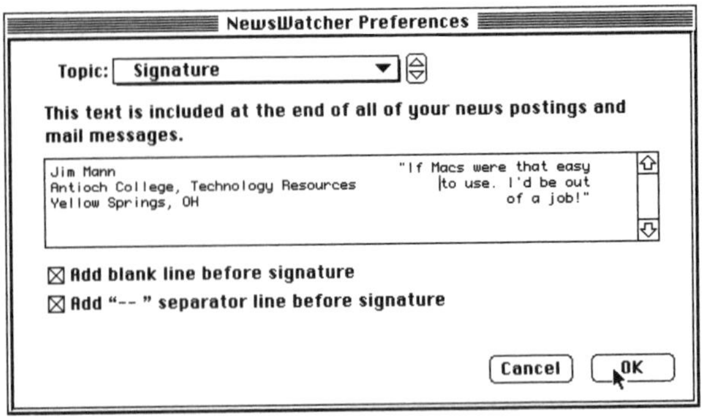

Fig. 16.11
Everyone wants a clever signature file. The Signature topic under the Preferences command lets you create one.

Fonts and screen color

Like Henry Ford's Model T, with NewsWatcher you get the choice of any color type you want as long as it's black. Likewise, you may have any screen color you wish, as long as it's white.

NewsWatcher can apply colors to icons, and lets you use the highlight color you've selected from the Colors control panel for your everyday operations.

Fig. 16.12
You can change your screen font and your printer font from the Font and Size topic.

NewsWatcher Preferences

Topic: | Screen Fonts

Group and Subject Lists:

Font: | Monaco

Size: | 9

This is the font and size in which NewsWatcher group and subject lists are displayed.

Article and Message Windows:

Font: | Monaco

Size: | 9

This is the font and size in which NewsWatcher article and message windows are displayed.

Cancel   OK

Fonts are something else. NewsWatcher lets you select your screen fonts—how you view news articles and your printer fonts.

To do this, select the Screen Fonts and/or the Printer Fonts topic from the Preferences menu, pull down the arrow, and select a font from your font list.

NewsWatcher defaults to 9 point Monaco. This font is easy to read, but you may want to change the font depending on the number of fonts in your system and your personal tastes.

Fig. 16.13
The font you choose is limited only by the number of fonts you have available on your Mac.

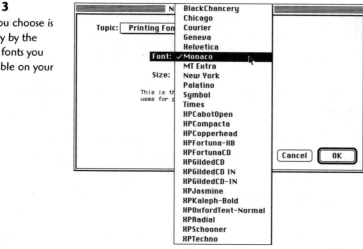

Topic: | Printing Fon

Font: | ✓Monaco

Size:

This is th
uses for

BlackChancery
Chicago
Courier
Geneva
Helvetica
✓Monaco
MT Extra
New York
Palatino
Symbol
Times
HPCabotOpen
HPCompacta
HPCopperhead
HPFortuna-HB
HPFortunaCD
HPGildedCD
HPGildedCD IN
HPGildedCD-IN
HPJasmine
HPKaleph-Bold
HPOxfordText-Normal
HPRadial
HPSchooner
HPTechno

Cancel   OK

Quitting NewsWatcher

To quit NewsWatcher:

1 First make sure you've saved any personal group list you created (see fig. 16.14).

Fig. 16.14
If you created a personal group list, make sure you save it before you quit NewsWatcher. Save it on your desktop or in some other easy-to-get-to place. Later, make an alias of it and put it in your Apple menu for faster access.

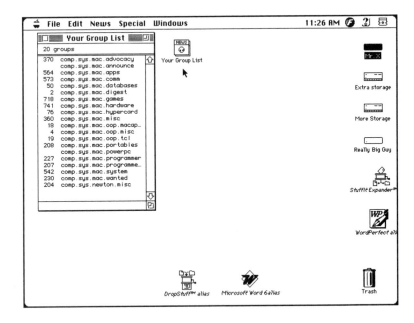

2 Open the File menu and choose Quit. Or use the keyboard shortcut ⌘+Q.

3 If you've read any articles from your personal group list, NewsWatcher will ask you if you want to save changes. If you say yes, the next time you open NewsWatcher, those articles will be marked as "read" and won't appear. This has the effect of reducing the number of articles available.

4 After NewsWatcher closes, select InterSLIP Setup and click the Disconnect button. This closes your connection to your news server and ends your first session.

17

Reading Articles in NewsWatcher

When you start NewsWatcher from Your Group List instead of from the program, NewsWatcher should gather a list of new articles right away.

I n chapter 16, we got most of the difficult things out of the way. Now, the second time you use NewsWatcher you should be able to quickly make your SLIP or PPP connection. And if you start NewsWatcher from Your Group List instead of from the main program, NewsWatcher should gather a list of new articles in much less time than when it gathered the full list of groups.

Follow these steps to make your second connection:

1 Open the Apple menu and choose InterSLIP Setup or open your PPP program.

2 Select the service you want to connect to (you'll probably only have the name of your service provider).

3 Click the Connect button or press Return.

4 When you're connected, InterSLIP displays a Disconnect button and the `Idle` notice at the top of the window changes first to `Dialing` and then `Connected`.

5 You can either close this window or hide InterSLIP. You won't need it again until you're ready to disconnect from the system.

6 Locate either the file (or alias) you created in chapter 16 and named as your personal group list. Double-click on the file to begin NewsWatcher.

NewsWatcher displays a message that it's looking for your host and gathering a list of articles and authors from Your Group List.

This process should take much less time than the first time you started NewsWatcher and gathered the Full Group List.

Subscribing and unsubscribing

Some good advice to keep in mind when using any computer program is to periodically ask yourself, "Where am I? What do I see?" (Don't be afraid to say it out loud!) The answer to your next question is usually right before your eyes!

NewsWatcher uses four different kinds of windows: Full Group List, New Group List, personal group lists, and Message windows. If you think in terms that you're taking a list of perhaps 10,000 topics and 50,000 articles and creating your personal newspaper, you'll need to learn to use three Group windows. What you'll want to do is start from the Full Group List and choose newsgroups that interest you. You may choose all computer topics or build a newspaper with current events, commentary, sports, entertainment, and classified ads. These topics become part of your personal group list. And, because news is always changing, NewsWatcher will periodically present you with a list of new groups that have been added since you last checked in.

Group windows

Group windows display lists of group names. There are three kinds of Group windows: the Full Group List; the New Groups List; and your personal group list (or lists, if you create more than one).

Each time you run NewsWatcher, it checks to see if any new groups have been created since the last time you ran the program. If there are any new groups, NewsWatcher adds them to your Full Group List and opens the New Groups window. This window lists just the names of the new groups. You can drag these new groups to Your Group List window if you wish to subscribe to them. If you don't wish to subscribe to any of them, you can just close the window.

You may disable new group checking by selecting Preferences from the File menu, choosing the Miscellaneous Options topic and removing the x from check for new groups. But, before you decide to do this, note that new groups are constantly added, and you may miss being notified of a group you'd like to read.

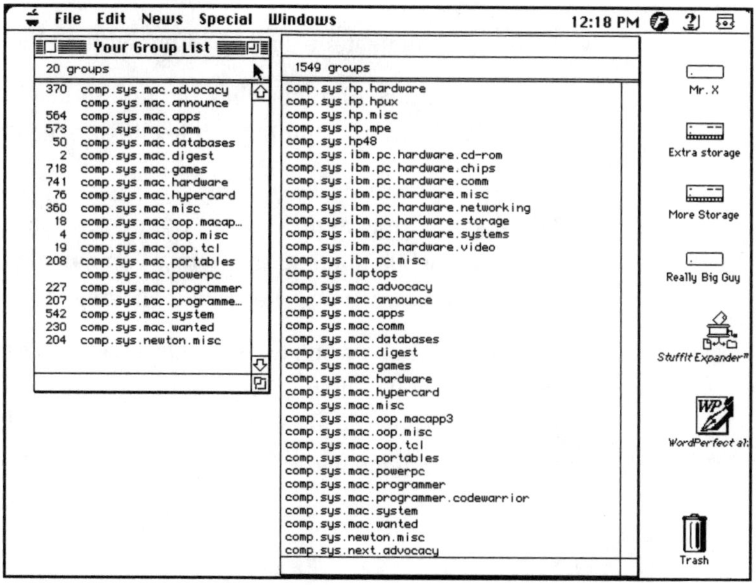

Fig. 17.1
NewsWatcher's Full Group List on the right, and Your Group List window on the left.

Your Group List is the list of groups to which you have subscribed. You can put the groups in any order you want within this kind of window. Use the mouse to drag a group name to any desired new position in the list.

When you use Your Group List to read articles, NewsWatcher keeps track of which articles you have read. NewsWatcher displays a continuously updated count of how many articles remain unread to the left of each group name. If there are no unread articles in a group, no count is displayed.

❋ {Note}

The Full Group List is retrieved from the news server the first time you run NewsWatcher. The Full Group List window is always available, although you may hide it by closing it or by opening the Windows menu and choosing Hide Full Group List.

If you have hidden the Full Group List and quit NewsWatcher, you have to open it again the next time you run NewsWatcher.

NewsWatcher uses the following standard conventions for selecting items in lists:

- To select a single item, click the item with no keys held down.

- To select a range of items, click the first or last item in the range, and then hold down the Shift key while clicking the item at the other end of the range.

- To select multiple items that are not in a continuous range, hold down the ⌘ key while clicking the items. You can also deselect a single item by holding down the ⌘ key while clicking the item.

- To deselect items when all the items in a list are selected, hold down the ⌘ key while clicking any item in the list. This deselects just that item. Then click the item again with no keys held down. This deselects all the other items in the list.

Searching for groups

By now you must be feeling overwhelmed. Here you have as many as 10,000 newsgroups with titles that don't make much sense. How do you find interesting groups without spending hours and/or days online?

NewsWatcher allows you to search through the Full Group List to find topics that might be of interest to you. Here's how:

1 Go to the Windows menu and select Show Full Group List.

2 Open the Edit menu and choose Find. A dialog box similar to figure 17.2 appears. In this dialog box, type the first two initials of the groups you're looking for. In our example, we typed **co.sy.ma** to locate the comp.sys.mac hierarchy of newsgroups.

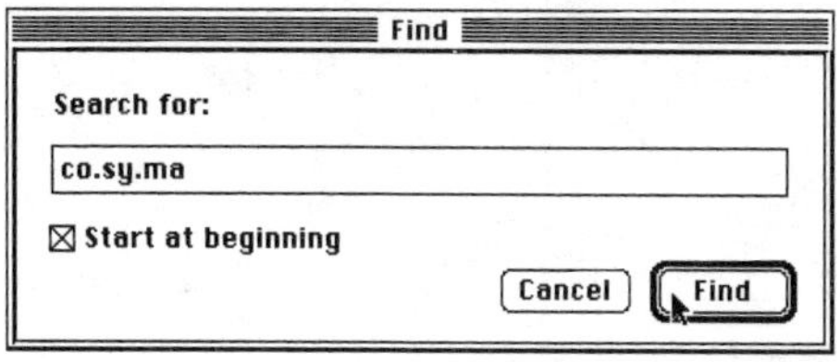

Fig. 17.2
NewsWatcher's Find feature lets you go quickly to a newsgroup or groups. To save time, you need only type the first two letters of the group you're looking for.

```
=================== Find ===================
  Search for:
  ┌──────────────────────────────────────┐
  │ co.sy.ma                             │
  └──────────────────────────────────────┘
  ☒ Start at beginning
                        ( Cancel )  ( Find )
```

3 Double-click the Find button and wait while NewsWatcher searches through the Full Group List.

Spend some time browsing through these groups to get a feel for what they're all about. In our example, you might conclude that you're interested in games and HyperCard, but have no interest in Object Oriented Programming or databases.

Selecting multiple groups

Once you've decided on one or more groups you'd like to read on a regular basis, you need to select them and drag them from the Full Group List to your personal list.

You may click a group and drag it; or, you may select a starting point and drag down to select several groups (you can also click the first group and Shift+click the last group); or, if the groups aren't next in line, you can use Option+click to select groups.

You continue to build your personal group list or subscribe to various groups by selecting them from the Full Group List and dragging them to Your Group List window.

When you're done making your selections, open the File menu and choose Save to save your subscription list.

When you're finished, you have a list similar to the one in figure 17.3.

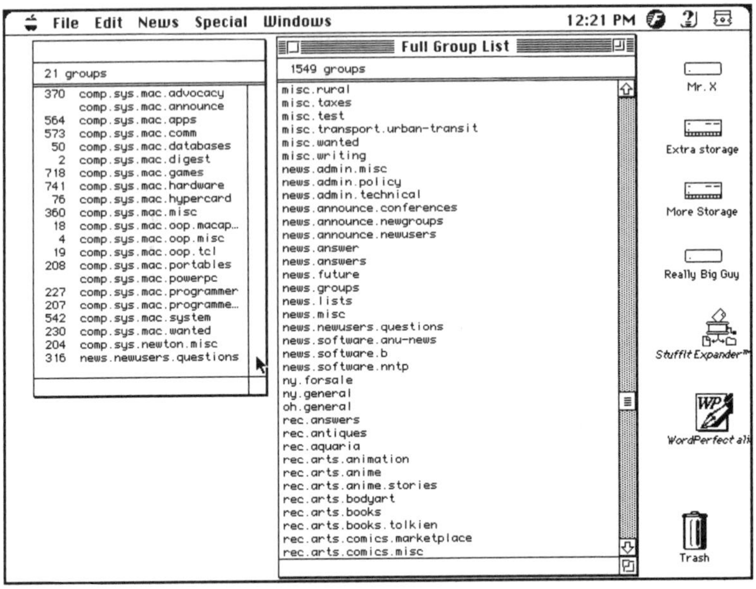

Fig. 17.3
You create your personal group list by dragging newsgroups from the Full Group List window to your personal group window and saving the result.

Moving subscribed groups to the top of the list

You can rearrange your personal group list by selecting the name of a group and dragging it from one location to another.

This technique is good if you have subscribed to a number of groups, but plan to check into only a few groups on a regular basis.

①(Tip)

In our example, we had only one personal group list, but you may create as many as you like using the techniques described above.

Open the File menu, choose New, and a new untitled window will open. You can then drag a selection of groups from the Full Group List to the new untitled window.

When you're done, save the list with a name that's useful to you such as "local groups," or "pictures."

Opening a group to read

Now that we have most of the details behind us, it's time to begin to seriously explore the world of UseNet news.

To open a group, double-click on its name. NewsWatcher will present you with a message that it's gathering a list of articles.

Figure 17.4 shows the window for **misc.test. misc.test** is a group designed to let UseNet newcomers post test messages. Reading from left to right, you'll see the number of messages in a thread and an arrowhead that, when selected and turned down, displays messages. (Check out the first item: This is a class project and 42 students responded to the original message!) Some messages have no replies and are indicated with a -(hyphen).

Fig. 17.4

This Group window is for **misc.test.** From left to right, arrowheads indicate more messages, number of messages in a thread, author's name, and the article title.

```
▤▯▤▥▥▥▥▥▥▥▥▥▥▥▥▥  misc.test  ▥▥▥▥▥▥▥▥▥▥▥▥▥▤▣
  273 articles, 273 unread
▷ 3       Neil Whiteside    blah
▷ 42      Neil Whiteside    test
-    ▸    Neil Whiteside    testing again
-         Neil Whiteside    again?
▷ 2       Neil Whiteside    test test test
-         Neil Whiteside    will this never end...
-         Ron Ritzman       Re: Bots/server/telnet/ops/FAQ
▷ 3       Operator          Please ignore.
▷ 16      gutiez@UNET.IBM…  ignore
-         Alf Green         Testing my homebrew poster
-         Gareth Rees       Ignore 890 1234567890 1234567890 1234567890 1234567890 12…
-         Gareth Rees       Ignore (iii)
-         *Katja*           I want to be tested
▷ 3       Jerry Kosko       +++++++++++++TEST2@@@@
-         Jerry Kosko       ||||||>>>>>> TEST 1
-         Samuel Gustaf S…  Re: Test misc.test
-         John Caruso       Re: test ignore no reply
-         Gilbert Baron     Tested 20 Jan 1156 0556 GMT IGNORE NO REPLY
-         Peter Gutmann     test of new news setup.
▷ 15      John Caruso       Test, ignore
-         Mark Nowak        test of it
-         Susanne B. Rams…  1/20/95
▷ 2       Richard T. Tarr…  Re: A test
-         Kevin Bluml       nata
-         The Sideliner     1234567890
▷ 2       Hollingsworth     testing--ignore
-         Paul J. Gooderh…  Re: Testing [IGNORE]
▷ 7       Christopher A. …  testing
-         Chester Bridal    newbie test
-         Margaret Byrd     ignore too
-         jughead           ignore please
-         Hollingsworth     vette.jpg (1/1) ignore
-         Internet Demo     -----Yes, its another one------
-         Internet Demo     yeah its another one
-         Internet Demo     test only
-         Internet Demo     This is Tracy's TEST
```

Next you see the author's name. Notice the variety of ways people choose to be represented on the Internet.

And finally the title of the message. Logic says that each title would simply say "test," but this is the Internet and topics in this group range from the precise to the profane. Don't be shocked.

 *{Note}*

In chapter 18, "NewsWatcher's Three Rs: Read, wRite, Reply," we learn to create a message and read messages, and we'll be using a test group.

If you haven't done so already, locate **misc.test** in your Full Group List and drag it to your personal group list.

Updating the article list

NewsWatcher's News menu allows you to get some control over what can be a huge amount of information. Open a newsgroup and use the following keyboard commands or News menu choices to practice navigating through the messages:

- You can use the keyboard shortcut +I to move to the next article in the window.

- Use +T to jump to the next thread.

- You can mark messages as read (or leave them unread) by using +M or +U.

These commands allow you to manage a newsgroup without spending the time to actually read every message.

Another feature is that NewsWatcher's News menu allows you to check for new articles on-the-fly. To do this, select either "Check for New Articles" or use the keyboard shortcut +Y. NewsWatcher then sends a query to your host to check for new messages. This helps if you're anxiously awaiting additional parts of a message that contains a binary file, or if you're curious to see if your last message was posted.

?Q&A _____

How long does it take for a message to make its way across the Net?

The answer is seconds, minutes, hours, or days depending upon your service provider's newsfeed and whether you're posting to a local group (a group only on your host computer) or an international group.

Many service providers have continuous newsfeeds. They constantly get new articles as news is passed from one computer to the next.

The best way to find out how often your service provider updates the news is to select a popular group such as **news.newusers.questions** and use +Y to check for new messages.

Another way to update your personal group list is to end your session by quitting NewsWatcher.

NewsWatcher asks if you want to save your changes. If you answer yes, NewsWatcher marks any articles you've looked at as read, and they won't show up the next time you read news.

18

NewsWatcher's Three R's: Read, wRite, Reply

In this chapter:

- How to start reading the news

- How and where to write your first article

- Where to post your first message

- Working smarter, not harder

Using NewsWatcher to read the news is as simple as selecting an interesting newsgroup and double-clicking.

Reading articles with NewsWatcher

It's easy to read the news using the Your Groups List window we created in chapter 16. The mechanics are straightforward, and once you get them under your belt, you can spend time getting involved with your favorite newsgroups.

Figures 18.1 through 18.3 illustrate the basics of opening a group, selecting an article, and reading it.

To open a group, double-click its name. This opens a window that lists the authors and the titles of the news articles in the group. To open an article, double-click on it in the group window.

Here's how:

1 Select a newsgroup from either Your Group List or the Full Group List and double-click on its name.

Fig. 18.1
You begin reading the news by selecting a newsgroup from either Your Group List or the Full Group List and double-clicking its name. We'll select **misc.test** for these examples.

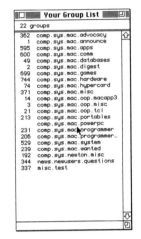

2 After you select the newsgroup, NewsWatcher will gather a list of subjects and authors. NewsWatcher then opens a window showing a list of articles in the group (see fig. 18.2).

3 To read an article, select it and double-click.

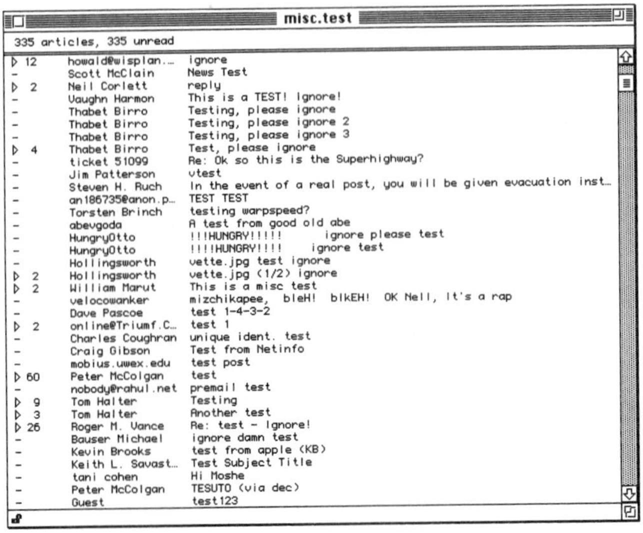

Fig. 18.2
NewsWatcher then opens a window that shows a list of articles in the group. To read an article, select it and double-click.

4 NewsWatcher opens an article window displaying the author's name, when the article was posted, what groups it was posted into, and in the lower panel, the article text.

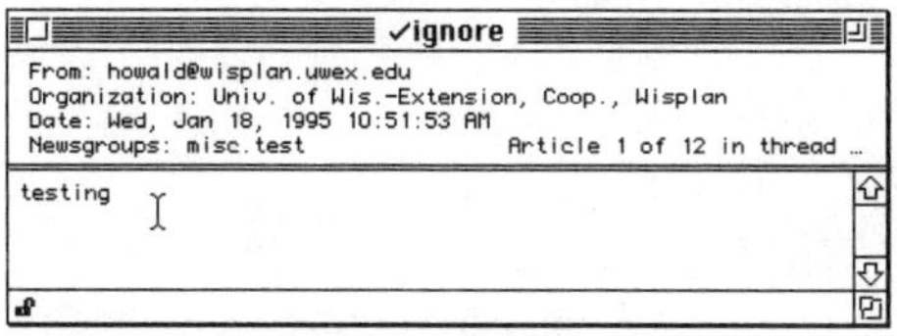

Fig. 18.3
NewsWatcher opens an article window that gives you all sorts of info.

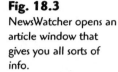

```
┌──────────────────────✓ignore──────────────────────┐
│ From: howald@wisplan.uwex.edu                      │
│ Organization: Univ. of Wis.-Extension, Coop., Wisplan │
│ Date: Wed, Jan 18, 1995 10:51:53 AM                │
│ Newsgroups: misc.test          Article 1 of 12 in thread … │
├────────────────────────────────────────────────┬─┤
│ testing  I                                      │⇧│
│                                                 ├─┤
│                                                 │⇩│
├─────────────────────────────────────────────────┼─┤
│ ♪                                               │▨│
└─────────────────────────────────────────────────┴─┘
```

Searching for articles

One of NewsWatcher's powerful features is its ability to search through the thousands of messages in Your Group List (or the Full Group List) and find articles by title, keyword, or author.

What's the benefit? It's quicker, and therefore cheaper, because you're saving online charges. Instead of browsing through hundreds or thousands of articles to find a reference to something, using Search will quickly narrow down the available choices for you.

Here's how you do it:

1 Open any newsgroup from Your Group List or the Full Group List.

2 Open the Special menu and choose Search. The Search dialog box appears.

3 Choose Subject from the Header drop-down list. Enter a one-word subject that describes the focus of your search in the Containing text box. Hit Return or click the Search button (see fig. 18.4).

Fig. 18.4
Define the criteria for
your search. You can
search by subject,
author, or keyword.
In this example, we
searched for the
subject SE.

Search
Search for articles with:
Header: Subject ▼
Containing: SE
Cancel Search

4 NewsWatcher will search through the group and answer your query
with the number of articles found.

5 Double-click the search result and NewsWatcher will open a list of the
articles.

6 Double-click an article and, as shown in figure 18.5, NewsWatcher will
open the article.

Fig. 18.5
After your search is
completed, you can
open the Search Group
and select an article to
read.

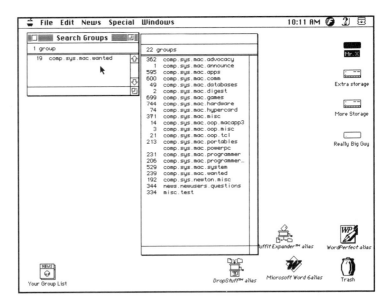

Following a thread

Sometimes someone will post a particularly provocative article or a general plea for help that will generate numerous responses. This is called a **thread**. You can tell when you're reading articles in a thread because they're entitled `Re: Something`.

Fig. 18.6

Here's an example of a number of threads. Notice how clicking on the arrowhead "opens" the thread to show additional messages.

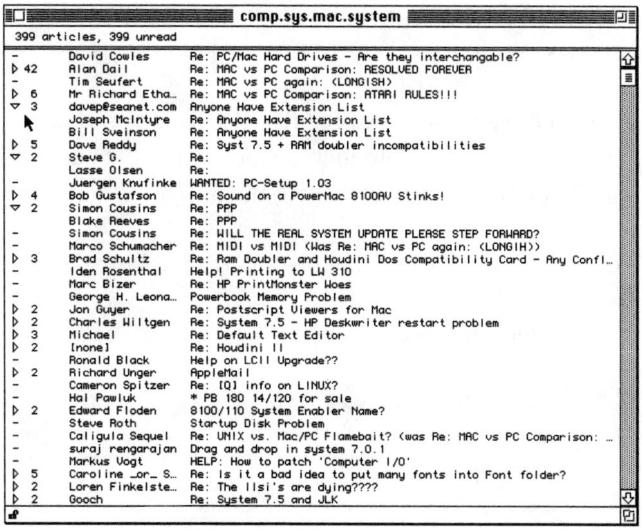

```
┌─────────────────── comp.sys.mac.system ───────────────────┐
│ 399 articles, 399 unread                                   │
│ -       David Cowles    Re: PC/Mac Hard Drives - Are they interchangable?  │
│ ▷ 42    Alan Dail       Re: MAC vs PC Comparison: RESOLVED FOREVER         │
│ -       Tim Seufert     Re: MAC vs PC again: (LONGISH)                     │
│ ▷ 6     Mr Richard Etha.. Re: MAC vs PC Comparison: ATARI RULES!!!         │
│ ▽ 3     davep@seanet.com Anyone Have Extension List                       │
│         Joseph McIntyre Re: Anyone Have Extension List                    │
│         Bill Sveinson   Re: Anyone Have Extension List                    │
│ ▷ 5     Dave Reddy      Re: Syst 7.5 + RAM doubler incompatibilities       │
│ ▽ 2     Steve G.        Re:                                                │
│         Lasse Olsen     Re:                                                │
│ -       Juergen Knufinke WANTED: PC-Setup 1.03                            │
│ ▷ 4     Bob Gustafson   Re: Sound on a PowerMac 8100AV Stinks!             │
│ ▽ 2     Simon Cousins   Re: PPP                                           │
│         Blake Reeves    Re: PPP                                           │
│ -       Simon Cousins   Re: WILL THE REAL SYSTEM UPDATE PLEASE STEP FORWARD? │
│ -       Marco Schumacher Re: MIDI vs MIDI (Was Re: MAC vs PC again: (LONGISH)) │
│ ▷ 3     Brad Schultz    Re: Ram Doubler and Houdini Dos Compatibility Card - Any Confl.. │
│ -       Iden Rosenthal  Help! Printing to LW 310                          │
│ -       Marc Bizer      Re: HP PrintMonster Woes                          │
│ -       George H. Leona.. Powerbook Memory Problem                         │
│ ▷ 2     Jon Guyer       Re: Postscript Viewers for Mac                     │
│ ▷ 2     Charles Hiltgen Re: System 7.5 - HP Deskwriter restart problem     │
│ ▷ 3     Michael         Re: Default Text Editor                           │
│ ▷ 2     [none]          Re: Houdini II                                    │
│ -       Ronald Black    Help on LCII Upgrade??                            │
│ ▷ 2     Richard Unger   AppleMail                                         │
│ -       Cameron Spitzer Re: [Q] info on LINUX?                            │
│ -       Hal Pawluk      * PB 180 14/120 for sale                          │
│ ▷ 2     Edward Floden   8100/110 System Enabler Name?                     │
│ -       Steve Roth      Startup Disk Problem                              │
│ -       Caligula Sequel Re: UNIX vs. Mac/PC Flamebait? (was Re: MAC vs PC Comparison: .. │
│ -       suraj rengarajan Drag and drop in system 7.0.1                    │
│ -       Markus Vogt     HELP: How to patch 'Computer I/O'                 │
│ ▷ 5     Caroline _or_ S.. Re: Is it a bad idea to put many fonts into Font folder? │
│ ▷ 2     Loren Finkelste.. Re: The IIsi's are dying????                     │
│ ▷ 2     Gooch           Re: System 7.5 and JLK                            │
└────────────────────────────────────────────────────────────┘
```

NewsWatcher offers you several choices on how to deal with a big thread, or any thread for that matter.

Open the News menu and you can mark the entire thread as read (⌘+M), or you can pick and choose articles and mark them as read.

It's a good idea to mark a thread as read if you want to manage a large discussion group like **comp.sys.mac.system**, but it's a bad idea if you're waiting for the remaining parts of a binary file to arrive. To preserve a thread in a binary group, you can open it and then use ⌘+U or Mark Unread. Binaries will be covered in more detail in chapter 19, "File Attachments."

Reading ROT13 encrypted articles

Often, especially in newsgroups like **alt.humor** or **alt.tv.melrose**, you'll open an article that contains nothing but a header and meaningless gibberish.

This is done for a couple of reasons; perhaps the article contains a particularly politically incorrect joke, or what are known as spoilers, which are articles giving away the plot of an upcoming episode of your favorite television program.

The technique used is called **ROT13**. This is sort of a simple code where each character is given a number, a=1, b=2, and the character is swapped with its neighbor 13 characters to the right, a=n, b=0, and so on, thus ROT13.

To translate an article that used ROT13, follow these steps:

1 Select the text.

Fig. 18.7

This is an example of a ROT13 encoded message.

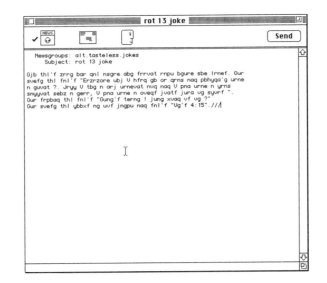

2 Open the Edit menu and choose Rot-13.

The message will instantly decode.

Fig. 18.8
The joke now
decoded.

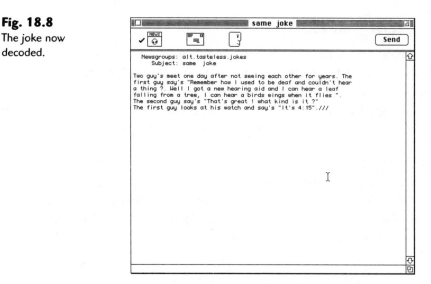

Saving articles

NewsWatcher's File menu contains most of the commonly used Mac features such as Save, Save As, and Print.

There are times when you may want to save an article for future reference. This can be a text file that you might read later with your word processor, a binary file awaiting additional parts, or just an interesting message you want to save for future reference. To do this, select the article, open the File menu, and choose Save (æ+S).

The usual Mac Save dialog box will open in which you can select a destination for your article.

You can also use Save As to save the article with another name. In addition, NewsWatcher adds two additional options: one allows you to save encoded messages and another allows you to save multiple files as either one file or separate documents. You would use this feature if you were saving multiple parts of a binary file into a single file, or if you were saving multiple messages as separate documents.

Printing articles

The fellow who delivers copier and printer paper at Antioch College in Yellow Springs, Ohio, recently remarked that he thought adding all the computers on campus to the network would mean less work for him, but it ended up generating more work and more paper. So much for the vision of computers creating a paperless society!

Even though NewsWatcher creates your personal cyber newspaper, you'll often find that you want to print a hard copy of an article. To do this, open the File menu and choose Print (æ+P). NewsWatcher will send the article to your printer and you'll get a typical Print dialog box based upon which printer you selected in your Chooser.

Writing articles with NewsWatcher

Writing your first article or posting your first message is an easy task with NewsWatcher. If you would like to try posting a few practice messages just to see how it works, use **misc.test** or a similar local .test group. It was created for just this purpose. Please don't post test messages to other groups—it's considered rude.

⊛ {Note}

The examples in the following figures were posted to a local newsgroup called **antioch.test**, which was set up so users on my system could post test messages and see an almost instantaneous result. Your service provider may or may not provide such a local group.

To compose a new posting starting a new thread, first click the name of the group to which you want to post the article, and then open the News menu and choose the Post New Article.

Here's how to write your first article:

1 Select the newsgroup you want to post in. You may either click once to select a group name from either Your Group List window or the Full Group List window, or double-click to open an individual group window.

2 Open the News menu and choose New Message (⌘+N).

3 A message window opens (see fig. 18.9). This is where you compose your message. If you created a signature file, NewsWatcher will automatically attach it to your message. If you haven't and want to now, you can open the File menu, select Preferences, pull down the Signature topic, and create a signature. Message windows are described in more detail in the next section.

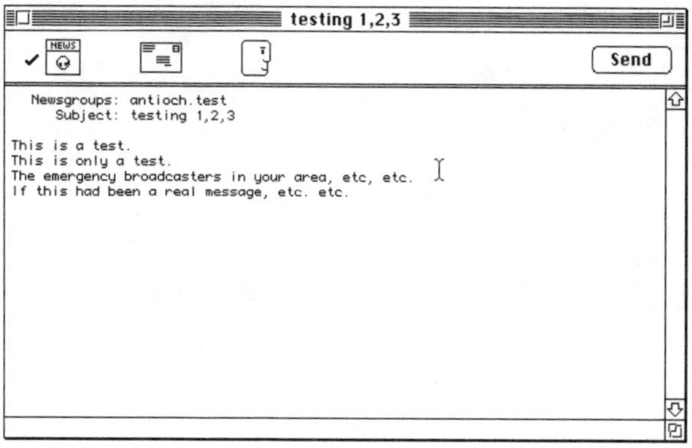

Fig. 18.9

This is an example of a new message ready to send to a test newsgroup. Notice that the News icon is checked, which means the message will be posted to the entire newsgroup.

4 When you're done, click the Send button.

5 Before your message is sent, NewsWatcher presents you with a warning message (see fig. 18.10). If you want to disable this message, you may go to the Preferences menu, open the Miscellaneous Options topic, and remove the Are You Sure alert on posts default.

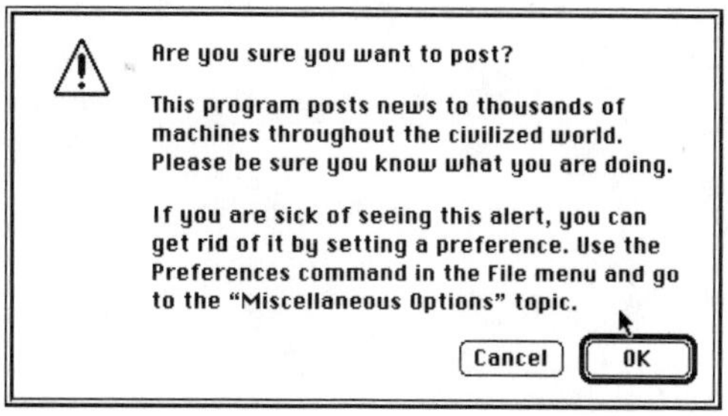

Fig. 18.10

NewsWatcher reminds you to think before you post.

If you want to post your message to multiple newsgroups, simply highlight the groups (or you can Shift+click or Option+click the desired groups), create a new message as above, and the message will automatically be addressed to multiple newsgroups.

Message windows

NewsWatcher does normal Mac word wrapping as you type paragraphs of text in message windows. When you actually send the message, NewsWatcher automatically breaks all your paragraphs into separate line lengths of 75 characters or less.

News icon
If this icon is checked, the message is posted as a news article. The article can then be read by anyone who reads the newsgroup.

Mail icon
If this icon is checked, the message is sent via e-mail. This allows you to reply or send a new message to only one person.

Self icon
If this icon is checked, a copy of the message is sent to you via e-mail. This option is valuable if you want to keep a record or copy of a message you have posted, or send an article from a newsgroup to your mail box for later reference.

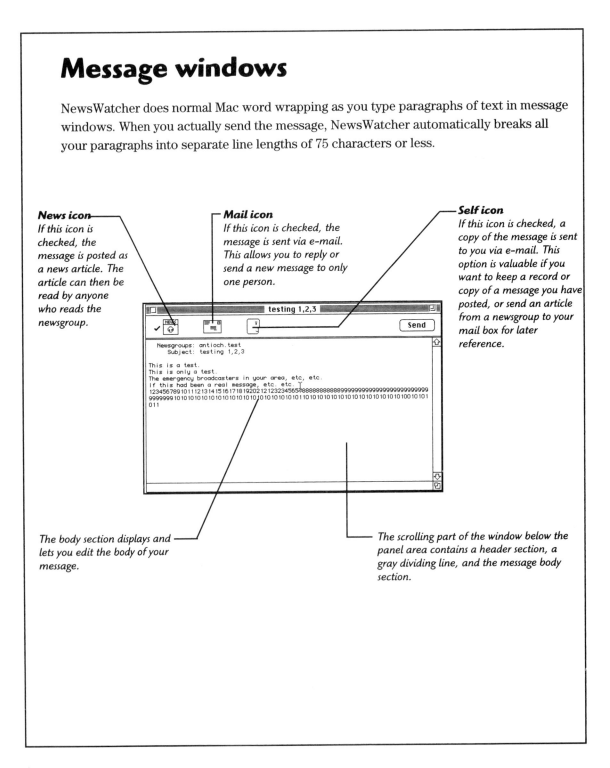

The body section displays and lets you edit the body of your message.

The scrolling part of the window below the panel area contains a header section, a gray dividing line, and the message body section.

Replying to an article

If you want to respond to an article, open the News menu and choose Reply. When responding to an article using this command, NewsWatcher opens a new window in which you compose your reply and choose whether you'll send the message to the group, to an individual, or to yourself. The difference between this and a New Message is that text from the original poster's message is included. When you're ready to send the reply, click the Send button in the window. The next section describes the various ways you can reply to a message.

Replying via e-mail

Let's suppose you're reading a newsgroup and you read a particularly interesting article. You think the author makes a good point, but you don't necessarily want to create a thread on the subject.

To reply to the author via e-mail, follow these steps:

1 Select the message.

2 Open the News menu and choose Reply (⌘+R).

A message window opens in which you can choose between the News icon or the Mail icon.

3 Select the Mail icon (see fig. 18.11). NewsWatcher will fill in the To: field with the author's e-mail address and the Subject line with Re: *Your message*.

4 Type your comments in the message area, edit the original message as necessary, and click the Send button to send the message via e-mail.

❋ {Note} Because one of the benefits—and disadvantages—of e-mail is that no real paper is involved, you might want to also click on the Self icon.

This will send a copy of the message to your mail box so that you have some record of the conversation.

Fig. 18.11
To reply to a
message via e-mail,
select the message,
open the News
menu, and choose
Reply. Then select
the Mail icon.

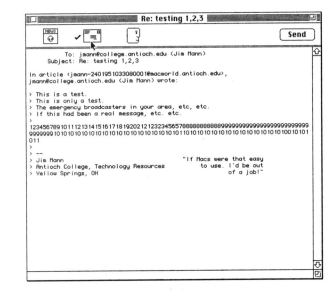

Posting a follow-up message

If you wish to post a follow-up message for the entire newsgroup to read,
select the original message, open the News menu, and choose Reply. When
the new message window opens, select the News icon (see fig. 18.12).

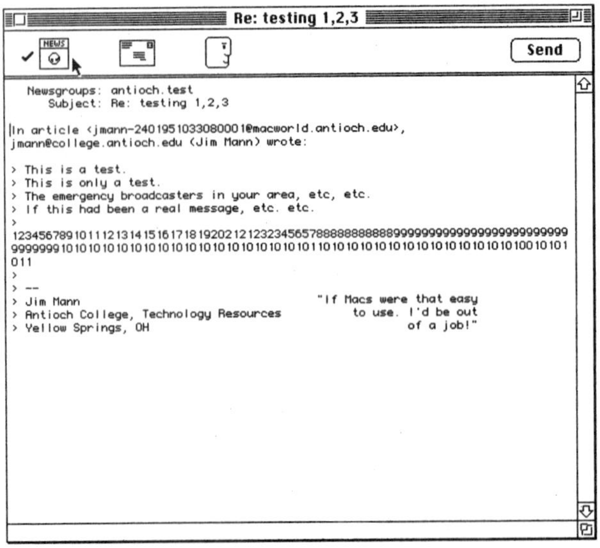

Fig. 18.12
To post a follow-up
message, open the
News menu and
choose Reply. Then
select the News icon.

NewsWatcher will automatically select the proper newsgroup, and add the
Subject line Re: *This message.*

Quoting

Editing your reply is called **quoting**. You can use the regular word processing techniques cut, copy, paste, and delete to clean up your replies and still
let the next reader know the main points the original poster made. In figure
18.13, you'll notice that the entire text, including signatures, of two previous
messages has been included and marked with greater than signs (>).

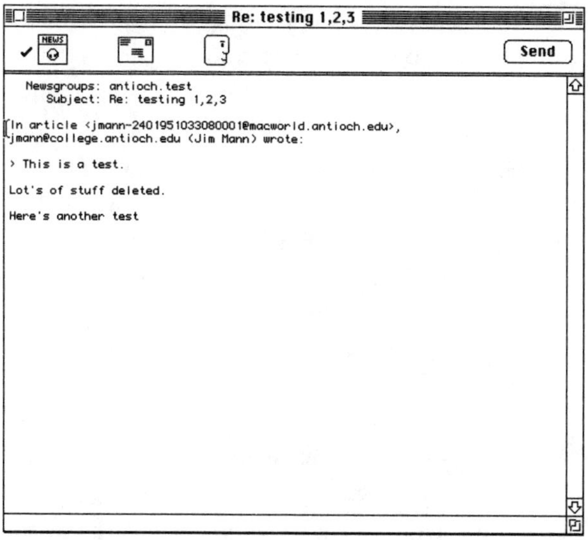

Fig. 18.13
Here's an example
of a reply that's been
edited to only include
the most important
points.

```
                          Re: testing 1,2,3

  NEWS
   ✓  ⊙          ⬚ ⬚         ?                        Send

     Newsgroups: antioch.test
       Subject: Re: testing 1,2,3

  In article <jmann-2401951033308000 1@macworld.antioch.edu>,
   jmann@college.antioch.edu <Jim Mann> wrote:

  > This is a test.

  Lot's of stuff deleted.

  Here's another test
```

There are five commands in the News menu that are used with message
windows:

- New Message (⌘+N). Opens a new message window.

- Reply (⌘+R). Replies to the current article.

- Forward (⌘+K). Forwards the current article via e-mail.

- Redirect (⌘+L). Redirects the current article via e-mail.

- Send Message (⌘+E). Sends the message (you can also click the Send
  button).

Forwarding and redirecting posts

The Forward command is appropriate for sending someone a copy of an article that you think they might find interesting, especially if you want to annotate the article with your own comments. The header and body of the article are copied to the new message body, with quoting (the original text is shown with > marks). When you mail the message, it is addressed from you.

The Redirect command is appropriate for sending yourself a copy of an interesting article, or for sending someone else a copy when you want replies to go to the poster rather than to you. The Subject and other header lines are copied from the article. The body of the article is copied to the new message body, without quoting (> marks). When you mail the message, it is addressed as from the original poster of the article, "by way of" you. If the recipient replies to the message, the reply is sent to the poster of the article. Unlike all other messages, your signature is not appended to redirected messages.

There are three commands in the Edit menu that are used with message windows:

- *Paste as Quotation.* This is the same as the Paste command, except that the pasted text is quoted as in message replies (the quote string is inserted in front of each pasted line). Paragraphs are wrapped before being quoted.

- *Wrap.* This wraps the selected text. Carriage returns are inserted to break paragraphs into 74-character or shorter lines. Paragraphs that are less than or equal to 80 characters are not wrapped. This is the same kind of wrapping that is done when messages are posted or mailed. You can use this command to see exactly what your text will look like when it's sent.

- *Unwrap.* This unwraps the selected text. Carriage returns at the end of lines inside paragraphs are removed (replaced by spaces). This can be useful if you paste in wrapped paragraphs of text from some other window or program and you want to edit the paragraphs. Unwrapping the paragraphs first makes editing much more pleasant.

A final thought on posting

You've no doubt heard the expression "think before you speak!" This holds 10 million times true on the Internet, especially in news. When you click the Send button, NewsWatcher presents you with a message warning you that what you are about to say will be read by thousands of people. Before you click the Send button, take another minute and think about whether you really want to post to the entire group, reply to the person via e-mail, or just forward the message to yourself.

Working smarter, not harder

NewsWatcher comes with a number of built-in features that can make even the newest user into a "power user." These features take advantage of the latest enhancements in Apple's System 7.5 and efforts to make programs like NewsWatcher work with other Macintosh TCP tools. In this section, we'll take a brief look at some of these features.

Drag and drop

If you hate to type, you'll love this feature!

NewsWatcher is **drag aware**, which means NewsWatcher takes advantage of a feature in System 7.5 that lets you drag selected bits of text or other objects from one application to another, or from one place in an application to another place (see figs. 18.14 and 18.15).

So how does this work, and what are the advantages? Well, the big advantage is that you'll never need to retype notes, or cut and paste again.

❋ *{Note}*

As this was being written, applications that take advantage of System 7.5's new features were still becoming available. If you haven't updated to the latest versions of your word processor and other programs, you can use SimpleText to experiment.

Using your word processor to edit posts

Let's say you're working on a long post and you'd rather use the features of a word processor like WordPerfect to correct spelling errors and so forth. You could create your article in WordPerfect, select all, copy and paste into a new message in NewsWatcher. But with drag and drop you just select the text in WordPerfect and drag it to NewsWatcher.

You can reverse the process and drag information from articles to your word processor.

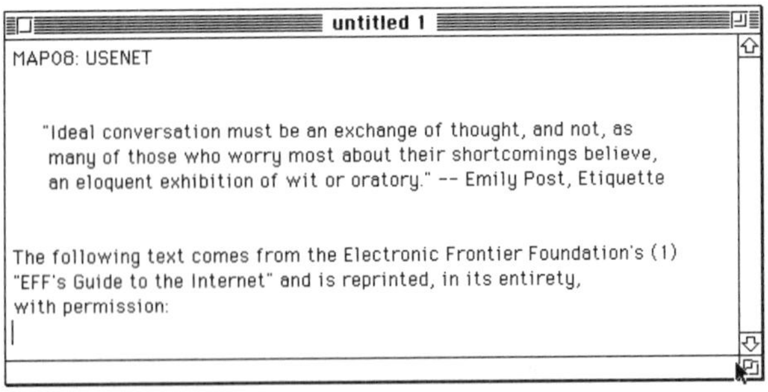

Fig. 18.14
Here's an example of a beginning of what will be a rather long post. It was created using SimpleText.

Fig. 18.15
The same message, dragged and dropped onto a new message that's ready to post.

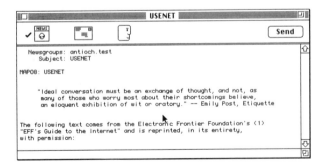

Making notes to yourself

One thing you could do with this information is create a **sticky** (System 7.5's "Postit Notes") and put it somewhere on your desktop for later reference. To do this, follow these steps:

1 Select the text you're interested in.

2 Hold down your mouse button and drag the text from NewsWatcher's window onto the sticky.

3 Release the mouse button and you have another wonderful sticky to clutter up your desktop!

Much like Apple's drop feature in System 7.x that allowed you to drop text or other types of documents onto the icon of drop aware programs, NewsWatcher's drag feature is an acquired taste. But, you say, why can't I just use copy and paste to accomplish the same thing? Good point, but if you think in terms of working smarter, not harder, why do something that requires four or five mouse clicks and keystrokes when one single process will do the same job?

The cluttered desktop is a sign of a...

From the author's standpoint, one of the most difficult parts of writing these chapters was following the instructions to clean up my desktop for the screen shots that illustrate these chapters.

I counted, and I have a screen shot to prove it, more than 30 aliases of drop aware applications, frequently used documents, plus about a dozen stickies that had to be hidden and put away in folders.

But, they eventually began to creep back, because once you get in the habit of dragging something from a document onto an icon of an application, or dropping a document on the icon of an alias, there's just no going back.

Someone once said that like "publish and subscribe," "drag and drop" is a technology waiting for a use. I disagree. Try it, you'll like it, and you'll find yourself working smarter not harder.

"Fetching" files

So far, we've avoided getting too techie about how NewsWatcher works its magic, but we must pause here for a brief moment and discuss what are known as URLs.

In simple terms, a **URL (Uniform Resource Locators)** is a pointer to something, someone, or someplace on the Net. The latest version of the NewsWatcher user manual spends several pages discussing URLs, and you should take the time to read it over if you want more information. Also, as this was being written, the authors of NewsWatcher and several of its Helper programs had developed a standard for making programs URL-aware, and in the future you should be able to take advantage of this powerful feature with more and more applications.

How do URLs work? Here's a very, very simple explanation. Suppose you're reading an article about the latest Apple software updates. In the article, you are referred to a source for these files. But, the poster says something like "it's at all the usual places." Not very helpful unless you know how to get to these "usual places." But, if the poster spent the time and provided the correct URL, you can get these files with a single mouse click.

This is an example of a correct URL: **ftp://abs.apple.com/pub/apple-internet-providers/**. This is a reference to something that can be obtained via FTP, at a site known as abs.apple.com in a directory named /pub/apple-internet-providers/.

The following are some examples of URLs:

> **news:j-doe-240687341230001@mac18.foo.edu (a message)**
>
> **news:comp.sys.mac.comm (a specific group)**
>
> **nntp://news.foo.edu/alt.groupname/5238**
>
> **mailto:j-doe@foo.edu**
>
> **ftp://ftp.foo.edu/pub/my-game/readme.txt**
>
> **http://www.foo.edu**

gopher://gopher.foo.edu

wais://wais.foo.edu:5520/usr/local/xxx/our-database

telnet://machine.foo.edu

tn3270://big-ibm.foo.edu

finger://j-doe@foo.edu

whois://j-doe@foo.edu

ph://ns.foo.edu/john%20doe

Let's say you want to get a copy of some files for future reference. To get these files, simply drag across the URL, ⌘+click on it, and Fetch, one of NewsWatcher's "helper" programs, will open up and go get the file for you.

When you find the file you're looking for, double-click on it and Fetch will bring it to your desktop.

✱ *{Note}*

Do you care how this works? Well, NewsWatcher uses an **Apple event** to send a call from NewsWatcher to Fetch. This is known as **multitasking**, and you can go back to NewsWatcher and continue reading the news while Fetch works in the background. Frankly, the only reason this would ever make any difference to you is if you're trying it from an SE with 4 MB of RAM and you don't have enough available memory to run two programs at once.

NewsWatcher's helpers

Here's a list of NewsWatcher's helper programs. Notice that the version numbers of these programs are subject to constant change, and it's a good idea to periodically check the NewsWatcher site for the most current versions. Some of these programs are shareware. Please send your shareware payments to the authors of the programs.

NewsWatcher uses **helper programs** to help open URLs and decode extracted binary files. These programs are also very useful for other purposes, and should be part of your collection of Internet tools. The helper programs are available via anonymous FTP at **ftp://ftp.acns.nwu.edu/pub /newswatcher/helpers/**.

uuUndo

uuUndo is a free program written by Aaron Giles of Cornell University Medical College. It was written specifically for use with NewsWatcher, although it's also useful on its own for doing uudecoding.

uuUndo is NewsWatcher's default helper program for extracting uuencode attached binaries. It has preferences to automatically delete or move the temporary input file to the trash after decoding it. To set one of these options, choose File, Preferences.

StuffIt Expander_ and DSEE

StuffIt Expander_ is a free program written by Leonard Rosenthol of Aladdin Systems. It's used to deBinHex files and expand both StuffIt and Compact Pro archives. StuffIt Expander_ is NewsWatcher's default helper program for extracting BinHex attached binaries.

There is a companion Aladdin product named DropStuff_ with Expander Enhancer (DSEE). DSEE is $30 shareware. When DSEE is installed, StuffIt Expander_ is able to decode uuencode files as well as BinHex files. If you have this product, you can configure NewsWatcher to use StuffIt Expander_ as your uudecode helper as well as your BinHex helper.

Fetch

Fetch is an FTP client written by Jim Matthews of Dartmouth College. Fetch is licensed free of charge for use in educational and nonprofit organizations. Users in commercial or government enterprises may obtain an individual license for $25. Multi-user licenses are also available.

Fetch is NewsWatcher's default helper program for fetching referenced files when you ⌘+click a file reference or use the Open URL command for a file reference. You need version 2.1.2 or later of Fetch to work properly with NewsWatcher.

Anarchie

Anarchie is an Archie and FTP client written by Peter Lewis in Australia. It's a $10 shareware program. You can use Anarchie instead of Fetch as your helper program for fetching referenced files. You need version 1.2.0 or later of Anarchie to work properly with NewsWatcher.

MacWeb

MacWeb is a World Wide Web client written by John Hardin of the Microelectronics and Computer Technology Corporation (MCC). It's licensed free of charge for academic, research, and personal use. It's NewsWatcher's default helper program for opening http URLs.

MacWAIS

MacWAIS is a WAIS client written by John Hardin of the Microelectronics and Computer Technology Corporation (MCC). It's $35 shareware and NewsWatcher's default helper program for opening WAIS URLs.

NCSA Mosaic

NCSA Mosaic is a World Wide Web client developed at the National Center for Supercomputing Applications and it's free. If you want to use NCSA Mosaic as a URL helper with NewsWatcher, you need version 2.0 or later. NCSA Mosaic is available at **ftp://ftp.ncsa.uiuc.edu/Mosaic/Mac/**.

Netscape

Netscape is a World Wide Web client developed at Netscape Communications Corporation. It is free for people at educational and nonprofit institutions. You need version 1.0 or later.

TurboGopher

TurboGopher is a Gopher client developed at the University of Minnesota and it's free. It's NewsWatcher's default helper for opening gopher URLs. You need version 2.0a1 or later.

NCSA Telnet

NCSA Telnet is a free Telnet client developed by Jim Browne and others at the National Center for Supercomputing Applications. It's NewsWatcher's default helper for opening Telnet URLs. You need version 2.4 or later of NCSA Telnet.

tn3270

tn3270 is a free tn3270 client developed by Peter DiCamillo of Brown University. It's NewsWatcher's default helper for opening tn3270 URLs. You need version 2.4d7 or later.

Finger

Finger is a Finger and whois client for the Mac written by Peter Lewis in Australia. It's a $10 shareware program and it's NewsWatcher's default helper for opening finger and whois URLs. You need version 1.5.0 or later.

Back to the preferences

If all your helper programs are unstuffed, and in the same folder as NewsWatcher, you don't have to configure the URL Helper Programs topic in the Preferences menu. NewsWatcher will default to it's favorite helpers and work just fine.

But, if you don't like the defaults or have a preference for say Anarchie over Fetch or Netscape over MacWeb, you'll want to change these preferences.

To do this:

1 Choose File, Preferences.

2 Open the topic URL Helper Programs 1.

3 Click on one of the "set" buttons and navigate to the correct program.

4 When you're done, open the URL Helper Programs 2 and 3 topics and make additional selections.

⊛ {Note} _____ If the helper programs are in the same folder as NewsWatcher, it will find them without resetting your preferences. Also, if NewsWatcher fails to find a helper program, you need to restart your computer and rebuild your desktop.

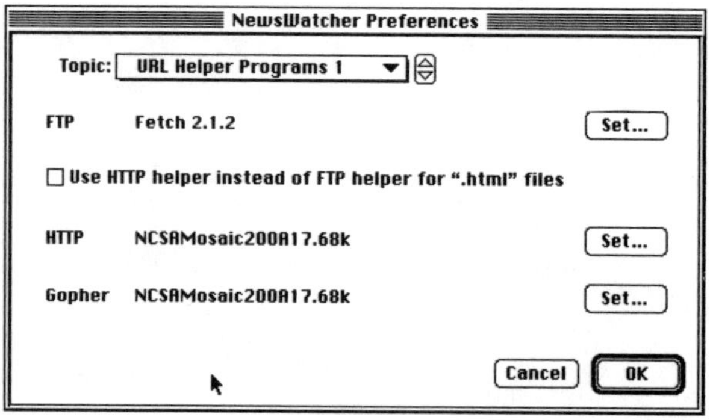

Fig. 18.16
The default choices for some of NewsWatcher's URL helpers.

```
═══════════════ NewsWatcher Preferences ═══════════════

   Topic: [ URL Helper Programs 1   ▼]⊜

   FTP       Fetch 2.1.2                              [ Set... ]

   ☐ Use HTTP helper instead of FTP helper for ".html" files

   HTTP      NCSAMosaic200A17.68k                     [ Set... ]

   Gopher    NCSAMosaic200A17.68k                     [ Set... ]

                                        [ Cancel ] [[ OK ]]
```

19

File Attachments

Depending on the newsgroup you're in, it seems that the two most frequently asked questions are "Where are the pictures?" and "How do I use these files?"

In chapter 18, you learned how to get involved in UseNet newsgroups by reading messages, posting your own messages, and replying via e-mail to other people on the Net.

In this chapter, you'll learn how to use some of NewsWatcher's powerful features to download binary files and how to use NewsWatcher as a tool to go to other exciting places on the Internet.

Before you get started, open the File menu, select Preferences, and open the topic for Extracting Binaries. Make sure your helper is set for uuUndo, and take a moment to open and configure uuUndo so it creates a default folder for saving binary files and deletes "temp" files. In uuUndo, open the File menu, select Preferences, and configure to suit your individual situation. You might also make sure that you've properly set up Stuffit or your GIF, JPEG, and MPEG viewers.

Typical viewers are Jpeg Viewer, GifConverter, or Sparkle. Information on downloading these files from your favorite FTP site is in chapter 8.

Extracting binaries

Depending on the newsgroup you're in, it seems that recently the two most frequently asked questions are "Where are the pictures?" and "How do I view these files?"

Most of these questions come from people using a command-line interface where downloading binary files is a challenge.

With NewsWatcher, there's really nothing to it. With NewsWatcher, extracting a binary file is as simple as one-two-three:

1 Locate a message containing a binary file.

2 Open the message.

3 Double-click the binary icon that appears in the upper right corner of the message.

You can also:

- Select the icon and drag it to your desktop.
- Select the message and type ⌘+**b**.
- Use Shift+click or Option+click to select a number of messages and type ⌘+**b**.

That's it. NewsWatcher makes extracting binary files as simple as double-clicking or remembering the keyboard shortcut ⌘+**b**.

If you prefer using menus, you select the message containing the binary file, open the Special menu, and select Extract Binaries.

The most difficult part of downloading binary files is having some patience. The time it takes to download a binary file depends upon the size of the file and your modem speed. A small file may take a couple of minutes; downloading every binary file in a group may take several hours.

If you've done everything correctly, i.e. properly configured your helper programs, the file will magically appear on your desktop. In fact, if you've got everything working correctly, uuUndo will pass the file off to Stuffit and Stuffit will unstuff it for you.

 **{Note}** ____ Despite rumors and misunderstandings to the contrary, binary files can be sounds or software, and not just pictures.

Fig. 19.1
If you haven't pre-configured uuUndo, you'll be prompted to select a name for the binary file and choose a location to save it.

Fig. 19.2
The end result: A few minutes later you have the binary file on your desktop. Note, because uuUndo wasn't configured, it added three parts to the file on the desktop: a temp.hqx, a Stuffit.sit file, and a folder for the application. With uuUndo and Stuffit working together, the file is unhqx'd and unstuffed for you.

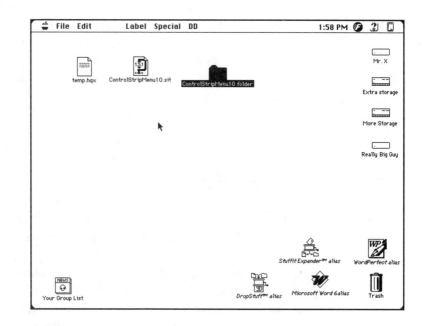

⊗<Caution> First, not all service providers offer binary groups. Second, binary files (and binary groups) are huge, and take up lots and lots of space on your host's server. So, many system administrators age binary newsgroups more rapidly than non-binary groups. This means that while your host may keep regular news messages for a week or more, it may begin to remove binary files after only a day or so. Third, binary files come in multiple parts and take a while to make their way across the Net. The caution is to download a binary file when you see it, and not to wait. The other caution is to be patient and make sure that all parts have arrived on your host. If you don't like the way your host handles binary groups, contact your system administrator.

There are pictures, clip art, movies, sounds, and you name it scattered across the Net. Some favorite places to look for pictures are **alt.binaries.clip-art** and **alt.pagemaker**. Both of these groups offer high-quality artwork to enhance your creations.

⊗<Caution> If you select all the files in a binary newsgroup, and NewsWatcher skips some of the files because parts were missing, you might not want to "save changes" to your group list when you quit NewsWatcher. If you save changes, NewsWatcher will mark all the messages as read and you won't see the files with missing parts the next time you log in.

Posting binary files

How do you post binary files with NewsWatcher? The bad news is that you don't, at least not until the author's complete version 2.1.

The good news is that there is another version of NewsWatcher available called "Value-Added NewsWatcher." It's a project by several people on the Net, including David Brewster, Bob Boonstra, and Brian Clark. And it is available via FTP from **ftp://grocne.enc.org/pub/V.A.NewsWatcher/**.

This version of NewsWatcher is for what might be considered more advanced users and includes some features like filtering, article sorting, digest handling, and posting binaries.

NewsWatcher.VA is so similar to the standard version of NewsWatcher that if you choose to use it, you'll find the setups are virtually the same. Or, you can have copies of both programs on your hard drive.

Much like downloading a binary file with standard NewsWatcher, posting a binary file with NewsWatcher.VA is not complicated.

To post a binary file, follow these steps:

1 Select the group or groups you wish to post in.

2 Open the News menu and select New Message.

3 Create a new message in the message window (see fig. 19.3).

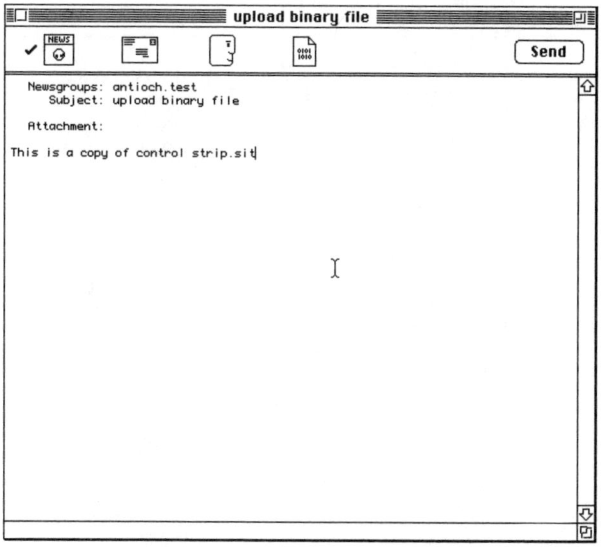

Fig. 19.3

The message window in NewsWatcher.VA is the same as you're used to, except a binary icon has been added.

4 Check the "binary" file icon.

5 Locate the binary file you want to post.

Fig. 19.4
The binary file is now contained in the message and ready to be sent.

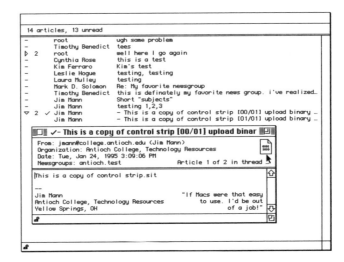

6 Send your message.

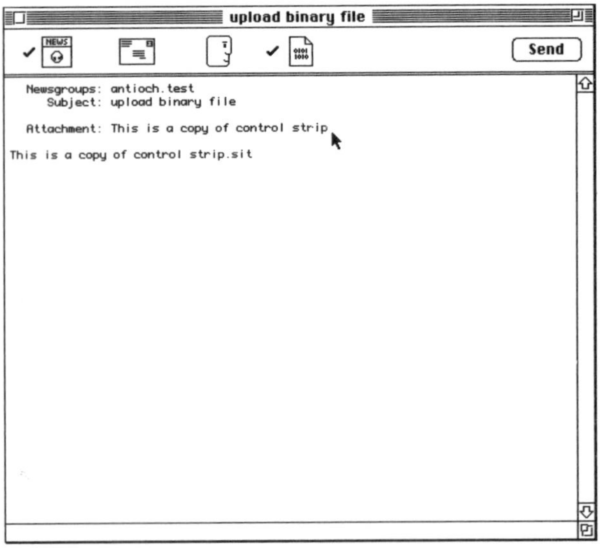

Fig. 19.5
When the message containing the binary file arrives in the newsgroup, it is shown as a multi-part thread. NewsWatcher users see it as a binary icon included in the message.

Surfing the Net with NewsWatcher

Now it's time to use URLs contained in news articles, to open HTTP sites on the WWW, and go Net surfing.

Even if you didn't have a clue what an HTTP site is or what the WWW is, you're only a mouse-click away from using NewsWatcher as an entry to a completely different part of the Net—the World Wide Web, where **home pages** offer even more access to information and pictures and movies.

How do you get there from here? Well, since this is a Mac—as opposed to computer science—the answer is that when you find an interesting reference to a Web site, select it,   +click on it and as if by magic you leave UseNet and are transported to someone's home page halfway around the world.

Fig. 19.6 comp.infosystems. www.announce is a good newsgroup to look for new "home pages."

```
┌──────────────────── comp.infosystems.www.announce ──────────────────┐
│ 32 articles, 27 unread                                               │
│ -    Jim Hurley       [PERSONAL][INFO][UPDATE] The Arachnaut's Lair │
│ -    Andrew Stephen …  PERSONAL: BOB(c)WEB!!!                        │
│ -    Carl Rogers      COMMERCIAL: Calypso Party Cruises              │
│ ✓    pbell@violet.be… SCIENCE EDUCATION - Computer as Learning Partner Web Site │
│ -    Patrick J. Chic… SHOPPING Kona Coffee Gift Baskets              │
│ -    Tom Neff         ENTERTAINMENT/MUSIC - The Dar Williams Web Page│
│ -    Peter Fraterdeus DESIGN: designOnline(tm) WWW resource for Design│
│ -    David Robertson… VISUALIZATION: Movies Added for Virtual Frog   │
│ -    Matthew H. Fiel… EDUCATION; MUSIC                               │
│ ✓    Daniel Hartung   INFO: Rotaract Home Page  [international service club] │
│ -    Stephen E. Coll… K-12 - WWW Site Registry                      │
│ -    SYSTEM@ko.hhs.dk EDUCATION: IfE home-page                       │
│ ✓    Chris Dent       Indiana University Honors Division + fun extras│
│ -    Juan Luis Bort … ANNOUNCE: INTER NATURA www pages               │
│ -    kaz iwami        NEWS:Shima Media Network                       │
│ -    Web business ca… PERSONAL: - Multi-Media Web Business Card, Resume', and Home … │
│ -    NetPost          SERVER                                         │
│ -    C Baral          El Paso, TX                                    │
│ -    Andrew MacRae    MAGAZINE Upside                                │
│ ✓    Richard Kaplan   SPORTS                                         │
│ -    John W. Keating  AUTO: Chesapeake Area Miata Club Home Page     │
│ -    Bradley M. Kuhn  MAGAZINE: Issue 2 of Crossroads                │
│ -    Tim Babb         ANNOUNCE EUROPEAN INTERACTIONS SERVICE         │
│ -    Julie Reese      PERSONAL homepage                              │
│ -    JFK              PERSONAL: JFK's page                           │
│ ✓    Barry Parr       INFO: Mercury Center from the San Jose Mercury News │
│ -    FlashBack SunFl… WEB WORLD: Multimedia Apps On The Internet (Orlando/Santa Cla… │
│ -    Glenn Davis      COMMERCIAL - Powerhouse Advertising            │
│ -    Jim Zwick        HISTORY LITERATURE Mark Twain & the Philippine-American War │
│ -    AlternaKids      ENTERTAINMENT: AlternaKids Records             │
│ -    HendersonThynne… SPORT: Karate                                  │
│ -    Ed Cohens - Hos… HEALTH-Florida Medical Newspaper               │
│                                                              ▶        │
└──────────────────────────────────────────────────────────────────────┘
```

Fig. 19.7

Here's an example of a message with a URL reference to a home page. If you drag your mouse across the URL and apple + click on it, NewsWatcher will open the WWW URL you've chosen and take you to the home page.

```
┌──────────── ✓Indiana University Honors Division + fun extras ────────────┐
│ From: cdent@yod.honors.indiana.edu (Chris Dent)                          │
│ Organization: Indiana University Honors Division                         │
│ Date: Fri, Jan 20, 1995 7:59:58 PM                                       │
│ Newsgroups: comp.infosystems.www.announce                                │
│                                                                          │
│ The Indiana University Honors Division is proud to announce the          │
│ unveiling of version two of its World Wide Web server. The server        │
│ provides information on the programs, policies and staff of the Honors   │
│ Division as well as distributing information for the National Collegiate │
│ Honors Council.                                                          │
│                                                                          │
│ Perhaps more interesting, and certainly more fun the server also house   │
│ the Labyrinth Electronic Publishing Project (LEPP), an interactive       │
│ poetry and art experience. LEPP includes poetry and artwork presented in │
│ an environment where readers and viewers can comment on the works and    │
│ view comments left by other people.                                      │
│                                                                          │
│ The Honors Division server can be reached at:                            │
│                                                                          │
│ <URL:http://www.honors.indiana.edu/index.html>                          │
│                                                                          │
│ While there, besides visiting the above you may also wish to visit       │
│ Chrome, the pale beginnings of what may prove to be a fun collection     │
│ of interactive web toys. Include are a graffiti wall, a hotlist          │
│ dynamo, various Star Trek dealies, and the oh so cleansing "When          │
│ the Revolution Comes." You can find Chrome at:                           │
│                                                                          │
│ <URL:http://www.honors.indiana.edu/%7echrome/index.html>                │
│                                                                          │
│ Enjoy!                                                                    │
│                                                                          │
│ --                                                                       │
│ Chris Dent cdent@indiana.edu http://www.honors.indiana.edu/~cdent/      │
│                                                                          │
└──────────────────────────────────────────────────────────────────────────┘
```

Fig. 19.8
We're surfing the net now! Here's a home page from Indiana University, using Netscape...all by just clicking on a URL.

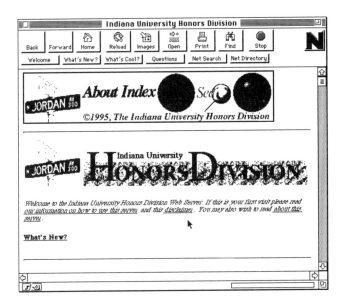

Once again, NewsWatcher is using an Apple event to send a call to a helper program, in this case MacWeb to open a WWW site.

Navigating or surfing the Web is the subject of another book, but since we're here, it's really as simple as double-clicking on items which show up in blue on your screen. Each reference is actually a pointer to somewhere or something else.

For more information about the WWW and various browsers you should read *Using Mosaic, Using the World Wide Web*, or *Using Netscape* from Que.

⊗<Caution> Surfing the Web with a 9600 baud modem (or connection) and a black-and-white computer is frustrating. Also, using NewsWatcher and a program like Netscape can quickly tax your computer's memory. If you're going to become a Web surfer you might consider more RAM, a faster modem, a better service provider, or saving up $10,000 to have a T-1 phone line installed in your home.

End Note: YMMV

In the process of writing these four chapters, I used five different versions of NewsWatcher and several different versions of the helper programs. Decisions to "freeze" the manuscript quickly changed when NewsWatcher came out with a fat version for Power Macintosh, and then a user's manual, and finally with an elegant implementation of using URLs and helper programs to link NewsWatcher with other parts of the Net.

Remember, NewsWatcher is "beta" software and subject to constant updates. Please make sure to check for the newsest versions of the software mentioned here.

So, as they say in news, YMMV: your mileage may vary.

Enjoy.

Part V:

Your Own Newsgroup or Site

20

Starting Your Own Groups

To learn the spirit of the rules for creating a newsgroup in the Big Seven, read news.groups for six months or so. During this time there is sure to be a group creation fiasco.

In this chapter:

- Why create another group?
- Creating a group in the Big Seven
- Creating a group in alt.*
- Creating a group in regional and national hierarchies
- After your group is created
- Creating and maintaining an FAQ

On many online services, forums or discussion areas are created by the people in charge. But on UseNet, there are no people in charge, and new groups are created by people just like you. If you think there should be another group on UseNet, you can make it happen. This chapter tells you how.

Why create another group?

There are five good reasons to create a new newsgroup to discuss a specific topic:

- There is no group to discuss that topic now. Be sure! Chapter 2, "How Newsgroups Are Organized," lists five ways to find a group that discusses your topic. Don't embarrass yourself trying to create a group that already exists.

- There are several groups that discuss a particular topic from time to time, but you'd like to pull all the discussions together in one place.

- The group for discussing your topic is too crowded with other topics, and you want to create a subgroup for your topic.

- The group for discussing that topic is moderated (or unmoderated) and you think there should be an unmoderated (or moderated) group as well.

- The group for discussing that topic is poorly named and you want to create a replacement group with a better name.

There are a number of bad reasons to create a new group too. If you can't come up with anything better than one of these, you're better off not trying to create a new group at all.

- There's an unmoderated group available to discuss your topic, but you don't like some of the traffic. You want to create another unmoderated group and you hope the unwanted traffic won't follow you there.

- There's a group available to discuss your topic, and the name makes sense, but some sites won't carry it because of the hierarchy it's in. You'd like to move it to a different hierarchy so it can get better propagation.

- People discuss the topic (which you don't care for) in a group you read, and you'd like them to go away into their own group.

Creating a group in the Big Seven

If you want to create a group whose name starts with comp, misc, news, rec, sci, soc, or talk, there are some very specific procedures you must follow. They take about three months to complete, and require you to follow not only the letter of the rules, but also the spirit. To learn the spirit of the rules, read **news.groups** for six months or so. During this time there is sure to be a group creation fiasco, and by reading all the flamage and accusations and counter-accusations, you'll learn a great deal about the way the Net works and the way you must work if you want to help build it.

⊗<Caution> Before you start, you should read "How to Create a New UseNet Newsgroup," and also "The UseNet Newsgroup Creation Companion," posted to **news.groups, news.announce.newgroups**, and **news.answers**, which help to explain why it's important to follow the procedures carefully. An early mistake can mean your group may not be approved.

The procedure for newsgroup creation in one of the main hierarchies is detailed in the periodic posting "How to Create a New UseNet Newsgroup," posted to **news.announce.newusers, news.groups, news.answers, news.announce.newgroups**, and **news.admin.misc** each month. This document, generally referred to as The Guidelines, uses the strict definition of UseNet: "groups in the Big Seven." The procedure involves three steps.

Request for discussion

The first step is to develop a document called an **RFD** (Request For Discussion), which describes the group you want to create. You give the reason for creation (one of the good ones listed in the previous section), the name and moderation status (and the name of the moderator), and a brief charter for the group.

❝❝ *Plain English, please!*

RFD is a **Request For Discussion**. By posting it to **news.groups**, you're asking for comments from people who will read your group if it's formed and also from people who've been around for many a group creation and will have some valuable advice for you. **❞❞**

Discussion of the proposed group

After you submit the RFD to the moderator of **news.announce.newgroups**, discussion of the new group will ensue. In the process of discussion, there will be lots of advice and ideas on suggested changes. Eventually, the RFD will be posted to **news.announce.newgroups**, **news.groups**, and any other groups you suggest.

About 30 days of discussion ensue, and you may change the name, moderation status, or charter of the group as a result of this discussion.

A **charter** is a paragraph or two explaining what the group is for and what it isn't for. It shouldn't explain why the topic is important or useful in the real world, nor list all the other places that the topic is being discussed now (that belongs elsewhere in the RFD). The charter will often be reposted for years, even decades to come, and used to guide people trying to decide what to post to the group. It needs to be written with care, and generally the shorter, the better.

Once your charter and group information has been finalized, you are ready to move on to the next step.

Call for votes

After discussion is over, a **CFV** (**Call For Votes**) is issued. An objective party must collect the votes. Anyone who has access to the CFV with an Internet address is eligible to vote. A vote passes if there are 100 more YES votes than NO votes and also if there are twice as many YES votes as NO votes. For example, a vote of 100:1 would fail (less than a hundred more YES votes than NO votes), a vote of 700:500 would fail (doesn't have twice as many YES votes as NO votes), and a vote of 250:120 would pass because it meets both requirements.

❝❝ *Plain English, please!*

The **Call For Votes** collects yes and no responses from everyone who sees the CFV. It is generally posted to the same newsgroups as the RFD. **❞❞**

Getting group creation help from a mailing list

There are two mailing lists that will help you reach people who can help you through the group creation process. **group-advice@uunet.uu.net** will help you decide whether or not your topic is a good one for a new group, and advise you on your name and moderation status. If group-advice thinks your proposal is seriously flawed, it will delay the posting of your RFD until the flaws are corrected. **group-mentors@amdahl.com** will connect you to a mentor and ally who will lead you through the group creation process. Your mentor will help write the RFD and provide you with valuable advice until the group is created, and even beyond.

✱ {Note}

It may seem at first glance that the procedures outlined in the previous sections are unnecessarily complex, and that the people involved are cliquish, elitist, and bureaucratic. But UseNet would be an unworkable mess if the names didn't make sense, and so a group of people volunteer to help ensure the names make sense.

Creating a group in alt.*

In contrast to the Big Seven, there are essentially no rules in alt.*. Some sysadmins (system administrators) won't create a new alt group unless it has been discussed in alt.config first. This gives inexperienced group creators a chance to learn a better name for their group, or to be told of an existing group for their topic. Many other sysadmins create all new alt groups, whether they were discussed or not.

If you think the two- or three-month process to create a group in the main hierarchies is just not worth it, start reading alt.config right away. When the periodic posting "So You Want to Create an Alt Newsgroup" arrives (it's posted every two weeks), read it carefully. It has some suggestions on names, and on the sorts of groups that shouldn't be created in alt.* (those of only local interest and those that already exist in the Big Seven).   Come up with a good name for your group, propose it in alt.config, and see what other people have to say. If no one has a valid objection, create the group.

When you get a group created in the Big Seven, someone else actually creates it for you, by sending out a special "control" article. Whenever this article arrives at a news site, it acts as a command to the local news system rather than just as an article. But if you want an alt group, you're the one who sends out that message. Finding out just how to do it isn't terribly difficult, but it's not public knowledge either. Several ways to find out are listed in "So You Want to Create an Alt Newsgroup."

Joel "will create newsgroups for food" Furr and Tim "No" Pierce

Joel and Tim are both famous throughout the Net. Among other things, they both moderate newsgroups, but in alt.config they are natural opposites. Joel is enthusiastic about any new group and tends to create a lot of them. Tim is skeptical about most new groups, and is so fed up with repeating the reasons why a new group would be a bad idea that he often just follows up with one word: No.

Joel has created so many new groups in alt that some sysadmins automatically ignore any group creation request from him. He even has his own group, **alt.fan.joel-furr**. He sells (for no profit) T-shirts, caps, and other Net.collectibles commemorating infamous Net people and events, like the Green Card Lawyers (see the sidebar in chapter 4).

Joel and Tim joined forces with Dave "tale" Lawrence (the moderator of **news.announce.newgroups**) and four other UseNet luminaries to develop a proposal for a us.* hierarchy. The plan wasn't accepted and the group disbanded, but in December 1994 Joel announced he was going to start just creating us.* groups, and treating it like alt. Time will tell what happens to the hierarchy.

❓Q&A___

If it takes three months to create a Big Seven group, and a week or two to create an alt group, why does anyone ever create Big Seven groups?

Because they think it's worth the wait. Some sites don't take groups in alt, so a main hierarchy group will have better propagation, and be taken more seriously. Some sensible and serious groups do exist in alt, but they are in the minority.

If the new group is to be moderated, it's definitely better to be an approved, voted-on group. That's because so many sites obey control messages from anyone and everyone for alt groups, and that means your group could be changed to unmoderated, or to moderated with a different moderator, by anyone at any time. In the Big Seven your group's moderation status will probably never change.

Creating a group in regional and national hierarchies

Many local and regional hierarchies use a *.config group to discuss new groups. For example, **tor.config** discusses possible new groups in the tor hierarchy, which is for topics specific to Toronto, Ontario, Canada. In general, hierarchies create groups in one of three ways:

- Anyone can issue a newsgroup control message, and each sysadmin decides whether to honor it or not.

- As above, but use of the appropriate *.config group is strongly encouraged, and many sysadmins will base their approval on the use of *.config.

- Only one (or a few) sysadmins can create groups, and control messages from other people are ignored. Suggestions to the sysadmin are conveyed by e-mail, posts in the appropriate *.config group, or non-electronic communication (such as stopping by the sysadmin's office to ask).

You can find out which way your hierarchy operates by reading the .config group, if it exists, or the .general group otherwise, and perhaps sending mail to someone who appears to be a well-informed regular.

> You'll know your group belongs in a local hierarchy if you can describe the people who'll read it using a geographic word or phrase. Expatriates can arrange a feed of the group to their new homes. So groups for "Canadians" go in can.*, and those for "Norwegians" go in no.*.

Sometimes you may want a local group that mirrors the name of a Big Seven group. For example, there is a misc.jobs hierarchy, five groups in all. Many regional hierarchies have jobs groups (one Toronto service provider carries 95 groups with "jobs" in their names).

Most hierarchies don't have enough traffic for multiple jobs groups: ont.jobs and nm.jobs carry both "I want a job" and "job available" postings in Ontario and New Mexico respectively. Where traffic warrants, some regional hierarchies have chosen to mimic the structure of misc.jobs.* (for example, ba.jobs.contract, ba.jobs.offered, and ba.jobs.misc for jobs in the San Francisco Bay Area). Some hierarchies place jobs under a second level hierarchy for commercial traffic: aus.ads.jobs and za.ads.jobs for Australia and South Africa, and de.markt.jobs for Germany, have taken this approach.

After your group is created

The most important thing to remember about "your" group is that it isn't really yours. You had the idea to create it, you got the process rolling, you wrote the RFD, you answered objections and changed the RFD during the discussion process, the group passed and now, well, now it's just a group like any other. If you're the moderator you can stop certain material from being posted in it, but moderator or not, you can't make material appear, or make people join and enjoy your group. You have to let it grow.

How to get your group off to a good start

There are a number of things you can do to get the group off to a good start. First, prepare a welcome posting as soon as the vote begins. This posting should include:

- A paragraph or so of charter (from the RFD)

- An indication of the date the group was created and the results of the vote (and your name too, if you'd like). This posting will probably be in use years from now, with minor changes

- A list of topics that are welcome in the group

- A list of topics that are not welcome, and an indication of where they might belong, if anywhere

- A list of Subject Line Conventions, if you have one (see chapter 9)

As soon as the group passes, update this Welcome with the vote results. When the group is created on your site, post this message. If anyone has posted already with a message like "Hey! Neat group! What's it for?" (most new groups see tons of messages like this in their first week or so) mail the poster a copy of the welcome message. Post the welcome again a few days later, before settling down to a once a week or every two week schedule. Mail it to everyone who posts something that suggests the welcome hasn't been read yet.

Try not to post public rebukes for transgressions during the early days. Be ready to send a lot of e-mail. Let the people who'll use the group feel their way around in it for a while without too much direction. Keep notes of what questions are asked most frequently for your FAQ. If you've already started one, be alert to the possibility that you'll need to add some questions or rearrange the order.

Creating and maintaining a FAQ

One of the nicest things a group creator can do is develop a FAQ. Chapter 5, "Frequently Asked Questions," discussed how to find the FAQ for other groups. In this section we discuss how to write your own. You don't have to have been the group's creator to write the FAQ. A group can have more than one FAQ with different authors, either as an exercise in teamwork or because people disagree on the "correct" questions or answers.

? Q&A

What belongs in a FAQ?

Read chapter 5 for extensive discussion of the sort of material you'll find in most FAQ's. Follow the instructions there to find hundreds and thousands of sample FAQ's for existing groups—you can use any one of them as a model.

Don't copy anyone's words though. If another group's FAQ has a great explanation of something, just refer to it in yours.

There are two sections to most FAQ's. The first part is the "preamble," containing most of the information in your welcome posting. If your group doesn't have a welcome posting, you'll need to put together a short description of the group, its topics, and any conventions or abbreviations you tend to use.

The second part is the question and answer section. You may have an idea which questions will be asked most frequently, but it's a good idea to actually take notes on the group for a month or so to confirm your impressions. If there's any controversy around these questions, you may want to put a team together to write balanced answers, or allow people from both sides of each issue to write point-counterpoint answers. Wherever possible, delegate! Get other people to draw up book lists, or research the more obscure points of a question, or summarize the huge file of answers that you've collected over the years. You may want to start a mailing list of volunteers to discuss and build the FAQ together for a few months.

Once you've got your material and you've arranged it into a format and structure that looks like most other FAQ's you've seen, post it to the group. Collect comments and corrections, and incorporate them into a new version. Post it again a few weeks later. Change your welcome posting to include a pointer to the FAQ: where it's archived, how often it's posted, and so on. Once the FAQ is relatively stable, you can settle into a regular pattern of posting every two weeks or once a month. Many groups post the welcome one week and the full FAQ the next.

After about six months you'll probably be ready to get your FAQ into *.answers. (If your group isn't in the Big Seven or alt, you may not have an answers group: check with your config or general group.) The procedure to get your FAQ posted regularly to *.answers is straightforward. It's described in the periodic posting "*.answers Submission Guidelines," posted to *.answers.

You'll probably update the FAQ regularly throughout the lifetime of the group, as new books are published, new versions of software are released, new abbreviations become common usage in the group, and so on. It's one of the most important of the many volunteer tasks on UseNet.

Setting Up Your Own News Server

In this chapter:

- How can you set your PC to download newsgroups?
- What hardware and software do I need?
- Alternatives to downloading a full newsfeed
- Using e-mail to get your news articles

Downloading an entire day's postings using a 9,600 baud modem would take about 40 hours.

Most people get their newsgroups through a direct connection to the Internet (such as through SLIP or PPP), or through a service provider (either a shell account or online service provider). For casual browsing of a few newsgroups, this is usually satisfactory. But if you get into UseNet in a big way and spend an hour or more reading newsgroups, the connection charges can be considerable. Also, if you want more control over how long articles are kept before deletion, you may want to consider an alternative: setting up your own newsgroup feed.

It doesn't matter whether you are receiving UseNet newsfeeds for yourself or an entire network, as the basic connection process is the same. When networks are involved, there are some protocol issues that may arise that can be solved through proper configuration of the software.

Setting yourself up to receive UseNet newsgroups is not a very complicated process. One of the hardest decisions to make is how you want to access UseNet. If you want to download some or all of the newsgroups to your personal machine, you better have sufficient resources to handle the high volume of traffic, in terms of both hard disk space and connection to a download site.

You can access UseNet without involving your own hardware very much by dialing in to a dedicated news distribution system. These services function much like an Internet shell account, except that you receive access to a downloaded newsfeed rather than access to all Internet services. As a consequence of the lower overhead involved, these newsgroup services are usually less expensive than full Internet service providers.

What you're going to need to download UseNet

Let's assume you've made the decision that you're going to download some or all of the newsgroups you are interested in to your PC, Macintosh, or other computer system. You need to concern yourself with the hardware, the software, a telephone connection, and the provider of the newsgroups. The following sections cover these in more detail.

Hardware

The most important hardware consideration if you want to download UseNet newsgroups is storage space. The math is quite simple: a daily download of all newsgroups amounts to between 90 MB and 100 MB. If you keep articles for five days, you need half a gigabyte of storage constantly dedicated to newsgroups.

Add to the half a gigabyte required for the newsgroup articles some extra space for the news access software and configuration information, as well as the rest of your operating system and application software. You can factor in an extra few hundred megabytes as a minimum hard disk configuration, boosting your disk requirements to about 700 MB.

Fortunately, the cost of high capacity hard disks is dropping all the time, so downloading all the newsgroups to your private PC is not as ridiculous as it may have been five years ago. With hard drives of 1 GB available for around $500, disk-hungry applications like UseNet are now available to any user who wants access.

⊛ {Note}

Want to download the entire UseNet newsfeed to your Windows PC everyday, as well as use it for the usual applications? Better assume a 1 GB hard drive as a minimum, preferably with fast access times on the order of 9ms.

The CPU in your machine is not as important a factor as most people would assume for newsgroup downloading. Even an 80386 is more than adequate to handle the communications, storage, and file processing required for a Windows-based UseNet download system. Of course, the faster your processor, the better, but you do not need a screamingly fast CPU to access UseNet.

The fast CPUs do have one advantage, though. They can process the newsgroups faster, giving you quicker access to different messages and newsreader features. The limiting factor on this kind of operation, more often than not, is the hard disk access speed.

In the same vein, RAM is often not an issue for newsgroup software. Because most DOS-based newsreaders require only a few hundred kilobytes of RAM and the download routines take about the same amount, even a 640 KB machine can handle a DOS-based UseNet system. Of course, if you run Windows, you need more memory just to run the graphical interface, and Windows applications are inherently larger than DOS-based versions. Still, a good rule of thumb is that most Internet access software will run with 8 MB, with some functioning well with 4 MB.

For Macintosh users, the same considerations apply. The CPU speed and amount of RAM is seldom a critical factor for newsfeeds. Instead, the hard disk space is often the bottleneck for Mac users. External hard drives are often the best solution to provide high capacity storage, either as a removable cartridge medium or a simple plug-in hard drive. Because Macintosh machines use the efficient and fast SCSI interface for most devices, you can add more storage to your Mac with little hassle.

So, the CPU, RAM, and hard disk are taken care of. After the hard disk, the next most important piece of hardware is the modem. In simple terms, the faster the modem, the better. Don't even think about using a modem slower than 9,600 baud for more than a few newsgroups. We look at modems again in the section "Connectivity" later in this chapter.

If you are setting up a news server for a network, the basic hardware requirement is the same but you should add a network board (or other method to allow other users access to the server). Most PC-based networks use a NetBIOS-based network protocol, although some rely on TCP/IP. You will have to ensure that your network card is compatible with the network operating system. Of course, every user on the network who wants to access the news server must also have a network card.

Software

To download newsgroups, you need the newsgroup software in general use, NNTP. Network News Transport Protocol (NNTP) was developed in 1986 and is now a standard method for transmission of netnews articles. You will have to find some software that provides NNTP-compatible download capabilities that work with your download site.

Fortunately, many Internet packages for the PC and Macintosh have NNTP already built-in. These software packages, such as MKS' Internet Anywhere, include NNTP, newsreaders, news posters, e-mail packages, and utilities like FTP.

Configuration is usually limited to telling the software the name and telephone number of the download site, and which newsgroups to request. Administration involves telling the system how long to keep the articles and where to store them. Figure 21.1 shows the newsgroup.

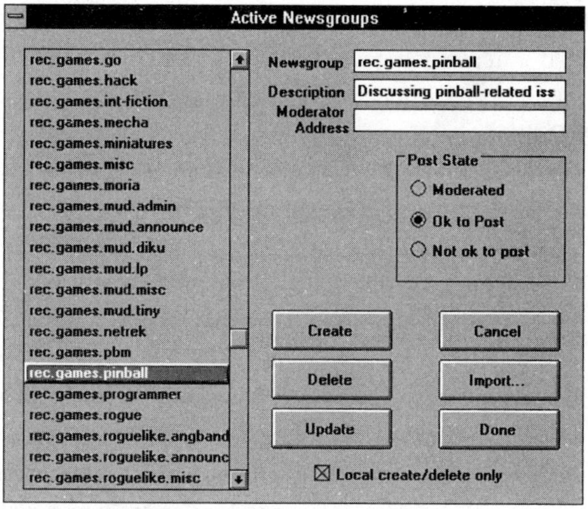

Fig. 21.1

MKS Internet Anywhere lets you select which newsgroups to download and whether they can be posted to. This is a good example of the simple Windows-based news access software available.

Connectivity

The last physical component you need for your newsgroup feed is a telephone line (not too difficult to arrange, as a regular household line can be used if you are downloading only a few newsgroups and won't mind tying up the line for a while) and a modem. As mentioned earlier, a fast modem is preferable.

As a minimum, you should plan on a 9,600 baud modem. Even better, use one of the faster modem speeds such as V.32 or V.FC. The faster the baud rate, the less time it takes to download the articles. When you subscribe to a lot of newsgroups, though, even the fastest asynchronous modem can take hours.

If you are downloading a lot of newsgroups (as you might for a network), you may want to consider synchronous modems that support speeds of 56k baud and higher, or a direct connection using ISDN, ATM, or similar high-speed link.

If you are downloading all the newsgroups for a network, standard telephone lines and an asynchronous modem won't cut it (you'll see why when we discuss the time involved, in the next section). A direct connection to either the Internet itself or an Internet service provider is necessary, and that means you have to set up service for the connection. If you are connecting to the Internet directly, you must contact the Internet Network Information Center and establish a domain, and then properly configure your system to handle TCP/IP. If you are using a service provider (like UUNET Technologies or NetCom), the process is usually faster and your connection options more varied. Before you commit to a service provider, talk to several and explain what you want to do. The better companies should be able to help you set your system up for easy UseNet access.

⊗<Caution> If you are using a fast, asynchronous modem with Windows, your serial port may not be able to keep up with the throughput of the fast speeds. Even the newest serial port designs with fast 16550 UARTs can't sustain high transfer rates in background, so you must not use your PC for anything else while transferring articles. An alternative is to use a communications accelerator, a board specially designed to sustain high background transfer rates under Windows. Hayes makes the ESP Communications Accelerator, which is claimed to support speeds up to 115,000bps while you use Windows for other tasks.

If speed is very important because you are transferring a lot of newsgroups, consider buying or leasing a synchronous modem. These devices require special software and tend to be expensive, but they can handle very high transfer rates. You may not be able to run a synchronous modem over a standard telephone line.

Time

So you want to download all the UseNet newsgroups. How long will that take? Of course, the answer depends on the speed of your connection. To give you an idea, downloading an entire day's postings over a 9,600 baud modem assuming a perfect transfer (no pauses or resends) would take just over 24 hours. Since transmission is never perfect, in reality the download would take about 40 hours.

Obviously, using a 9,600 baud modem is not the answer to daily downloadings. Those numbers do give you an idea of the time problem, though. Even with the fastest modems in general use today running at 28.8kbps (which requires a perfect telephone connection), a full download of all newsgroups will still take eight hours of perfect transmission, or a more realistic 13 hours.

Given those numbers, using a standard modem to download a full day's UseNet postings is ridiculous. Even with high-speed asynchronous lines running at 56kbps, a full download takes a real seven hours. High-speed direct links are the only answer for full downloads. An ISDN line can download the entire day's newsgroup postings in just under 45 minutes of real connect time. The actual amount of time will vary depending on the effect throughput of the connection, but it still is an appreciable time investment on a daily basis. ISDN lines are quite expensive, too, so this approach is best left to the large networks that can justify the expense spread over many users.

How about downloading just a few newsgroups, though. That is certainly feasible with a slower modem. If you were to download your 20 favorite newsgroups at 9,600 baud, you would probably have to spend 20 to 30 minutes. As the speed increases, the time drops. A V.FC modem running at 28.8kbps will take 10 minutes to download those newsgroups.

To calculate your download time, check the newsgroups for the amount of postings each day. As a general rule, UseNet newsgroups generate an average of 10 KB of data per day. Multiply the numbers (factoring in extra space for heavily used newsgroups—about double the space—and those which allow binaries—about 1 MB per newsgroup) and divide that by your modem speed. That will produce the ideal number of minutes needed. Then, factor in a 40% loss for reality.

For example, suppose you want to download 30 newsgroups, two of which handle binaries. That's 2 MB for the binaries and 2.8 MB for the other 28 newsgroups for a total of 4.8 MB. A 9,600 baud modem can transfer 4.12 million bytes per hour, so at 9,600 baud you have an ideal transfer time of about one hour, 10 minutes. Add the loss factor, and you have one hour, 45 minutes. With a 28.8kbps modem, the number drops to one third, or just over half an hour.

The point is, downloading more than a couple of newsgroups isn't a quick process. If you are going to download newsgroups you have to be prepared to let the system run for a while. Individual users may be happy with 20 newsgroups, but if you are downloading for a network you may have to multiply that many times.

Accessing news on a UNIX system

Since NNTP and the Internet are intimately connected with the UNIX operating system, it is quite easy to download newsgroups onto UNIX machines. Most versions of UNIX, including the SCO UNIX system for Intel-based PC architectures, provide the basic software as part of the distribution system.

More advanced download software and newsreaders are readily available for UNIX from many public sites. SCO users, for example, can get the new InterNet News transport (INN) system for downloading newsgroups. One site of the SCO source code is **ftp.uu.net**, which also includes full instructions for building a newsfeed machine and setting up the feed itself.

UNIX workstations generally act as newsfeed servers very well, primarily because UNIX machines tend to be supplied with fast CPU and lots of disk space.

Accessing a remote newsfeed

If all the bother of downloading your own newsfeed seems to be too much trouble or expense, why not consider using a remote news service? Many of these services are springing up around the country, in many cases from individuals who download the newsgroups for their own use and decide to share with others (partly to subsidize the expenses).

Usually, a remote newsfeed is a dial-in system much like a typical Bulletin Board System (BBS), except it has newsgroups online. You use it as you do any other online service (such as CompuServe, America Online, or Delphi). You dial in, supply a login name and password, and then read the newsgroups as you would when attached to a local news machine.

You are usually faced with a monthly fee, with some systems adding a small connect charge. In most cases, these fees are considerably less than you would pay if you belonged to an online service and requested newsgroup access. This would make newsfeeds financially attractive.

What do you give up? You don't get control of the newsgroups themselves; you can't decide to keep messages around for an extra few days when you go on holiday. On the other hand, you don't have to worry about the configuration of the system or the daily connection routine. You also don't get auxiliary services like those provided by CompuServe and America Online. You may get some other Internet services, such as e-mail, depending on the site.

To find a local newsfeed system, check with a local computer magazine (usually distributed free of charge by computer stores), ask other UseNet users at work or at a user group, or post a question on UseNet itself.

Alternative ways to get newsgroups

You can access newsgroups in several ways most people don't immediately think of, such as through e-mail, FTP, World Wide Web, and other Internet services. Few of these services (other than e-mail) provide timely delivery. Most systems like FTP and World Wide Web lead to archives of older information.

E-mailed newsgroups

If you only want to monitor a few newsgroups, you can get them e-mailed to you. Most customers of e-mailed newsgroup articles use a service provider, just as if they were going to download the newsgroups directly. However, because e-mail only is transferred, rates may differ. Many service providers, such as UUNET Technologies, can supply newsgroups by e-mail on request.

✱ {Note} Most people recommend the following rule of thumb: if you receive more than 5 MB of newsgroup articles by e-mail (about 100 articles), consider setting up an NNTP feed. NNTP is much more efficient with this quantity of traffic.

A problem with getting newsgroups by e-mail is posting. Not all service providers have the software to allow e-mail posts to newsgroups. If you have any problems, several mail-to-newsgroup sites are available on the Internet. A few commonly used sites are **decwrl.dec.com**, **pws.bull.com**, and **news.cs.indiana.edu**.

Posting to a newsgroup through e-mail requires you to use the newsgroup name as the destination user. For example, sending e-mail to **rec.audio.high-end@pws.bull.com** sends your e-mail to the newsgroup rec.audio.high-end. Before using this type of service, though, you may want to ensure that they still provide the conversion capability and that they don't mind if you use it. A simple e-mail to the system's UseNet account or the postmaster (such as **usenet@pws.bull.com** and **postmaster@pws.bull.com**) will help make sure you do not annoy system administrators with unauthorized access.

News filtering services

In chapter 6, we briefly mentioned that the Computer Science department at Stanford University has developed "the Database Project." This project provides a news filtering services for UseNet that lets you get selected articles from UseNet e-mailed to you.

To use the filtering service, you create a user profile on the system that includes all the keywords of subjects in which you are interested. The system will e-mail you all the articles that match your keywords. For information about the Stanford news filtering service, send e-mail to **netnews@db.stanford.edu** with the word "help" as the body.

Some other systems are also beginning to provide newsgroup filtering capabilities. Check for FAQs in the general newsgroups, or post a question in news.answers asking for site names.

Most filtering services require you to have an e-mail account that can be reached through Internet. Some services offer message mail-out through the postal service, but costs are quite high.

News server options for a BBS

Most bulletin board system (BBS) system operators (sysops) try to provide as many features are they can for their users, and UseNet newsgroup access has become a popular feature among BBSs. Adding newsgroup access to a BBS requires two pieces: the newsfeed itself, and software to allow BBS users access to the newsgroups.

Getting the newsfeed for a BBS is no different than for any other system, except many BBSs can afford high-speed connections. Depending on the type of machinery the BBS runs on, there may be alternatives for direct connection to the Internet using UNIX's UUCP program, for example. Downloading newsgroups to the BBS is the usual approach to providing the service, although a few sysops now allow a link to a news server, through a network or dedicated connection (much like hyperlinks in the World Wide Web).

Providing newsgroup access to the system users is a little more difficult, as some BBS software doesn't allow deviations from the message base format. Most BBS software has been revised in the last few years to either include an optional newsreader package or permit the sysop to create a tie to a reader package outside the BBS system itself. With the popularity of the Internet, some BBS software systems now include several different readers (for command line and GUIs), as well as control systems for handling postings from users.

If you are running a BBS and want to provide newsgroup access, check with your BBS software vendor. If it doesn't provide an expansion product for newsreading, you may still be able to create a menu option that jumps to any commercially available newsreader. However, security issues will have to be considered, as some commercial newsreaders will allow a user to access the operating system directly.

Part VI:

Hot Newsgroups

Chapter 22: Hot Newsgroups

22

Hot Newsgroups

In this chapter:

- What are the best groups for information about the Internet and computers?

- Where to find information about your favorite hobby or recreation

- Groups dealing with current important social issues

- Groups that discuss business issues

- Flying saucers, bad jokes, and Beavis

- How do I find a more complete list of groups?

With the many newsgroups and the constant creation of new groups, you'll need to take care to follow only the groups that interest you the most.

UseNet newsgroups are one of the most popular and often controversial aspects of the Internet. With over 10,000 groups, there are very few topics of passing or lasting importance that go untouched. Some groups that deal with how to use UseNet, computer topics, and the Internet have been in service since the early days of UseNet. Other groups are created almost instantly in the wake of a major news item of public interest and then fade into oblivion after the event passes from the public eye (**alt.fan.oj-simpson** and **alt.fan.tonya-harding.whack.whack.whack** are examples of this phenomenon).

With the many newsgroups and the constant creation of new groups, you'll need to take care to follow only the groups of most interest to you. Following more than a dozen active groups is a sure way to be a victim of information overload.

To help you avoid the pitfall of over-subscribing, this chapter presents a short list of the best of UseNet. Even though these listings are highly subjective, they should help you narrow your search for the groups you need.

Internet-related groups

If you're reading this book, you must have some interest in the Internet. There are quite a few good newsgroups where you can find out more about all aspects of the Net, from Archie to WHOIS.

News

It only seems natural that there are several newsgroups related to UseNet news. Here are a few of the most important ones.

news.announce.newusers

This is a moderated group that posts informative articles for new users. (We can thank the moderators for keeping the postings to this group to the truly essential, even though a staggering 800,000 people read it.) If you're new to UseNet, there is no reason not to read this group for a few months. If you have a question about UseNet that isn't answered here, you can post it to **news.newusers.questions**. (For information on moderated groups, see Chapter 2, "How Newsgroups are Organized.")

news.answers

This is another highly useful moderated group. Here you find all of the periodic postings to the Net, such as FAQs for the various groups and lists of active newsgroups. You'll also find some technical information like an International standards FAQ and a summary of LAN Mail Protocols.

news.groups

A visit to this group shows what a democratic and chaotic world UseNet is. Newgroups, group splits, and the validity of groups are all discussed and debated here with the enthusiasm usually reserved for politics and religion.

news.list

If you're interested in up-to-date lists of available newsgroups, news sites, and top groups by number of readers or by megabyte of postings, this is the place to look. It's a moderated list, so don't expect to be able to post a list of your favorite groups here.

news.software.readers

If you're having problems with your newsreader, here's a good place to look for answers. Chances are, someone else has had the same problem and will be able to help you. (If you use the WinVN newsreader, you also may want to post questions to **alt.winsock**.)

Other Internet Topics

In addition to newsgroups about UseNet, there are quite a few good groups that discuss other parts of the Internet.

alt.cyberspace

Cyberspace is a loosely defined term that has come to encompass all areas of online activity. In this group, you'll find a wide variety of opinions on the state of the Internet, BBSs, and the online world.

alt.gopher

If you're using Gopher for the first time or setting up your own Gopher server, this is a group with all the Gopher news. Of related interest is **comp.infosystems.gopher** (mostly for more advanced needs).

alt.internet.services

Here's a group where you can ask questions about any Internet service. You'll find questions here about service providers in a given area code, new Web sites, questions about specific Internet programs like WAIS or Gopher, and just about every other Internet topic.

alt.irc

Internet Relay Chat (IRC) can be very intimidating if you don't know what you're doing. This group gives you an opportunity to ask questions in a more relaxed setting than the fast-paced IRC world. Subgroups here include **alt.irc.announce**, **alt.irc.hottub**, **alt.irc.ircii**, **alt.irc.opers**, **alt.irc.questions**, and **alt.irc.undernet**.

alt.online.service

Do you have questions about CompuServe, AOL, and the other major online services? You'll find advice from experts here. There also is a subgroup for each of the five major services and Freenet.

alt.test

One sure way to prove you're a newbie is to post a test message in a general-use newsgroup. (Uh. Ignore this post. I'm just testing my news program.) Luckily, there is a group where you can give your newsreader a whirl without embarrassing yourself: **alt.test**. It's there. Please use it!

alt.winsock

If you're connecting to the Internet using Windows, chances are you'll have questions about Windows Sockets (WinSock) at some point. (If you don't, go buy a lottery ticket as you are truly lucky!) This group is a good place to start your search for answers.

alt.zines

Zines, the online equivalent of magazines, have exploded onto the scene in the last few years. Here you can find discussions of popular zines, announcements of new zines, and requests for contributors.

comp.infosystems.www

The Web is the hottest topic there is on the Net, but there are surprisingly few newsgroups that discuss it. This group and its subgroups **comp.infosystems.www.misc**, **comp.infosystems.www.providers**, and **comp.infosystems.www.users** are all good Web resources.

comp.mail.*

✹ *{Note}* Here we're using the * as a wild card. There is no group with the name comp.mail, but there are several that begin with comp.mail.

Do you have questions about Internet mail? There are about a dozen mail-related groups that begin with comp.mail. Some of the specific categories are **comp.mail.elm**, **comp.mail.mime**, and **comp.mail.uucp**.

halcyon.general

NorthWest Nexus (their domain name is Halcyon) is one of the biggest Internet service providers in the U.S. This group exists to help customers with any questions or problems. Related groups are **halcyon.slip** and **halcyon.test**.

Computer-related groups

By default, everyone participating in UseNet on the Internet has access to a computer. But not everyone is interested in computers. If you're like me, though, computer groups are right at the top of your "newsgroups subscribed to" list with Internet topics. This section presents the best computer groups.

alt.bbs

Here's the newsgroup for BBS sysops and users to discuss everything about the topic including BBS operating systems, new boards, and BBS hardware. Related subgroups include **alt.bbs.ads**, which has ads for various BBSs; **alt.bbs.allsysop**, which discusses Sysop concerns of all networks and technologies; **alt.bbs.doors**, which is about BBS add-on executables, or **doors**; **alt.bbs.internet**, which lists and discusses BBSs that are hooked up to the Internet; and **alt.bbs.lists**, which posts regional BBS listings. There also are several subgroups discussing the most popular BBS systems, including WildCAT! and The Major BBS.

alt.cad

Computer-aided design (CAD) experts and novices converge here to discuss general drafting concerns and questions about specific CAD products. Of related interest are **alt.cad.autocad** and **comp.cad.autocad**.

alt.cd-rom

This group discusses every CD-ROM topic imaginable. There are regular posts ranging from "How do I install a CD-ROM?" to "Where can I find ISO-9660 standards for CD-ROMs?" You'll also see new product announcements, individuals selling used drives and CDs, and mail order companies advertising their catalogs.

alt.soft-sys.corel.draw

CorelDRAW! users worldwide unite here to share problems and solutions with this popular drawing/painting/presentation/animation package. (Another Corel-related group, **alt.corel.graphics**, is inactive. Don't expect to find anything there!)

alt.sys.pc-clone.dell, alt.sys.pc-clone.gateway2000, alt.sys.pc-clone.zeos

These three PC clone makers have dominated the clone market in recent years. They've sold enough of their clones to have their buyers start these groups that are dedicated to discussions of the hardware from these vendors.

comp.apps.spreadsheets

Discussions here mostly focus on the PC-based spreadsheet giants Excel and Lotus 1-2-3. You'll find occasional questions and answers of a more general nature and about other spreadsheet applications as well.

comp.answers

This moderated list contains postings of FAQs and other periodic postings from the comp newsgroups.

comp.benchmarks

This group has discussions of benchmark performance measures for every imaginable computer system and peripherals from a lowly 8088-based PC to the CRAY supercomputer.

comp.fonts

Discussions here range from problems and solutions with TrueType fonts in Windows to typography and service bureau issues.

comp.graphics

Graphics software tips and tricks, graphics hardware reviews, and product announcements can be found here anytime. If it has to do with generating or processing graphics on a computer, it's fair game here. Also, check the 10 subgroups ranging from **comp.graphics.algorithms** to **comp.graphics.raytracing** and finally **comp.graphics.visualization**.

comp.os.ms-windows.announce

This is a moderated group with announcements of interest to Microsoft Windows users. There are 25 other groups that begin with **comp.os.ms-windows** (see table 22.1). If you have any questions or answers about Microsoft Windows, you are sure to find a group that discusses them here. Make a real effort to confine your posts to the appropriate groups. These subgroups exist to help with specific areas.

Table 22.1   Microsoft Windows groups

Group name	Discussion topics
comp.os.ms–windows.advocacy	Speculation and debate about Microsoft Windows
comp.os.ms–windows.announce	Announcements relating to Windows (moderated)
comp.os.ms–windows.apps.comm	MS-Windows communication applications
comp.os.ms–windows.apps.financial	MS-Windows financial and tax software
comp.os.ms–windows.apps.misc	MS-Windows applications
comp.os.ms–windows.apps.utilities	MS-Windows utilities
comp.os.ms–windows.apps.word–proc	MS-Windows word-processing applications
comp.os.ms–windows.misc	General discussions about Windows issues
comp.os.ms–windows.networking.misc	Windows and other networks
comp.os.ms–windows.networking.tcp–ip	Windows and TCP/IP networking
comp.os.ms–windows.networking.windows	Windows' built-in networking
comp.os.ms–windows.nt.misc	General discussion about Windows NT
comp.os.ms–windows.nt.setup	Configuring Windows NT systems
comp.os.ms–windows.programmer.controls	Controls, dialog boxes, and VBXs
comp.os.ms–windows.programmer.drivers	Drivers and VxDs no driver requests!
comp.os.ms–windows.programmer.graphics	GDI, graphics, and printing
comp.os.ms–windows.programmer.memory	Memory management issues
comp.os.ms–windows.programmer.misc	Programming Microsoft Windows
comp.os.ms–windows.programmer.multimedia	Multimedia programming
comp.os.ms–windows.programmer.networks	Network programming
comp.os.ms–windows.programmer.ole	OLE2, COM, and DDE programming
comp.os.ms–windows.programmer.tools	Development tools in Windows
comp.os.ms–windows.programmer.win32	32-bit Windows programming interfaces

Group name	Discussion topics
comp.os.ms-windows.programmer.winhelp	WinHelp/Multimedia Viewer development
comp.os.ms-windows.setup	Installing and configuring Microsoft Windows
comp.os.ms-windows.video	Video adapters and drivers for Windows

❊ {Note}_____ The groups that begin with comp.windows discuss operating systems other than MS-Windows with a window-based structure. Don't post questions about MS-Windows to these groups!

comp.os.msdos.apps

MS-DOS doesn't get quite the coverage in newsgroups that its flashy Windows counterpart does. There are only a handful of MS-DOS groups. This one is most useful to end users who have questions about DOS applications. There's also a group for programmers (**comp.os.msdos.programmer**) and a miscellaneous category for questions that don't fall into the specific MS-DOS groups (**comp.os.msdos.misc**).

comp.sys.mac.*

Table 22.2 is a short list of Mac-related groups that are all nestled together with names beginning with comp.sys.mac. You'll find that most of these group names are self-explanatory. You may also be interested in the groups that begin with misc.forsale.computers.mac-specific if you're looking to buy or sell Mac computers or components, or comp.binaries.mac for Mac software.

Table 22.2 Macintosh groups

comp.sys.m ac.advocacy	comp.sys.mac.misc
comp.sys.mac.announce	comp.sys.mac.oop.macapp3
comp.sys.mac.apps	comp.sys.mac.oop.misc
comp.sys.mac.comm	comp.sys.mac.oop.tcl
comp.sys.mac.databases	comp.sys.mac.portables

Table 22.2   Continued

comp.sys.mac.digest	comp.sys.mac.programmer
comp.sys.mac.games	comp.sys.mac.programmer.codewarrior
comp.sys.mac.graphics	comp.sys.mac.scitech
comp.sys.mac.hardware	comp.sys.mac.system
comp.sys.mac.hypercard	comp.sys.mac.wanted

comp.security.misc

This group hosts discussions of data security issues of interest to computer users. Encryption and hacking are popular topics here. Of related interest are the groups **alt.privacy.clipper** and **alt.security.pgp**.

comp.sys.ibm.pc.*

Table 22.3 lists a slew of groups related to the IBM-PC. Games, games, and more games, as well as hardware issues, dominate this category.

Table 22.3   IBM-PC groups

Group name	Discussion topics
comp.sys.ibm.pc.demos	Demonstration programs which showcase programmers' skills
comp.sys.ibm.pc.digest	The IBM PC, PC-XT, and PC-AT (moderated)
comp.sys.ibm.pc.games.action	Arcade-style games for PCs
comp.sys.ibm.pc.games.adventure	Adventure (non-rpg) games for PCs
comp.sys.ibm.pc.games.announce	Announcements for all PC gamers (moderated)
comp.sys.ibm.pc.games.flight-sim	Flight simulators for PCs
comp.sys.ibm.pc.games.marketplace	PC clone games wanted and for sale
comp.sys.ibm.pc.games.misc	Games not covered by other PC groups
comp.sys.ibm.pc.games.rpg	Role-playing games for the PC
comp.sys.ibm.pc.games.strategic	Strategy/planning games for PCs

Group name	Discussion topics
comp.sys.ibm.pc.hardware.cd-rom	CD-ROM drives and interfaces for the PC
comp.sys.ibm.pc.hardware.chips	Processor, cache, memory chips, etc.
comp.sys.ibm.pc.hardware.comm	Modems and communication cards for the PC
comp.sys.ibm.pc.hardware.misc	Miscellaneous PC hardware topics
comp.sys.ibm.pc.hardware.networking	Network hardware and equipment for the PC
comp.sys.ibm.pc.hardware.storage	Hard drives and other PC storage devices
comp.sys.ibm.pc.hardware.systems	Whole IBM-PC computer and clone systems
comp.sys.ibm.pc.hardware.video	Video cards and monitors for the PC
comp.sys.ibm.pc.misc	Discussion about IBM personal computers
comp.sys.ibm.pc.rt	Topics related to IBM's RT computer
comp.sys.ibm.pc.soundcard.advocacy	Advocacy for a particular soundcard
comp.sys.ibm.pc.soundcard.games	Questions about using soundcards with games
comp.sys.ibm.pc.soundcard.misc	Soundcards in general
comp.sys.ibm.pc.soundcard.music	Music and sound questions using soundcards
comp.sys.ibm.pc.soundcard.tech	Technical questions about PC soundcards

comp.unix.questions

If you have some basic questions about the UNIX operating system, this is the place to start. More advanced issues are discussed in related groups, such as **comp.unix.programmer**, **comp.unix.wizards** (moderated), and many others.

Hobby and recreation groups

We all know that the Net isn't just bytes and byteheads. There's a fun side to the Net too. While most employers probably frown on their employees spending their working hours reading **rec.beatles** (unless you're a disk jockey), we all know that these are some of the best groups. So, when your boss isn't looking, or after hours, spend a few hours browsing some of these groups.

rec.arts.books

Discuss your favorite authors, books, and the publishing industry in general. Of specific related interest are **alt.books.isaac-asimov** and **alt.books.stephen-king**. If computer and other technical books are your interest, try **alt.books.technical**.

rec.arts.movies

Can't wait to hear what the critics and movies are saying about Stallone's latest? Got something to say about your favorite foreign film? Here is the group to discuss all aspects of movies and movie-making. Of related interest are the moderated groups **rec.arts.cinema** and **rec.arts.movies.reviews** and the group **alt.cult-movies**.

rec.arts.sf.starwars

I find it difficult to believe how much traffic this group generates. On average, expect to see several hundred messages per week. Topics range from discussion of the original movies to speculation on sequels or prequels, the popular series of books, and the actors from the movies.

rec.arts.startrek

Here's another group with a large following and a high volume of messages. All four Star Trek TV series, the movies, the books, and the actors are discussed here. Of related interest are **alt.shared-reality.startrek.klingon**, **alt.startrek.creative**, **alt.startrek.klingon**, **alt.sexy.bald.captains**. And of course, don't miss the ever-popular **alt.ensign.wesley.die.die.die**.

rec.audio

Here's where to ask questions and discuss hi-fidelity stereo systems and components with other audio buffs. For high-tech video buffs, take a look at **alt.video.laserdisc**.

rec.birds

You'll find many posts about bird watching, as well as issues that affect captive and pet birds. Of related interest is **rec.pets.birds**.

rec.games.misc

There are more game groups here than I care to count. Suffice it to say, if you play board games, computer games, video games, or role-playing games, you'll find a group related to your interests in table 22.4. If your specific game isn't listed, try **rec.games.misc**.

Table 22.4 rec.games groups

Group name	Discussion topics
rec.games.abstract	Perfect information, pure strategy games
ec.games.backgammon	Discussion of the game of backgammon
rec.games.board	Discussion and hints on board games
rec.games.board.ce	The Cosmic Encounter board game
rec.games.board.marketplace	Trading and selling of board games
rec.games.bolo	The networked strategy war game Bolo
rec.games.bridge	Hobbyists interested in bridge
rec.games.chess	Chess and computer chess
rec.games.chinese–chess	Discussion of the game of Chinese chess, Xiangqi
rec.games.corewar	The Core War computer challenge
rec.games.deckmaster	The Deckmaster line of games
rec.games.deckmaster.marketplace	Trading of deckmaster paraphernalia
rec.games.design	Discussion of game design-related issues
rec.games.diplomacy	The conquest game Diplomacy
rec.games.empire	Discussion and hints about Empire
rec.games.frp.advocacy	Flames and rebuttals about various role-playing systems
rec.games.frp.announce	Announcements of happenings in the role-playing world (moderated)
rec.games.frp.archives	Archivable fantasy stories and other projects (moderated)
rec.games.frp.cyber	Discussions of cyberpunk-related role-playing games

continues

Table 22.4 Continued

Group name	Discussion topics
rec.games.frp.dnd	Fantasy role playing with TSR's Dungeons and Dragons
rec.games.frp.live-action	Live-action role-playing games
rec.games.frp.marketplace	Role-playing game materials wanted and for sale
rec.games.frp.misc	General discussions of role-playing games
rec.games.go	Discussion about Go
rec.games.int-fiction	All aspects of interactive fiction games
rec.games.mecha	Giant robot games
rec.games.miniatures	Tabletop wargaming
rec.games.misc	Games and computer games
rec.games.mud.admin	Administrative issues of multiuser dungeons
rec.games.mud.announce	Informational articles about multiuser dungeons (moderated)
rec.games.mud.diku	All about DikuMuds
rec.games.mud.lp	Discussions of the LPMUD computer role-playing game
rec.games.mud.misc	Various aspects of multiuser computer games
rec.games.mud.tiny	Discussion about Tiny muds, like MUSH, MUSE, and MOO
rec.games.netrek	Discussion of the X window system game Netrek (XtrekII)
rec.games.pbm	Discussion about Play by Mail games
rec.games.pinball	Discussing pinball-related issues
rec.games.programmer	Discussion of adventure game programming
rec.games.roguelike.angband	The computer game Angbandr
ec.games.roguelike.announce	Major info about rogue-styled games (moderated)
rec.games.roguelike.misc	Rogue-style dungeon games without other groups
rec.games.roguelike.moria	The computer game Moria
rec.games.roguelike.nethack	The computer game Nethack
rec.games.roguelike.rogue	The computer game Rogue

Group name	Discussion topics
rec.games.trivia	Discussion about trivia
rec.games.video.3do	Discussion of 3DO video game systems
rec.games.video.advocacy	Debate on merits of various video game systems
rec.games.video.arcade	Discussions about coin-operated video games
rec.games.video.arcade.collecting	Collecting, converting, repairing, etc.
rec.games.video.atari	Discussion of Atari's video game systems
rec.games.video.cd32	Gaming talk, info, and help for the Amiga CD32
rec.games.video.classic	Older home video entertainment systems
rec.games.video.marketplace	Home video game stuff for sale or trade
rec.games.video.misc	General discussion about home video games
rec.games.video.nintendo	All Nintendo video game systems and software
rec.games.video.sega	All Sega video game systems and software
rec.games.xtank.play	Strategy and tactics for the distributed game Xtank
rec.games.xtank.programmer	Coding the Xtank game and its robots

rec.humor

Have you heard a good joke that you want to share? Are you looking for a good joke? We can't guarantee that everything in this group is actually funny, but someone thinks it is. You may also want to see **alt.humor.best-of-usenet** (moderated).

alt.music and rec.music

These two collections of groups (see table 22.5) are a music lover's paradise. Whether your musical tastes are fairly common (like classical or alternative) or more specialized (like ska or Swedish pop), you'll find something of interest in one of these groups. The group names are self-explanatory.

Table 22.5 alt.music and rec.music groups

alt.music.a-cappella	alt.music.sonic-youth
alt.music.alternative	alt.music.sophie-hawkins
alt.music.alternative.female	alt.music.soul
alt.music.amy-grant	alt.music.swedish-pop
alt.music.barenaked-ladies	alt.music.sylvian
alt.music.beastie-boys	alt.music.synthpop
alt.music.bela-fleck	alt.music.techno
alt.music.big-band	alt.music.the-doors
alt.music.billy-joel	alt.music.the.police
alt.music.bjork	alt.music.tmbg
alt.music.blues-traveler	alt.music.todd-rundgren
alt.music.bootlegs	alt.music.type-o-negative
alt.music.brian-eno	alt.music.u2
alt.music.canada	alt.music.ween
alt.music.chapel-hill	alt.music.weird-al
alt.music.complex-arrang	alt.music.who
alt.music.counting-crows	alt.music.world
alt.music.danzig	alt.music.yes
alt.music.deep-purple	rec.music.a-cappella
alt.music.def-leppard	rec.music.afro-latin
alt.music.dream-theater	rec.music.beatles
alt.music.ebm	rec.music.bluenote
alt.music.ecto	rec.music.bluenote.blues
alt.music.elo	rec.music.cd
alt.music.enya	rec.music.celtic

alt.music.fates-warning	rec.music.christian
alt.music.filk	rec.music.classical
alt.music.fleetwood-mac	rec.music.classical.guitar
alt.music.genesis	rec.music.classical.performing
alt.music.hardcore	rec.music.compose
alt.music.independent	rec.music.country.western
alt.music.james-taylor	rec.music.dementia
alt.music.jethro-tull	rec.music.dylan
alt.music.jewish	rec.music.early
alt.music.jimi.hendrix	rec.music.folk
alt.music.kylie-minogue	rec.music.funky
alt.music.led-zeppelin	rec.music.gaffa
alt.music.leonard-cohen	rec.music.gdead
alt.music.lor-mckennitt	rec.music.indian.classical
alt.music.makers.woodwind	rec.music.indian.misc
alt.music.marillion	rec.music.industrial
alt.music.ministry	rec.music.info
alt.music.misc	rec.music.makers
alt.music.monkees	rec.music.makers.bass
alt.music.moody-blues	rec.music.makers.builders
alt.music.nin	rec.music.makers.guitar
alt.music.nirvana	rec.music.makers.guitar.acoustic
alt.music.orb	rec.music.makers.guitar.tablature
alt.music.paul-simon	rec.music.makers.marketplace
alt.music.pearl-jam	rec.music.makers.percussion
alt.music.peter-gabriel	rec.music.makers.piano

continues

Table 22.5   Continued

alt.music.pink–floyd	rec.music.makers.synth
alt.music.prince	rec.music.marketplace
alt.music.producer	rec.music.misc
alt.music.progressive	rec.music.movies
alt.music.queen	rec.music.newage
alt.music.roger–waters	rec.music.phish
alt.music.rush	rec.music.reggae
alt.music.seal	rec.music.rem
alt.music.ska	rec.music.reviews
alt.music.smash–pumpkins	rec.music.tori–amos
alt.music.smiths	rec.music.video

rec.pets.herp

Quick! What is herpetology? The study of reptiles, of course. If you already knew that, you may want to check out this group. All sorts of reptiles from common green iguanas to exotic snakes and gators are discussed here. For those of you with a more common taste in pets, check out **alt.pets.rabbits**, **rec.pets.birds**, **rec.pets.cats**, and **rec.pets.dogs**.

rec.travel

Planning your next vacation? Or maybe you just like to read about travel. Regardless of your travel interests, this is a good group to follow. Also, see the related groups **rec.travel.air**, **rec.travel.cruises**, and **rec.travel.europe**.

alt.fan

This is one of the largest categories of newsgroups. It seems like everyone wants to discuss the actors, rock stars, and politicians they like (or dislike).

There are even groups for fans of things, such as a brand of gum or beverage. Table 22.6 lists these groups. Most of the names are self-explanatory. As always, there is a good chance that some of these groups will be inactive by the time you read this and that there will be other new groups not listed.

Table 22.6   alt.fan groups

alt.fan.actors	alt.fan.leningrad.cowboys
alt.fan.addams.wednesday	alt.fan.letterman
alt.fan.alan-lowell	alt.fan.linus-torvalds
alt.fan.art-bell	alt.fan.lion-king
alt.fan.asprin	alt.fan.madonna
alt.fan.authors.stephen-king	alt.fan.marcia-clark
alt.fan.barry-manilow	alt.fan.mel-brooks
alt.fan.big-red-gum	alt.fan.michael-bolton
alt.fan.bill-gates	alt.fan.mike-jittlov
alt.fan.blues-brothers	alt.fan.monty-python
alt.fan.brie	alt.fan.mr-kfi
alt.fan.british-accent	alt.fan.mst3k
alt.fan.bruce-campbell	alt.fan.nathan.brazil
alt.fan.cecil-adams	alt.fan.noam-chomsky
alt.fan.ceiling	alt.fan.oingo-boingo
alt.fan.chris-elliott	alt.fan.oj-simpson
alt.fan.conan-obrien	alt.fan.oj-simpson.die.die.die
alt.fan.courtney-love	alt.fan.oj-simpson.gas-chamber
alt.fan.cult-dead-cow	alt.fan.ok-soda
alt.fan.cult.of.the.dead.cow	alt.fan.paul-bernardo
alt.fan.dan-quayle	alt.fan.penn-n-teller

continues

Table 22.6   Continued

alt.fan.dave_barry	alt.fan.pern
alt.fan.david-bowie	alt.fan.philip-dick
alt.fan.debbie.gibson	alt.fan.piers-anthony
alt.fan.devo	alt.fan.pratchett
alt.fan.disney.afternoon	alt.fan.q
alt.fan.don-n-mike	alt.fan.ren-and-stimpy
alt.fan.douglas-adams	alt.fan.rickie-lee.jones
alt.fan.dr-bronner	alt.fan.road-work
alt.fan.dr.william-annis	alt.fan.robert-jordan
alt.fan.dragonlance	alt.fan.ronald-reagan
alt.fan.dragons	alt.fan.rush-limbaugh
alt.fan.dune	alt.fan.schwarzenegger
alt.fan.eddings	alt.fan.serdar-argic
alt.fan.fabio	alt.fan.seth-cohn
alt.fan.fan-man	alt.fan.shostakovich
alt.fan.frank-zappa	alt.fan.skinny
alt.fan.furry	alt.fan.spinal-tap
alt.fan.furry.muck	alt.fan.sting
alt.fan.g-gordon-liddy	alt.fan.super-big-gulp
alt.fan.gene-scott	alt.fan.surak
alt.fan.goons	alt.fan.tank-girl
alt.fan.greaseman	alt.fan.tarantino
alt.fan.greg-kinnear	alt.fan.teen.idols
alt.fan.hello-kitty	alt.fan.teen.starlets

alt.fan.holmes	alt.fan.tlc
alt.fan.howard-stern	alt.fan.tolkien
alt.fan.james-bond	alt.fan.tom-clancy
alt.fan.jay-leno	alt.fan.tom-robbins
alt.fan.jello-biafra	alt.fan.tom-servo
alt.fan.jen-coolest	alt.fan.tonya-harding.whack.whack.whack
alt.fan.jerky-boys	alt.fan.u2
alt.fan.jesus-christ	alt.fan.vic-reeves
alt.fan.jimi-hendrix	alt.fan.warlord
alt.fan.jimmy-buffett	alt.fan.wavey.davey
alt.fan.joel-furr	alt.fan.wayne-dolesman
alt.fan.john-palmer	alt.fan.wedge
alt.fan.john-winston	alt.fan.weird-al
alt.fan.karla-homolka	alt.fan.winona-ryder
alt.fan.kroq	alt.fan.wodehouse
alt.fan.laurie.anderson	alt.fan.woody-allen
alt.fan.lemurs	

Sports groups

There are so many sports groups that this topic merits its own section. Whether you need to find someone to share your grief over the canceled World Series, or if you're interested in a less publicized sport, such as fencing, you'll find a group to share your discussions. Tables 22.7 and 22.8 provide a laundry list of the main categories of sport groups. The group names are self-explanatory.

Table 22.7 rec.sport groups

rec.sport.baseball	rec.sport.football.misc
rec.sport.baseball.analysis	rec.sport.football.pro
rec.sport.baseball.college	rec.sport.golf
rec.sport.baseball.data	rec.sport.hockey
rec.sport.baseball.fantasy	rec.sport.hockey.field
rec.sport.basketball.college	rec.sport.misc
rec.sport.basketball.misc	rec.sport.olympics
rec.sport.basketball.pro	rec.sport.paintball
rec.sport.basketball.women	rec.sport.pro-wrestling
rec.sport.billiard	rec.sport.rowing
rec.sport.boxing	rec.sport.rugby
rec.sport.cricket	rec.sport.soccer
rec.sport.cricket.info	rec.sport.swimming
rec.sport.disc	rec.sport.table-tennis
rec.sport.fencing	rec.sport.tennis
rec.sport.football.australian	rec.sport.triathlon
rec.sport.football.canadian	rec.sport.volleyball
rec.sport.football.college	rec.sport.water-polo
rec.sport.football.fantasy	rec.sport.waterski

Table 22.8 alt.sport and alt.sports groups

alt.sport.racquetball	alt.sports.football.pro.cinci-bengals
alt.sport.squash	alt.sports.football.pro.cleve-browns
alt.sports.baseball.atlanta-braves	alt.sports.football.pro.dallas-cowboys
alt.sports.baseball.balt-orioles	alt.sports.football.pro.denver-broncos

alt.sports.baseball.bos-redsox	alt.sports.football.pro.detroit-lions
alt.sports.baseball.calif-angels	alt.sports.football.pro.gb-packers
alt.sports.baseball.chi-whitesox	alt.sports.football.pro.houston-oilers
alt.sports.baseball.chicago-cubs	alt.sports.football.pro.kc-chiefs
alt.sports.baseball.cinci-reds	alt.sports.football.pro.la-raiders
alt.sports.baseball.cleve-indians	alt.sports.football.pro.la-rams
alt.sports.baseball.col-rockies	alt.sports.football.pro.miami-dolphins
alt.sports.baseball.detroit-tigers	alt.sports.football.pro.ne-patriots
alt.sports.baseball.fla-marlins	alt.sports.football.pro.no-saints
alt.sports.baseball.houston-astros	alt.sports.football.pro.ny-giants
alt.sports.baseball.kc-royals	alt.sports.football.pro.ny-jets
alt.sports.baseball.la-dodgers	alt.sports.football.pro.phila-eagles
alt.sports.baseball.minor-leagues	alt.sports.football.pro.phoe-cardinals
alt.sports.baseball.mke-brewers	alt.sports.football.pro.pitt-steelers
alt.sports.baseball.mn-twins	alt.sports.football.pro.sd-chargers
alt.sports.baseball.montreal-expos	alt.sports.football.pro.sea-seahawks
alt.sports.baseball.ny-mets	alt.sports.football.pro.sf-49ers
alt.sports.baseball.ny-yankees	alt.sports.football.pro.tampabay-bucs
alt.sports.baseball.oakland-as	alt.sports.football.pro.wash-redskins
alt.sports.baseball.phila-phillies	alt.sports.hockey.fantasy
alt.sports.baseball.pitt-pirates	alt.sports.hockey.nhl.boston-bruins
alt.sports.baseball.sd-padres	alt.sports.hockey.nhl.hford-whalers
alt.sports.baseball.sea-mariners	alt.sports.hockey.nhl.la-kings
alt.sports.baseball.sf-giants	alt.sports.hockey.nhl.mtl-canadiens
alt.sports.baseball.stl-cardinals	alt.sports.hockey.nhl.nj-devils
alt.sports.baseball.texas-rangers	alt.sports.hockey.nhl.ny-islanders

continues

Table 22.8 Continued

alt.sports.baseball.tor-bluejays	alt.sports.hockey.nhl.ny-rangers
alt.sports.basketball.ivy.penn	alt.sports.hockey.nhl.phila-flyers
alt.sports.basketball.nba.boston-celtics	alt.sports.hockey.nhl.pit-penguins
alt.sports.basketball.nba.chicago-bulls	alt.sports.hockey.nhl.sj-sharks
alt.sports.basketball.nba.denver-nuggets	alt.sports.hockey.nhl.tor-mapleleafs
alt.sports.basketball.nba.gs-warriors	alt.sports.hockey.nhl.vanc-canucks
alt.sports.basketball.nba.hou-rockets	alt.sports.hockey.nhl.wash-capitals
alt.sports.basketball.nba.la-lakers	alt.sports.hockey.nhl.winnipeg-jets
alt.sports.basketball.nba.mn-wolves	alt.sports.hockey.rhi
alt.sports.basketball.nba.orlando-magic	

Social and political groups

UseNet isn't all fun, games, and computers. There are a few groups out there that discuss profound moral and social issues with which we should all be concerned. If you're inclined to enter into public debates about politics, are interested in issues that complicate the lives of men and women, or are interested in the culture of another country, check out the listings in this section.

alt.activism

Activists pursuing a variety of goals meet here to discuss legalizing marijuana, civil rights, prison reform, and more.

alt.missing.kids

Here's an example of the better side of newsgroups. Help find missing children through these postings.

alt.politics.*

Here's a surprise. There are more than 20 groups beginning with alt.politics. Most of these groups are related to political issues in the U.S., but you'll also find **alt.politics.british**.

alt.recovery

Participants discuss recovery from various addictions. Recovery programs also are hotly debated. There are several subgroups for people recovering from specific problems.

alt.president.clinton

Do you have an opinion about the President? After all, almost everyone in the U.S. has something to say about Bill (and Hillary).

soc.culture.*

Discussions here focus on the cultures of dozens of other countries and different ethnic groups. This is a great way to learn about countries ranging from **.afghanistan** to **.yugoslavia**. (Someone please add a group about Zaire so that we can truly have an A-to-Z listing.)

soc.men

No, this isn't a place for men to socialize. Rather, discussions here involve topics that affect men. You will find discussions of gender bias, sexual discrimination, the Daddy Track, and father's rights.

Business groups

Depending on what line of work you're in, many of the other groups listed in this chapter will relate to your business. For instance, the Internet and computer listings are all related to my work at Que Corporation. If you work in the entertainment biz, you may find some of the **alt.fan.*** or **alt.tv.*** listings pertinent to business.

However, for the purpose of this section, we're going to look at business as something related to jobs, the economy, stock markets, and finance.

⊛ {Note}

There also are many good business-related groups in the clari hierarchy. Remember from chapter 2, "How Newsgroups Are Organized," that the clari hierarchy is a subscription-based service. You'll need to check with your service provider or news administrator to see if you have access to these groups.

alt.business.multi-level

Amway and other multilevel business opportunities are discussed here by both advocates and opponents. While many of the offers on this group are on the level and legitimate, use some common sense and beware of anything that sounds too good to be true. Just as in any other arena, there are scam artists lurking here.

alt.computer.consultants

If you're selling your services as a computer consultant or are looking to hire one, this is a good group to follow. You'll also find that some of the folks are willing to answer computer questions of a general nature.

biz.jobs.offered

The bad news is that the job I am really waiting for (Commissioner of Major League Baseball) still hasn't been posted. But, if you have somewhat more realistic goals, especially in the computer industry, here's a good place to get a leg up on the non-wired job-seeking populace. Expect to see a few hundred postings a week here. Of related interest, take a look at **misc.jobs.offered**, **misc.jobs.offered.entry**, and **misc.jobs.resumes**.

misc.entrepreneurs

Are you looking to start your own business? Or maybe you already run a business and need some advice. You'll find discussions related to these topics and more. As in the **alt.business.multilevel** group, keep an eye on your wallet until you get to know this group well.

misc.int-property

Anyone in business in the information age should be interested in the topic of intellectual property. Follow discussions here of current intellectual property issues, as well as those of a historical nature.

misc.invest

As with **misc.entrepreneurs** and **alt.business.multilevel**, you'll find investment opportunities here. What sets this group apart, though, are the discussions of news relevant to investors such as economic indicators, stock reports, and more. Also of interest are the subgroups **misc.invest.canada**, **misc.invest.funds**, **misc.invest.real-estate**, **misc.invest.stocks**, and **misc.invest.technical**.

misc.taxes

Discuss tax problems, voice your opinion about tax laws, and ask tax experts for advice. Of related interest is **clari.news.gov.taxes**.

Some off-the-wall groups

There are some groups that are just too strange to warrant a comment. This section presents a small sample of some of the most unusual corners of the alt hierarchy of UseNet.

alt.alien.visitors

Are you convinced aliens are holding Elvis hostage? Well, not everything in this group is quite that farfetched, but you'll see an occasional post that strains the credibility of the poster. Also of interest would be **alt.tv.x-files**, **alt.bigfoot**, and **alt.paranormal**. (And if you're worried about the whereabouts of the King, check out **alt.elvis.king**.)

alt.cows.moo.moo.moo

I quote: "Is there anyone in this newsgroup that has had an extrasensory perception of a cow? That had a paranormal experience with cows?

Or maybe, in your previous life, you were a cow?" In addition to serious subjects like this, you will find discussions of the ever-popular sport of cow tipping. Along these same lines, see **alt.duck.quack.quack.quack**.

alt.hi.are.you.cute

Not sure if you qualify as cute? Post a description of yourself here and let the rest of the cute world vote on you!

alt.flame

No, **alt.flame** is not where you go to complain if you've been flamed. Rather, this is flame-central. In a typical week, you'll see several hundred mostly pointless flames posted here. If you need to practice being rude on the Net, this is the place. Be forewarned that most posts involve language not suitable for publication.

alt.personals

Not to sound judgmental, but is this really the best way to meet that "special someone?" Apparently several hundred people of every imaginable sexual orientation think so. There are several interesting related subgroups too, including **alt.personals.ads** and **alt.personals.spanking** (using an anonymous remailer to post here would be a good idea).

alt.out-of-body

Do you have an out-of-body experience to share with the Internet world? Or maybe you need to know what your body does while you're out of it. In either case, you're likely to find this group eager to hear your story or answer your questions.

alt.satanism

Where do you turn on the Net if you need to know the difference between Wiccans and Satanists? What if you're looking for an experienced exorcist in your part of the world? This would be the place to check.

alt.sex

This group has dozens of subgroups. It's a very popular unmoderated group, so there is a large volume of postings on a wide variety of topics. Topics range from sincere questions about the subject to what most polite readers would classify as rude. We won't list them all. If you're mature enough to be discussing these topics, you should be able to find the right groups on your own!

alt.tasteless.jokes

Don't take the "tasteless" part of this name lightly. If you're easily offended, this group is not for you. On the other hand, if you think Eddie Murphy's stage humor is too tame, you'll be right at home here.

alt.tv.barney

Most of the posters in this group are fans of the purple dinosaur. You'll mostly find posts defending his character.

alt.tv.beavis-n-butthead

"Uh huh huh huh uh uh huh uh huh." What list of strange newsgroups would be complete without mentioning MTV's senseless simpletons? In case you don't know, you can find discussions of the show's episodes, characters, the characters' assessments of music, as well as bootleg graphics, and sound clips.

More groups than you can imagine

We've just scratched the surface of the available groups. If this isn't enough for you, or if you're looking for a specific group that isn't listed here, this section should help you find what you need.

Use your newsreader subscribe feature

If you're using either of the newsreaders discussed in Part 3, "Using WinVN," or Part IV, "Using NewsWatcher," you can get a list of available newsgroups through the subscribe feature. You can browse through the list to find a group you want. With well-named groups, it's fairly simple to determine the topic, based on the group names.

Subscribe to news.lists

Lists of all the available newsgroups are regularly posted here. These lists also are posted in **news.group**, **news.answers**, **news.announce.newusers**, and **news.announce.newgroups**. You'll find lists of the standard hierarchies, in addition to separate lists of the alt hierarchy. Most of these lists are broken into several parts.

You also can get these lists via FTP. The best source for these is **rtfm.mit.edu** in the directory /pu/usenet-by-group/. From here, change directories to one of the group names listed in the paragraph above.

{ Index }

Symbols